USING HIGHER-ORDER THINKING TO IMPROVE
READING COMPREHENSION

Reading Detective® Series
📖 Beginning 📖 A1 📖 B1 📖 R$_x$

Math Detective® Series
📖 Beginning 📖 A1 📖 B1

Science Detective® Series
📖 Beginning 📖 A1

World History Detective® Series
📖 Book 1

U.S. History Detective® Series
📖 Book 1

Written by
Cheryl Block, Carrie Beckwith,
Margaret Hockett, and David White

Pen and Ink Illustrations by
Susan Giacometti

© 2014, 2005, 2001
THE CRITICAL THINKING CO.™
www.CriticalThinking.com
Phone: 800-458-4849 • Fax: 541-756-1758
1991 Sherman Ave., Suite 200 • North Bend • OR 97459
ISBN 978-0-89455-768-2

TABLE OF CONTENTS

NONFICTION ARTICLES and ACTIVITY PAGES

POSTTESTS

ANSWERS

GLOSSARY

LITERATURE CITATIONS

TEACHER OVERVIEW

This program uses higher-order thinking skills to develop students' reading comprehension. The reading skills are based on state reading standards and assessment tests for Grades 7 and 8.

The goal of the program is to teach students how to analyze what they read. Students answer questions based on a passage then provide supporting evidence from the text for their answers. Each sentence is identified with a superscripted number; each paragraph has a letter. Students use these numbers and letters to cite specific sentences and paragraphs as evidence.

The purpose in asking for evidence is to:
- encourage students to go beyond simple recall of information.
- require students to support their answers by drawing on specific information from the passage.
- clarify for the teacher a student's thinking about and understanding of the material.
- require students to analyze the passage in greater depth.

Contents

The book contains three types of reading passages:
- Nonfiction articles on a variety of topics in the different content area
- Fictional stories in a variety of writing styles
- Literature excerpts from award-winning and well-known authors frequently read in school

Each exercise provides a passage the student must read followed by a series of questions. Most of the questions are multiple choice or short answer, the formats used on state reading assessments. Each question requires students to use one of the skills listed on the reading skills matrix. Definitions are given for key vocabulary words and technical terms.

Pre- and posttests are included to offer a general assessment of students' skills before starting the program and after completing it. Two passages, one fiction and one nonfiction, are offered for each. These tests are NOT intended as a diagnostic tool to assess an individual student's reading abilities. They are simply meant to give you an idea of your students' general level in reading comprehension. They should be used only for determining which skills and lessons to focus on.

We have included student lessons to introduce and/or review some of the higher level skills that students may not be as familiar with, such as inference. All the lessons can be given prior to starting the program, or specific lessons can be used based on pretest results.

A key component in this book is discussion of answers. The teacher's manual gives suggested answers with supporting evidence. However, many of the questions (inference and prediction, for example) are open to interpretation. It is important to discuss with students how they came up with their answers and how the evidence supports their answers. If you feel a student has made a good case for his response, accept that answer. The key to this program is encouraging students to think about what they read in order to better understand it. We give what we consider to be the best possible answer based on the evidence, but this does not mean that there is only one right answer. The evidence that a student gives is the key to pinpointing his understanding, and some of the evidence is subtle and open to interpretation.

The Use of Inferences in this Book

Students can be taught to make good inferences without actually knowing the word "inference." In this book, most of the inference questions in the student activities do not use the term "inference." However, it is a good idea to introduce the terminology *and* the concept.

The Use of Generalization in This Book

Students can be taught to make good generalizations without actually knowing the words "generalization" and "generalize." In this book, the questions requiring generalization in the student activities do not use the term "generalization." However, it is a good idea to introduce the terminology along with the concept, as shown below. The following lesson material is part of the student lesson on making generalizations. Any notes to the teacher or answers are shown in bolded text.

Look at the following example. What general statement could you make about Lisa based on the information given below?

> [1]Every day, Lisa greeted the neighbors on her way to school. [2]She waved at the milkman and brought old Mrs. Newcomb her morning paper. [3]She smiled at the joggers as they ran through the park. [4]She knew the doorman at the hotel and the crossing guard by name. [5]Everyone knew and liked Lisa.

Lisa was a friendly person. She greeted people. She helped people. She made friends with people, and they liked her.

The Use of Figurative Language in This Book

This level of the *Reading Detective®* series includes specific questions about simile, metaphor, personification, idiom, and analogy. The following material is part of the student lesson on figurative language. Any notes to the teacher or answers are shown in bolded text.

Simile and Metaphor

Can you identify which kind of figurative language is used in the following sentences?

> [1]New green leaves appear on the trees. [2]The leaves slowly unfold like the tiny fingers on a newborn baby's hands. [3]Pink and white blossoms burst open like popcorn popping on the branches. [4]Each tree is a lovely lady dressed in her finest gown. [5]Spring is here!

Both sentences 2 and 3 use similes. Sentence 2 compares new leaves unfolding to a baby's fingers. Sentence 3 compares blossoms opening to popcorn popping. Sentence 4 is a metaphor comparing trees to ladies dressed in their finest gowns.

Idiom

Identify which phrase is used as an idiom in the following passage. What do you think the phrase means?

> [1]Mom was fit to be tied when she heard I was going to be late for dinner. [2]I tried to explain, but she wouldn't listen.

Sentence 1 uses the expression "fit to be tied." It means that Mom was mad.

Personification

Sometimes a writer will describe an object or an abstract idea in human terms. This is called personification. Can you tell how personification is used in the next passage?

[1]I watch the daffodils poke their sleepy heads through the soil. [2]In a matter of days, bright yellow daffodils are nodding cheerfully in the garden. [3]Clusters of purple hyacinth stand at attention between them.

The writer describes the spring flowers in human terms, or personifies them. The daffodils "poke their sleepy heads" and "nod cheerfully." The hyacinths "stand at attention."

Analogy

A writer may compare two things that are normally quite different in order to make you see something in a new way. This comparison is called an analogy. It gives several similarities between the two items. What is the analogy used below? How might the two things be alike?

[1]She said he had a rock for a heart, cold and hard. [2]She said it would take a strong chisel ever to open it up and see what was inside.

An analogy is drawn between his heart and a rock. In this comparison, the author is referring to the person's feelings. A rock is physically cold and hard; it has no feelings. A person with a hard heart or a cold heart is considered unfeeling. You may have to chisel a rock open just as you may have to force someone to open his heart.

The Use of Literary Devices in This Book

This level of the *Reading Detective®* series introduces the literary devices of flashback, foreshadowing, symbolism, and irony.

The Use of Vocabulary Using Context Clues in This Book

Quite often, students will come across new or unfamiliar words while reading a passage. It is important for them to understand how to use the context of the word to determine its meaning.

Using Context Clues Within the Sentence

Context is the words or sentences that surround an unfamiliar word. If you understand the other words in a sentence, you can often figure out the meaning of an unfamiliar word.

[1]The evening finally *culminated* with the arrival of a huge, flaming dessert carried in on a silver tray by two waiters.

The dinner *ended* or *climaxed* with dessert. The word *finally* is a clue that this is the end of the evening. Students also know that dessert is usually last.

The Use of Fact/Opinion in This Book

At this level of the *Reading Detective®*, students must determine that something can be a fact not only if *they* could actually verify it, but if, by nature, it could be verified by reliable sources, such as a dictionary or encyclopedia. It should be emphasized that we are trying not necessarily to find whether or not a thing is *true*, but whether it is possible to *verify* its truth or falsehood.

The Use of Summary in This Book

The practice of summarizing passages teaches a student to focus on the important points and understand connections between main ideas, details, and conclusions. It allows a student to become a more critical reader by learning to put examples and supporting evidence into their proper perspective.

SKILLS FOR READING COMPREHENSION/LITERARY ANALYSIS GRADES 7–8 LITERATURE

READING COMPREHENSION SKILLS

READING

Skill	The Cay	Sparrow Hawk Red	El Güero	The Moon by Night	The Giver	Under the Sun	View From Saturday	Trolley to Yesterday	Rhinoceros Skin	Face to Face	Bronze Bow
Compare/contrast		■		■		■			■	■	
Define vocabulary in context			■		■		■	■		■	■
Distinguish cause/effect	■		■	■	■		■	■	■	■	
Distinguish fact/opinion						■					
Draw conclusions	■		■	■	■	■		■		■	
Find supporting details		■									
Identify author's purpose											■
Identify main idea											
Make inferences	■	■	■	■	■	■	■	■	■	■	
Make generalizations		■							■		
Make predictions								■			
Read for details					■	■		■			■
Summarize information			■						■		
Use tables, illustrations, etc.											

LITERARY ANALYSIS

Skill	The Cay	Sparrow Hawk Red	El Güero	The Moon by Night	The Giver	Under the Sun	View From Saturday	Trolley to Yesterday	Rhinoceros Skin	Face to Face	Bronze Bow
Analyze author's style							■				
Analyze character traits	■		■		■		■	■	■		■
Analyze figurative language	■	■		■				■			
Identify key events in plot		■				■			■		
Identify setting	■	■	■								■
Identify theme					■						
Predict outcome/resolution				■							
Recognize conflict		■			■	■	■				■
Recognize literary devices	■			■							■
Recognize literary form				■					■	■	
Recognize mood or tone				■			■	■			
Recognize point of view		■		■	■					■	
Sequence events	■		■	■					■		

SKILLS FOR READING COMPREHENSION/LITERARY ANALYSIS GRADES 7–8 FICTION

READING COMPREHENSION SKILLS	Ancient Greece	The Prime Suspect	Comeback Can	Diving In	A Flood of Help	15 Minutes of Fame	Sketches of Summer	Amazon Adventure	The Way of the Wild	Dramatic Plea	Middle School	Old Woman of the Oak	A Test of Friendship	The Game Winner	My Most Embarrasing Day	He Said, She Said	Sea Otter Attack	Race for Pepper	Camp Gitchigoomi	Head Chef at 14
READING																				
Compare/contrast	●	●			●		●		●		●	●			●					●
Define vocabulary in context				●		●						●						●	●	
Distinguish cause/effect		●	●		●			●	●	●	●	●		●		●	●	●	●	
Distinguish fact/opinion	●		●		●			●		●							●			
Draw conclusions	●	●		●	●	●	●		●	●	●			●	●	●	●	●	●	
Find supporting details		●			●						●			●		●				
Identify author's purpose																				
Identify main idea											●									
Make inferences			●		●	●	●	●	●	●		●	●	●	●	●	●	●	●	●
Make generalizations	●		●		●											●				●
Make predictions					●			●			●				●		●	●	●	
Read for details			●							●		●		●						●
Sequence steps																				●
Summarize information			●							●						●				
Use tables, illustrations, etc.						●					●									
LITERARY ANALYSIS																				
Analyze author's style																				
Analyze character traits		●						●	●			●	●	●		●	●	●	●	●
Analyze figurative language		●	●			●		●	●		●	●	●	●		●			●	
Identify key events in plot									●			●	●	●			●			
Identify setting		●				●	●								●			●		
Identify theme	●												●							
Predict outcome/resolution		●					●		●			●	●					●		
Recognize conflict													●							
Recognize literary devices				●									●							
Recognize literary form				●				●												
Recognize mood or tone				●	●		●	●	●			●								
Recognize point of view															●				●	●
Sequence events				●			●							●		●	●			

SKILLS FOR READING COMPREHENSION/LITERARY ANALYSIS GRADES 7–8 NONFICTION

READING COMPREHENSION SKILLS

Lesson	Compare/contrast	Define vocabulary in context	Distinguish cause/effect	Distinguish fact/opinion	Draw conclusions	Find supporting details	Identify author's purpose	Identify main idea	Make inferences	Make generalizations	Make predictions	Read for details	Sequence steps	Summarize information	Use tables, illustrations, etc.	Analyze character traits	Analyze figurative language	Identify key events in plot	Identify setting	Identify theme	Organization of material	Predict outcome/resolution	Recognize conflict	Recognize literary devices	recognize literary form	Recognize mood or tone	Recognize point of view	Sequence events
Making of Constitution	■		■	■	■			■				■																
Secret Codes		■			■		■		■	■				■	■													
Superman to X-Men	■	■	■		■				■	■																■		■
Training for the Ballet				■				■	■	■		■	■		■													
Finding a Career				■								■	■				■										■	
Latitude & Longitude	■	■		■	■		■	■				■			■						■							
Is Earth Heating Up?	■		■		■			■				■																
Kublai Khan			■		■	■	■	■								■												■
Special Effects	■					■	■	■				■			■													
Sports Stats			■		■			■	■		■	■			■													
Electro-Magic	■					■				■					■													
Measuring Time	■		■		■	■		■	■	■	■	■			■													
Soccer: Mia Hamm					■	■						■				■										■	■	
Researching the Renaissance	■		■		■	■				■		■		■														
Making Mountains	■		■		■	■		■	■			■			■													
Making Apple Pie	■	■	■			■						■	■		■													
Long, Short of Color	■	■	■			■				■	■				■												■	
Goalsetting	■	■	■			■		■			■		■	■												■		
Galileo's Vision	■		■	■		■		■				■																
Put Your Heart Into It	■							■	■		■	■									■							

WHAT IS *READING DETECTIVE*®?

Reading Detective® has stories and questions that will help you read and think better. After reading a story, you will answer questions that will help you improve not only your basic reading skills (such as reading for detail), but also your thinking skills. One of the best ways to learn is by discussing your answers with your teacher and other students. By comparing your interpretation of the story with other people's ideas, you will learn to see new relationships (between story events and characters, for example).

Types of Reading Passages

There are three types of stories: (1) literature passages from books written by highly acclaimed authors you may have read before; (2) factual articles; and (3) a variety of short fiction stories. The passages include a variety of story types: mystery, science fiction, humor, adventure, etc.

Types of Questions

Each activity asks you 7–10 questions about the passage. Types of questions include multiple choice, short answer, and fill-in-the-blank. Multiple choice questions include four choices. Usually, you pick only one. Once in awhile, there will be more than one correct answer, and you must list all answers that are correct.

Reading for Evidence

When you answer questions, you will often be asked to list sentences or paragraphs from the story to support your answer choice. When giving evidence, you must choose the best evidence to support and explain your answer.

The sentences in each passage are numbered with a small number at the beginning of the sentence. In some stories, a letter is used to indicate each paragraph in the story. You will use these numbers and letters to identify your evidence.

Key vocabulary words and technical terms in some of the passages are highlighted with a star (asterisk). A definition of the word is then given at the end of the passage.

Using the Glossary

At the end of the book is a glossary of terms you will need to know when answering the questions. You may refer to this glossary at any time.

MAKING INFERENCES

Inferences and Facts

In many of the activities in this book, you will be asked to draw a conclusion from information that is suggested in the passage. This is called *making an inference*. There is a difference between making an inference and identifying a fact. When you identify a fact, you are simply finding information that is stated in the passage. When you make an inference, you are drawing a conclusion based on information that is not directly stated in the passage.

In the following passage, see if you can tell the difference between an inference and a fact.

1.   ¹The sun was shining; the birds were singing. ²He could see out the bus window that there wasn't a cloud in the sky. ³It was going to be a beautiful day. ⁴"A perfect spring day to be biking," thought Eli, as his bus pulled into the school parking lot.

Fact: Birds were singing.
Fact: Eli was on a bus.

Inference: Eli is a student.
Inference: Eli would rather be biking.

The facts are stated in the passage. The inferences require the reader to use the facts to draw a conclusion suggested by the story.

Examine the Evidence

When you make an inference about information from a story, look at the events described and the actions and words of the characters. Often an author uses the events and characters to lead you toward an inference he or she wants you to make. The events described and the characters' words and actions become evidence for your inferences. The more evidence you have to support your inference, the more likely your inference will be true. However, you must be careful when making inferences to identify and carefully examine your evidence. Otherwise, you may make an inference that turns out to be false.

For instance, in the passage above, the author never directly says that Eli is a student who is riding to school in a school bus, but you can infer this. Your inference may be true. However, another possibility is that Eli is the bus driver. You need more evidence to determine who Eli is.

Read the next passage. What can you infer (or conclude) about Charlie's behavior?

2.   ¹Charlie had taken my lunch box again and was holding it over his head. ²"Come on, kid," he said. ³"Try and get it."
⁴We'd been through this before. ⁵I knew it was no use trying to get it, but Charlie just loved to keep playing this game. ⁶As I grabbed for the box, Charlie tripped me, and I went sprawling on the concrete.
⁷"Missed again, loser!" yelled Charlie, as he dumped the contents of my lunch box on top of me.

The passage doesn't state that Charlie is acting like a bully. However, the author gives you evidence in the words and actions of both Charlie and the narrator. In sentence 1, Charlie takes the narrator's lunch box. Both sentence 1 and 4 tell us he has done this before. In sentence 6, Charlie trips the narrator. In sentence 7, Charlie dumps the boy's lunch on his head. You can also infer that Charlie is a bully from his comments. He teases the narrator in sentences 2 and 3. In sentence 7, he calls him a name.

Using Your Own Knowledge

Sometimes when you make an inference, you combine your own knowledge with the information that is suggested or given in the text. It is common knowledge that some snakes eat rodents. In the following passage, can you make an inference about what happened to the gerbils? Is there enough evidence to support your inference?

3. [1]Amanda was pet-sitting Alejandro's pet boa constrictor. [2]When she went to check on him in the morning, the snake was missing. [3]There also seemed to be fewer gerbils in the next cage.

It is possible that the snake and the gerbils escaped together. It is more likely that the snake escaped and ate the gerbils. It is a fact that boa constrictors eat small animals. Although the author doesn't give us this fact, we can use our own knowledge of boas to support this conclusion. In this case, our inference is probably true, but could be false. There is not enough evidence to make a definite conclusion about the gerbils.

MAKING GENERALIZATIONS

Generalizations

Some of the questions in this book ask you to make a general statement about a group of things. This is called making a *generalization*. When you make a generalization, you take specific information about something and apply it to *all* similar things. For example, let's say you've never tasted Brussels sprouts. You try one Brussels sprout, and it tastes bad to you. What do you decide about Brussels sprouts? Do you figure they *all* taste bad and decide not to eat them again? Such a decision is a generalization, but it may not be a good generalization.

A Good Generalization

To make a good generalization, you need plenty of evidence. Could you be sure all Brussels sprouts taste like the one you ate? Maybe the sprout you got was spoiled. How could you be sure about the taste of Brussels sprouts in general? Let's say you tried all the sprouts in the batch and they all tasted bad. Would that mean all Brussels sprouts taste bad? What if that whole batch had been spoiled? Or what if your sense of taste was "off" because of illness? To make a good generalization, you should try Brussels sprouts at different times and from different places.

Read the following passage. Could you make a general statement about all cats, based on the information given?

1. [1]Whenever Nancy has a bowl of yogurt, her cat Archie wants to share it. [2]He comes running when he hears her open the refrigerator. [3]If she pulls out the yogurt, he meows until she gives him some.

Even though Nancy's cat likes yogurt, this does not mean that *all* cats like yogurt. Saying that all cats like yogurt would not be a good generalization. One cat is not a large enough sampling to make a general statement (a generalization).

The following passage gives information about several similar animals. What general statement might you make about all animals of this kind?

2. ¹Squirrels are rodents that use their strong front teeth for breaking nuts. ²Beavers are rodents that use their front teeth for gnawing wood. ³Rats and mice are rodents that can use their front teeth for gnawing through plaster walls. Even pet rodents, like hamsters and gerbils, chew on sticks of wood to keep their teeth strong.

Since all of these animals are rodents and all of them use their front teeth for gnawing on hard objects, you might decide that all rodents have strong front teeth. You would be making a generalization about these animals. Since your statement is based on more than one type of rodent, it is probably a good generalization.

Besides making general statements about groups of things, you can also make a general statement about an individual. For example, you can make a generalization about a character's traits based on his or her actions. When you do this, you are applying what you know about the character's actions in one or more situations to his or her behavior in all other similar situations. What might you decide about Amanda after reading the following description?

3. ¹Amanda prepared dinner every night this week. ²She did all her homework. ³She scrubbed the kitchen floor, cleaned the bathrooms, and delivered papers each morning.

From her actions, you might decide that, in general, Amanda is a hard-working person. When you do this, you are making a broad statement about Amanda's behavior in all similar situations. However, it is possible that she worked hard only this week. The more evidence you have to support your general statement, the stronger it is.

Look at the following example. What general statement could you make about Lisa based on the information given below?

4. ¹Every day, Lisa greeted the neighbors on her way to school. ²She waved at the milkman and brought old Mrs. Newcomb her morning paper. ³She smiled at the joggers as they ran through the park. ⁴She knew the doorman at the hotel and the crossing guard by name. ⁵Everyone knew and liked Lisa.

USING FIGURATIVE LANGUAGE

Using Figurative Language

Sometimes writers use words in a special way to make their writing more interesting or to create an image in the reader's mind. Often, figurative language uses words to mean something other than their dictionary or *literal* meaning. Literal language describes how something actually looks, feel, or sounds. For example:

Literal: He looked strong.
Literal: She is flying through the air on her hang glider.

Figurative language describes something by comparing it to something else or by using words in creative ways.

Figurative: The muscles in his arms looked like bowling balls.
Figurative: She is a bird riding gently on the breeze.

Of course, his arms are not really the size of bowling balls, and she is not *really* a bird. Figurative language helps the writer to make a point and to make the writing more imaginative.

Simile and Metaphor

Two specific kinds of figurative language are used in the activities in this book.

Simile: A simile uses the word "like" or "as" to compare two things.

Metaphor: A metaphor makes a comparison by suggesting that one thing is the other.

Look at the two examples below. Which one is a simile? Why?

1. She floated in the air like a feather.

2. Her lined face was a map of her life.

Sentence 1 is a simile. It says she floated *like a feather*. Sentence 2 is a metaphor. Can you identify which kind of figurative language is used in the following sentences?

3. [1]New green leaves appear on the trees. [2]The leaves slowly unfold like the tiny fingers on a newborn baby's hands. [3]Pink and white blossoms burst open like popcorn popping on the branches. [4]Each tree is a lovely lady dressed in her finest gown. [5]Spring is here!

Idiom

Figurative language is more than similes and metaphors. There are other ways an author might use figurative language to describe something. When you say, "My father blew his stack last night," you don't really mean that your father has a stack on his head or that he blew up. You mean he was angry. There are many common phrases that use words to mean something other than their literal meaning, such as "keep tabs on" or "lost track of." These are called *idioms*.

Identify which phrase is used as an idiom in the following passage. What do you think the phrase means?

4. [1]Mom was fit to be tied when she heard I was going to be late for dinner. [2]I tried to explain, but she wouldn't listen.

Personification

Sometimes a writer will describe an object or an abstract idea in human terms. This is called personification. Can you tell how personification is used in the next passage?

5. [1]I watch the daffodils poke their sleepy heads through the soil. [2]In a matter of days, bright yellow daffodils are nodding cheerfully in the garden. [3]Clusters of purple hyacinth stand at attention between them.

Analogy

A writer may compare two things that are normally quite different in order to make you see something in a new way. This comparison is called an analogy. It gives several similarities between the two items. What is the analogy used below? How are the two things alike?

6. [1]She said he had a rock for a heart, cold and hard. [2]She said it would take a strong chisel to open it up and see what was inside.

USING LITERARY DEVICES

Flashback

A flashback is a jump from the present to the past: it describes events that happened at an earlier time. For example, the story may get our interest by showing a very exciting event in present time. Later on, when we are already hooked on reading the story, the author may have the main character remember, or "flash back," to an earlier time to give us information to help our understanding of the plot. The following excerpt follows a scene in which a boy is beaten in a fight. Which sentences represent a flashback?

1. ¹The pain now was bad, and he wished he could turn back the clock. ²Only a year ago, he was walking this same path when the bad boys called his name. ³They had taunted him and had even thrown pebbles. ⁴And he just ignored them; he kept plodding along the broken sidewalk. ⁵He wished he could have done the same today.

Sentences 2, 3, and 4 describe what happened earlier than the present time. Sentences 1 and 5 are in present time.

Foreshadowing

Sometimes an author wants to give you a hint of what is going to happen later in the story. This early suggestion of things to come is called foreshadowing. In the following excerpt, decide how the author gives you a clue about the storm that will occur later the same day.

2. ¹Banny Frye was starting to bore me with his opinion of last year's Bear Club party. ²As I looked around, things seemed unnaturally still. ³No stirring breeze, no robin's chirp. ⁴Probably just the sense of time-standing-still I always got when Banny went on and on. ⁵I shook off a feeling of unease and left him—I had to get ready for tonight's club festivities!

The words "unnaturally still" in sentence 2 and all of sentence 3 suggest that something is different with the environment. Those, along with the feeling of unease mentioned in sentence 5, give us a clue that something big may be coming.

Irony

Authors sometimes use a special kind of humor called irony. When an author is being ironic, her real meaning may be the opposite of what her words literally mean, or an outcome may be the opposite of what is expected. A well known story by O. Henry, "The Gift of the Magi," gives a classic example of irony. A poor couple sacrifice to buy each other presents. The man sells his watch to buy the woman a comb for her hair, but she has sold her hair to buy him a chain for his watch. The irony is in the unexpected outcome—the sacrifice makes their gifts useless.

Irony is based on contradiction. Things are not as they seem, they do not turn out as they should, or there is a discrepancy between the intent and the effect. See if you can explain the irony in the following passage:

3. ¹Feldsters Department Store was having a clothing sale, so Mr. Draper drove the 50 miles beyond his regular store to get there. ²By the time he finished shopping, he had saved only $10 on his purchases. ³He had also spent the same amount, $10, on the gas he used to drive the extra miles.

The irony is that the man who made an effort to save money saved nothing in the end; he spent $10 to save $10. Things did not turn out as they should have.

Symbolism

An author will sometimes use a simple object to represent a more complex idea. For example, a rock can be used to symbolize strength. The Statue of Liberty represents freedom and democracy and is often used as a recurring theme or idea.

In the following excerpt, what object could be thought of as a symbol? Explain what it symbolizes.

4. [1]I had been beaten down for so long. [2]First losing my job, and then my family. [3]Yet, I was beginning to feel hopeful. [4]Things were going to change. [5]Maybe today's job interview would turn out okay. [6]Just then I saw the bud of a fresh crocus poking its head defiantly through the dying blanket of old snow.

The crocus could be a symbol: it stands for the renewed hope felt by the narrator. Its defiance echoes the narrator's declaration that things will be better. Also, the "dying blanket of old snow" could be taken as a symbol of the narrator's previous bad circumstances.

DEVELOPING VOCABULARY USING CONTEXT

Using Context Clues Within the Sentence

Context is the words or sentences that surround an unfamiliar word. If you understand the other words in a sentence, you can often figure out the meaning of an unfamiliar word.

1. Long *festoons* of flowers were strung along the railings of the balconies as decorations.

In the sentence above, we know that the festoons were long, made of flowers, and were strung up as decorations. The word *strung* also gives you a clue that a festoon is probably a kind of string or garland of something, in this case, flowers.

Sometimes a sentence will describe the meaning of the word for you, as in this example:

2. She spoke in such a soft whisper that her voice was barely *audible*, and I had to bend down to hear her.

The second part of the sentence helps to define the word for you. Since the person had trouble hearing her, the word *audible* probably means able to be heard. The definition is also supported by the fact that since she spoke in a whisper, she was barely heard.

Using clues in the sentence, what do you think the word in italics in the following sentence means?

3. The evening finally *culminated* with the arrival of a huge, flaming dessert carried in on a silver tray by two waiters.

Using Context Clues Within the Passage

The surrounding sentences in a passage can also give you clues as to the meaning of an unfamiliar word. Look at the following example:

> 4. [1]The phone had rung unexpectedly very early that morning. [2]It was a short call, but Uncle Art seemed *perturbed* after the call. [3]He wouldn't talk to anyone. [4]He just kept lighting one cigarette after another and pacing back and forth in the kitchen.

The sentence using the word *perturbed* does not give you much information about the word's meaning. However, there are clues in the surrounding sentences that can help you define the word. In sentence 1, we know that it was the unexpected phone call that caused Uncle Art to be perturbed. In the last two sentences, we learn that Uncle Art reacted to the call by not talking, by smoking constantly, and by pacing. This information suggests that Uncle Art was upset or disturbed by the phone call. So upset or disturbed would be a good definition for the word *perturbed*.

DETERMINING FACT VS. OPINION

Fact or Opinion?

Being able to tell the difference between facts and opinions can help you make good judgments about events or people. Opinions can give you information about individuals and help you get to know them. Facts can help you form good judgments and make decisions. For example, suppose you are trying to decide which movie to see: "The Sharpie" or "Crier Joseph." Sherry saw "The Sharpie" and says she hated it and that it was a musical having at least five major dance numbers. Pat tells you he loved "Crier Joseph," and that there were three buildings blown up and an excellent car chase scene through a crowded city. If you know you have enjoyed musicals in the past but dislike action and violence, you would probably go against the opinions. You listen to the facts— things that can be proven, such as the number of dance scenes or the number of chase scenes— and choose "The Sharpie."

It is not always easy to decide what is based on fact rather than opinion. For example, suppose you and Sam are surprised to find a frog on your chair. Sam says, "This has got to be Fernando's idea of a joke. He put a snake in his brother's bed last month, and I heard some girls complaining that he stole their books last week." Do you decide that it is a fact that Fernando put the frog on your chair? Can you prove it? There may be evidence that he did the other things, but so far, you have only an opinion about Fernando and the frog.

Read the following and decide which are facts and which are opinions.

> [1]He was a wonderful leader. [2]His orders were forceful and direct. [3]He held his followers to a strict code of conduct, but he was compassionate, too. [4]For example, when Darian's mother was ill with pneumonia, he signed a request for two days' leave for visitation.

That he was a wonderful leader is an opinion. Even though many might agree, there is no objective way to prove anyone is "wonderful." It is also opinion that his orders are forceful and direct or that he holds followers to a strict code of conduct. Different people have different ideas of what makes something forceful, direct, or strict. On the other hand, the idea that Darian's mother has pneumonia is classified as fact, since it can be proved that she either has it or doesn't have it. Also, it can be proved whether or not he signed a request for leave.

SUMMARIZING INFORMATION

Summary

A good summary combines a main idea, key supporting ideas, and a conclusion. A summary can be a single sentence or several sentences. To write a summary, put the author's main idea in your own words. The main idea will often include the information in the passage title, so take the title into consideration when writing a summary. (Do not include all the examples and other supporting evidence the author uses to round out the passage.) Add just one or two key points to support the main idea.

Answer the following questions to help you write your summary: What is the passage about? What does the author want you to know about the topic? What is she or he trying to convince you of? What is the ending and what is its connection to the main idea?

Keeping the above information in mind, summarize the passage below in two sentences.

1. [1]Making your own shirt takes some time and effort but is worth it, since you'll have a shirt in a color you like and that fits. [2]First, you'll need to go to the fabric store. [3]Get a pattern in your size and in a style you like. [4]Then choose material you like (consult the pattern envelope to buy the necessary amount). [5]At home, fold your material so it's doubled and lay it out on a table. [6]Pin your pattern pieces onto the cloth and cut them out. [7]Follow the pictures and instructions on the pattern envelope to sew the pieces together on your sewing machine. [8]Pull the results over your head. [9]Enjoy the rewards of your labor and show off your brand new, custom-made shirt.

A good summary will include the main idea, key supporting details, and a conclusion, as follows:

2. [1]To make your own pullover shirt [main idea], you must first buy a pattern and material, and then cut out and sew the pieces together [supporting details]. [2]It requires effort, but will be worth it because you will have a new shirt you like [conclusion].

pretests_____

FICTION PRETEST
Billy Brussels Sprouts

A ¹"Seven!" ²Two boys gave each other high-fives as groans and cries of wonder echoed from one corner of the cafeteria.

B ³"Eight!" someone close to Billy Pierce crowed. ⁴Billy stopped to catch his breath and stared for a few heartbeats at the pile of Brussels sprouts still on his plate.

C ⁵It wasn't *his* big mouth that had started the whole thing. ⁶The culprit was Sevy Gonsalves, his up-until-this-moment best friend. ⁷But when Sevy had claimed in front of 16 other guys that Billy could eat 16 Brussels sprouts at one sitting, Billy couldn't just walk away, especially since the other guys were waiting to call him a wimp if he did walk away (not to mention give him their Brussels sprouts).

D ⁸He liked Brussels sprouts, sort of. ⁹He didn't *detest* them, like some of the other kids did. ¹⁰Whenever the cooks offered them, which seemed to be about every two weeks, Billy got more than his fair share from his "friends."

E ¹¹"Nine!" Sevy called, his smile stretching from ear to ear. ¹²"Want some mustard?" ¹³He slapped Billy on the back. ¹⁴Billy coughed and rolled his eyes.

F ¹⁵In the few seconds between number nine and number ten, Billy blamed his mother. ¹⁶She was the nutrition nut who had fed him these things since he was five years old. ¹⁷

"Eat your Brussels sprouts, and good nutrition will be as easy as ABC," she liked to say. ¹⁸Billy didn't really care how many vitamins the little cabbages had in them, especially now that number ten was making its way into his stomach.

G ¹⁹"I don't believe it!" one girl called. ²⁰

"Ooh!" another said. ²¹"They smell bad. ²²I don't see how he does it."

H ²³To Billy's total dismay, Maria Hernandez was telling her best friend, Cynthia Greenstreet, that the whole thing was gross and disgusting. ²⁴Billy wanted to stop right then and there and plead coercion. ²⁵He wanted to smile his winning smile at Maria and tell her that he was forced into it, that he wasn't really as weird as he seemed. ²⁶He knew in his heart that it was more than just a bet. ²⁷He really needed that money to buy her a present, the kind that would make her see that he was the guy for her, no matter what he looked like with Brussels sprouts juice running down his chin.

I ²⁸"Eleven!"

J ²⁹The teachers were on to them now, though. ³⁰Billy hurriedly tried to finish the pile in front of him, determined to collect his winner's wage of $16. (³¹Each of the guys had chipped in a dollar.)

K ³²Too late!

L ³³Mrs. Wertheimer and Mr. Greene were breaking up the crowd. ³⁴His arms behind his back and his mouth and belly full, Billy resigned himself to losing the money, the respect of Maria Hernandez, and his appetite for Brussels sprouts.

M ³⁵What would his mother say?

DIRECTIONS: Choose or write the best answer to each of the following questions using the evidence provided in the passage. When required, list specific sentence numbers or paragraph letters from the story to support the answer.

1. How often were Brussels sprouts on the menu?

   _____

   _____

   Give the number of the sentence that best supports the answer. _____

2. Why did the author describe Billy's fellow students as "friends" in sentence 10?

   _____

   _____

   _____

3. In general, Billy is the kind of person who:
   A. wants to be liked.
   B. likes to get into trouble.
   C. prefers to eat healthy foods.
   D. backs away from a challenge.

   List the numbers of the 2 sentences that best support the answer. _____, _____

4. Which of these best describes why Billy agreed to *finish eating* all of the Brussels sprouts?
   A. He valued his friendship with Sevy.
   B. He wanted to make his mother proud of him.
   C. He wanted money to buy a present for Maria.
   D. He thought other people would look at him differently.

   List the numbers of the 2 sentences that best support the answer. ____, ____

5. Label these phrases from paragraphs F and G as fact (F) or opinion (O).

   _____ They smell bad.

   _____ They are little cabbages.

   _____ They contain vitamins.

   _____ Good nutrition will be as easy as ABC.

6. What does the word coercion mean, as used in sentence 24?

   _____

   _____

   _____

   Give the number of another sentence that best supports the answer. _____

7. Number the following according to the actual order of events.

   _____ Billy agrees to eat a plate full of Brussels sprouts.

   _____ Billy blames his mother.

   _____ Billy's mother praises the nutritional value of Brussels sprouts.

   _____ Teachers step in.

   _____ Sevy claims Billy can eat 16 Brussels sprouts at one sitting.

   _____ Maria Hernandez tells her friend how gross the whole thing is.

8. What is meant by the phrase "on to them," as used in sentence 29?

   A. They wanted to watch.
   B. They were attacking them.
   C. They discovered what was going on.
   D. They were counting along with the crowd.

9. What does the statement that Billy wanted to "collect his winner's wage" (sentence 30) mean?

   _____

   _____

   _____

   List the numbers of 2 sentences (other than sentence 30) that best support the answer. ____, ____

5

NONFICTION PRETEST
The Hidden Cost of Buried Treasure

A ¹When we hear of hidden treasure, our eyes may light up with excitement. ²We may even be tempted to take up pick and shovel and head for the hills. ³But will extracting the bounty be worth the price it extracts from us? ⁴Here are just some of the things that have happened to people who heeded the call of the treasure.

B ⁵1560: Antonio de Sepulveda tries to retrieve offerings of gold that are said to lie at the bottom of Colombia's volcanic Lake Guatavita. ⁶He uses thousands of workers and digs through the rim of the crater to start draining the lake. ⁷A few precious items surface, so he digs deeper. ⁸The rim fails, and many workers are killed in the collapse. ⁹Sepulveda dies poor.

C ¹⁰1795: Nova Scotian Daniel McGinnis finds a shaft more than 90 feet deep. ¹¹A stone is found whose markings tell of treasure below, but the shaft has a complex system of booby traps and flood channels. ¹²McGinnis and others sink their savings into a hole that refuses to give up its prize. ¹³During attempts to block the floods and reach the treasure, accidents claim at least six lives.

D ¹⁴1937: Milton Noss finds a cave holding coins, jewels, and gold in southeastern New Mexico. ¹⁵He removes some of the gold and hides it elsewhere. ¹⁶Later, he tries to widen the cave opening by blasting with dynamite. ¹⁷Instead, the blast starts a landslide that seals the cave. ¹⁸In an argument over the gold that had been retrieved, a partner shoots him to death.

E ¹⁹1968: Tom Gurr finds the wreck of the *San José de las Animas* after searching diligently for four years. ²⁰Boundary rules change, and a judge decides that the state of Florida has a right to half the treasure. ²¹After court battles, the man is so frustrated he dumps the money back where he found it. ²²Facing a lawsuit for larceny, he is forced to retrieve it again. ²³But after spending so much time and effort for so little, he loses the desire to ever do any more treasure hunting.

F ²⁴Undoubtedly, there are stories of more successful treasure hunts. ²⁵But who can tell what hidden costs the finders may eventually incur?

DIRECTIONS: Choose or write the best answer to each of the following questions using the evidence provided in the passage. When required, list specific sentence numbers or paragraph letters from the story to support the answer.

1. The word *extract* means to draw or pull out. Explain the meaning of the words "price it extracts from us," as used in sentence 3.

   _____

   _____

   _____

   _____

2. The author's main purpose is to:
   A. persuade you that searching for treasure may cost a lot.
   B. give examples of times and locations of finding treasure.
   C. entertain you with the adventures of treasure seekers.
   D. describe the details of difficulties suffered by particular men.

   Give the number of the sentence from paragraph A that best supports the answer. ____

3. According to paragraphs B through E, all of the following were lost as a result of seeking treasure EXCEPT:
   A. money.
   B. lives.
   C. effort.
   D. land.

4. The word *heeded*, as used in sentence 4, most nearly means:
   A. refused to hear.
   B. looked for.
   C. paid attention to.
   D. required.

5. Write the phrase in sentence 12 that shows personification.

   _____

   _____

   _____

6. What cause and effect are suggested in sentence 6?

   _____

   _____

   _____

7. Choose the best summary for the passage.
   A. Many of us are attracted to treasure, but whether in a lake, a cave, a shaft, or at the bottom of the sea, finding a fortune can carry a high price tag.
   B. Some people do find money and live happily ever after, but chances are strong that most of us will never even have the opportunity to hunt for treasure.
   C. Though it costs a lot to find buried or hidden riches, human greed has remained the same from the 1500s to the 1900s.
   D. If you are tempted to search for hidden fortunes, it is best not to go looking in lakes, caves, shafts, or shipwrecks.

8. What made Tom Gurr's search different from the other treasure hunts?
   A. He got to keep all the money.
   B. No treasure was found.
   C. No people were killed.
   D. The treasure was underwater.

   Give the numbers of the 3 sentences from paragraphs B, C, and D that best support the answer. _____, _____, _____

9. Based on the examples given, what generalization is the author trying to convey?
   A. Treasure hunting is a successful activity.
   B. Most buried treasure lies in the oceans.
   C. Seeking hidden treasure is not worth the effort.
   D. Treasure is always hidden intentionally.

10. Explain why the first statement is a fact but the second is an opinion.
    A. Some treasure hunts have ended in death. (fact)
    B. Treasure hunting is not worth the cost. (opinion)

    _____

    _____

    _____

    _____

    _____

    _____

    _____

literature excerpts___

1.   *The Cay* (Excerpt)
by Theodore Taylor

A [1]In twenty or thirty minutes, the wind picked up sharply and Timothy said that we must stand against the palm again. [2]Almost within seconds, the full fury of the storm hit the cay* once more. [3]Timothy pressed me tightly against the rough bark.

B [4]It was even worse this time, but I do not remember everything that happened. [5]We had been there awhile when a wave that must have reached halfway up the palms crashed against us. [6]The water went way over my head. [7]I choked and struggled. [8]Then another giant wave struck us. [9]I lost consciousness then. [10]Timothy did, too, I think.

C [11]When I came to, the wind had died down, coming at us only in gusts. [12]The water was still washing around our ankles, but seemed to be going back into the sea now. [13]Timothy was still behind me, but he felt cold and limp. [14]He was sagging, his head down on my shoulder.

D [15]"Timothy, wake up," I said.

E [16]He did not answer.

F [17]Using my shoulders, I tried to shake him, but the massive body did not move. [18]I stood very still to see if he was breathing. [19]I could feel his stomach moving and I reached over my shoulder to his mouth. [20]There was air coming out. [21]I knew that he was not dead.

G [22]However, Stew Cat was gone.

H [23]I worked for a few minutes to release my arms from the loops of rope around the palm trunk, and then slid out from under Timothy's body. [24]He slumped lifelessly against the palm. [25]I felt along the ropes that bound his forearms to the trunk until I found the knots.

I [26]With his weight against them, it was hard to pull them loose, even though they were sailor's knots and had loops in them. [27]The rope was soaked, which made it worse.

J [28]I must have worked for half an hour before I had him free from the trunk. [29]He fell backwards into the wet sand, and lay there moaning. [30]I knew there was very little I could do for him except to sit by him in the light rain, holding his hand. [31]In my world of darkness, I had learned that holding a hand could be like medicine.

*cay: a small, low island made largely of coral or sand

DIRECTIONS: Choose or write the best answer to each of the following questions using the evidence provided in the passage. When required, list specific sentence numbers or paragraph letters from the story to support the answer.

1. What natural disaster does the passage describe?
    A. a tornado
    B. a hurricane
    C. an avalanche
    D. an earthquake

    List the letters of the 2 paragraphs that best support your answer. ____, ____

2. The narrator proved that he was:
    A. resourceful.
    B. helpless.
    C. lucky.
    D. adventuresome.

3. Put the following events from the story in their proper time order.

    ____ Narrator unties Timothy.

    ____ Narrator stands against palm tree.

    ____ Narrator holds Timothy's hand.

    ____ Wind dies down.

    ____ Narrator unties himself.

    ____ Narrator regains consciousness.

4. Explain how the roles of the narrator and Timothy changed from the beginning of the passage to the end.

    _____

    _____

    _____

    _____

5. What caused the narrator and Timothy to faint?
    A. being tied to a tree
    B. being struck by waves
    C. being battered by wind
    D. being so close together

    Give the letter of the paragraph that best supports the answer. ____

6. Which of these does the narrator probably feel toward Timothy?
    A. anger
    B. jealousy
    C. indifference
    D. compassion

    Give the letter of the paragraph that best supports the answer. ____

7. Name two things that made it difficult for the narrator to untie the ropes around Timothy and himself.

    _____

    _____

    _____

    _____

    List the numbers of the 2 sentences that best support the answer. ____, ____

8. Explain the simile used in sentence 31.

    _____

    _____

    _____

2. *Sparrow Hawk Red* **(Excerpt)**
by Ben Mikaelsen

A [1]"Hey! Wait for me," he shouted.

B [2]She stopped and turned.

C [3]When he caught up, he glanced about, embarrassed to be seen with the grubby little girl. [4]But people passed them by on the street, hardly noticing. [5]Ricky saw his reflection in a store window and his embarrassment deepened. [6]He did not recognize himself. [7]Not until he smiled and made a funny face did the image look familiar. [8]He had not wanted to be recognized. [9]But this bothered him. [10]Here he felt invisible, like a piece of dirt on the street.

D [11]"Do you like good food?" Soledad asked. [12]She started out again.

E [13]"Of course," Ricky said, following. [14]"Why?"

F [15]She answered by angling across the street. [16]A large new car raced toward her, blaring its horn. [17]She walked slower, forcing the car to swerve abruptly. [18]A smug smile creased her lips. [19]As it passed she turned and stuck out her tongue.

G [20]Ahead the thrum of Spanish guitar floated from inside a fancy restaurant. [21]A trumpet sounded clear through the air. [22]Blinking lights surrounded a huge sign over the arched doorway. [23]Restaurante del Sol.

H [24]"We'll eat here," Soledad announced.

I [25]Ricky stared in disbelief as Soledad passed by the front door and continued around the side of the building to the back door. [26]She walked directly toward two garbage cans swarming with flies.

J [27]"You can have that one," she said, pointing to the fullest can.

K [28]Ricky stared at the can and at Soledad in numbed silence. [29]Already she had started burrowing through her can, stuffing chunks and bits into her mouth. [30]She glanced up briefly. [31]"Hurry," she exclaimed, "or he'll catch us!"

DIRECTIONS: Choose or write the best answer to each of the following questions using the evidence provided in the passage. When required, list specific sentence numbers or paragraph letters from the story to support the answer.

1. In paragraph C, what bothered Ricky?
   A. He wanted to go home.
   B. He was barely noticed.
   C. He was worried about the girl.
   D. He didn't like the attention.

   Give the number of the sentence that best supports the answer. _____

2. Which of the following statements can be made about Soledad?
   A. She is familiar with street life.
   B. She cares only for herself.
   C. She lives alone.
   D. She likes Spanish music.

   List the letters of the 3 paragraphs that best support the answer.
   _____, _____, _____

3. List the numbers of the three sentences that best support the idea that Soledad did not like the car racing towards her and honking. _____, _____, _____

4. Which of the following is NOT a key event of the passage?
   A. Ricky watches Soledad eat food from the garbage.
   B. Ricky is bothered by his appearance.
   C. Soledad leads Ricky to the restaurant.
   D. Ricky catches up to Soledad.

5. Write the sentence that uses a simile in paragraph C. Underline the simile.

   _____

   _____

   _____

6. Why was Ricky surprised when Soledad headed for the back of the restaurant?

   _____

   _____

   _____

   _____

   Give the number of the sentence that best supports the answer. _____

7. Compare Soledad's attitude about eating from the trash with Ricky's attitude.

   _____

   _____

   _____

   _____

   _____

8. Describe the Restaurante del Sol.

   _____

   _____

   _____

   _____

   _____

   _____

   List the letters of the 2 paragraphs that best support the answer. _____, _____

3. *El Güero* (Excerpt)
by Elizabeth Borton de Treviño

A ¹Some of the adobe bricks were already drying in the sun. ²There was a pit where the clay was thick and oozy, and this the Indians formed into bricks, with straw from the dry grasses. ³They had made frames of wood, into which they patted the mixture, and there the bricks took shape.

B ⁴"Ho! When it rains, they will all melt!" I cried.

C ⁵David, who had never spoken to me, said, "No. ⁶They will dry firm and strong. ⁷You will see. ⁸My people have known how to do this for many years."

D ⁹"Your people?" I asked. ¹⁰He was a white boy, like me. ¹¹Yet he pointed to the Indians and called them his people.

E ¹²"Yes, I lived with the Indians for a long time," he said, "and I know their language and their ways. ¹³I have an Indian name, too. ¹⁴El Coyote. ¹⁵That name was given me because I can run very fast."

F ¹⁶"Let's see how fast!" I challenged, and we had a good race down to the beach. ¹⁷He beat me easily.

G ¹⁸I told my parents about El Coyote.

H ¹⁹"Yes," Papa told me. ²⁰"Don David Zarate, the boy's father, told me the story. ²¹The child was kidnapped when he was an infant. ²²No, not kidnapped exactly, but taken away to the hills by his Indian nurse.

I ²³"It seems that Don David is a miner, frequently away looking for gold and silver in the hills, and then he tried to interest the Americans on the other side of the border to invest in his mines. ²⁴Once when he was gone to the north, his wife took sick and died, and the daughter, a girl of about sixteen, decided to go to San Diego and try to find him. ²⁵She left, probably on a boat with some fishermen going toward the north, and the Indian nurse,

finding herself alone with the boy, simply started out for the hills and her own people, taking the baby with her. ²⁶The child was brought up with the tribe.

J ²⁷"Somehow the girl located her father and he tried for six or seven years to find the nurse and his son. ²⁸But the tribes moved about, and never gave white men any information.

K ²⁹"At last he did the only thing he knew to do… ³⁰He offered gold for any information as to the whereabouts of the woman and the boy.

L ³¹"Eventually he found them. ³²The boy was afraid and reluctant, but the old Indian nurse brought him back, and remained with the family until she died, a year or so ago.

M ³³"The boy is an Indian in everything but looks and blood. ³⁴He must learn to be white."

N ³⁵"I will teach him!" cried Tia Vicky. ³⁶"And he can teach us. ³⁷We can learn much from him. ³⁸All of us."

O ³⁹That is how we three, Brazo Fuerte, El Coyote, and I, became companions, and best friends.

DIRECTIONS: Choose or write the best answer to each of the following questions using the evidence provided in the passage. When required, list specific sentence numbers or paragraph letters from the story to support the answer.

1. What does Don David's search for his son suggest about his character? He was:
   A. an indifferent father.
   B. a cruel man.
   C. a good provider.
   D. a determined man.

2. What did Papa mean when he said David "must learn to be white"?
   A. He must learn to live among his own people.
   B. He must change his skin color.
   C. He must learn how to cook.
   D. He must learn to speak his family's language.

3. What does the reference to David's *blood* mean in sentence 33?

   _____

   _____

4. Why was David afraid to go with his father?

   _____

   _____

   _____

   List the numbers of the 3 sentences that best support the answer. ____, ____,

   ____

5. Why was the narrator surprised when David called the Indians *his* people?

   _____

   _____

   Give the number of the sentence that best supports the answer. ____

6. Where does most of the story take place?
   A. San Diego
   B. Mexico
   C. Spain
   D. Canada

   List the numbers of the 2 sentences that best support the answer. ____,

   ____

7. Why did it take Don David so long to find his son?

   _____

   _____

   _____

   Give the number of the sentence that best supports the answer. ____

8. Which of the following is a good summary of young David's (El Coyote's) history?
   A. When his mother died, his father went to look for gold, and the Indian nurse took him to live with her tribe.
   B. While his father was gone, his mother and sister died, but the Indian nurse stayed until his father returned.
   C. While his father was gone, his mother died. His sister left to find his father, and the Indian nurse took him to live with her tribe.
   D. While his father was gone, the Indian nurse took the boy to live with her tribe. Then his mother died.

4. *The Moon by Night* **(Excerpt)**
by Madeleine L'Engle

A ¹It was a most peculiar feeling. ²The solid ground under my feet gave a shudder. ³I stood still. ⁴It kept on feeling as though the ground were shivering. ⁵Then suddenly there was a jerk under me. ⁶It was something like when you go water skiing and someone cuts the motor and then suddenly speeds up again, trying to throw you.

B ⁷The next jerk did throw me. ⁸It was a much bigger jerk, and I fell flat on my face in the soft grass of the field. ⁹Underneath me the ground seemed to heave the way your stomach does when you're terribly, terribly sick. ¹⁰I clung to the grass because there wasn't anything else to cling to. ¹¹It was as though the whole Earth, the whole planet, were jerking out in space, veering wildly out of course, and I was on its back clinging to its mane.

C ¹²Behind me there was terrible noise. ¹³It was louder than thunder and it seemed to keep on and on until I thought my head would burst. ¹⁴Then the noise began to break into separate parts, a sound like thunder, a roar like the ocean in a storm, great crackings, crunchings, and finally all the noises got smaller and with spaces of quiet in between, and then they stopped. ¹⁵The silence was so complete that it was as frightening as the noise had been. ¹⁶I managed to turn my head, and the top of the mountain wasn't there any more. ¹⁷It didn't seem to be anywhere.

D ¹⁸Then I remembered the town of Frank in Alberta, the mountain that had fallen on the town. ¹⁹I pressed my face into the grass of the field, and, as the earth heaved beneath me, I thought I was going to throw up, too, from terror. ²⁰But I didn't.

E ²¹I looked around again. ²²The top of the mountain was still gone. ²³Everything looked different. ²⁴I realized that most of the mountain had fallen into the field, because the mountain was much closer to me and the field was much narrower than it had been before.

F ²⁵I lay there, clutching the grass, not daring or even able to move, even if the rest of the mountain should fall on me. ²⁶But after a while I realized that the tremors were less violent, that Earth was becoming quiet again. ²⁷I staggered to my feet. ²⁸The ground seemed quite solid beneath them. ²⁹I looked for Zachary. ³⁰The pile of rock was still there, but it was a different shaped pile. ³¹I didn't see Zachary.

DIRECTIONS: Choose or write the best answer to each of the following questions using the evidence provided in the passage. When required, list specific sentence numbers or paragraph letters from the story to support the answer.

1. What probably caused the shivering mentioned in paragraph A?

   _____

   _____

   _____

2. Fill in the following blanks to describe the metaphor used in sentence 11.

Metaphor		Represents
_____	:	the planet
The mane	:	_____

3. Explain what two things are being compared in the analogy given in sentence 6.

   _____

   _____

   _____

4. The narrative form of the passage could best be classified as:
   A. humorous.
   B. tragic.
   C. suspenseful.
   D. fantastic.

5. In paragraph E, the words "the mountain was much closer to me" mean that:
   A. she had moved towards the mountain.
   B. the mountain had literally moved towards her.
   C. she was speaking figuratively.
   D. the field had risen into a mountain.

6. Based on paragraph F, where is Zachary most likely to be found?

   _____

   _____

   _____

   Give the numbers of the 2 sentences that best support the answer. ____, ____

7. Which of the following most likely describes the narrator's point of view?
   A. The earth is a monster she must tame.
   B. The earth is a partner; she is at ease with it.
   C. She is vulnerable to the earth's terrifying forces.
   D. She is not affected by the natural forces of the earth.

8. Number the following events in the order of the narrator's experience.

   ____ Looked for Zachary.

   ____ Heard loud noises.

   ____ Felt like vomiting.

   ____ Clung to the grass.

   ____ Saw the mountain was closer.

9. How does the narrator compare herself to Earth in paragraph D?

   _____

   _____

   _____

5. *The Giver* (Excerpt)
by Lois Lowry

A [1]"But I want them!" Jonas said angrily. [2]"It isn't fair that nothing has color!"

B [3]"Not fair?" [4]The Giver looked at Jonas curiously. [5]"Explain what you mean."

C [6]"Well..." Jonas had to stop and think it through. [7]"If everything's the same, then there aren't any choices! [8]I want to wake up in the morning and *decide* things! [9]A blue tunic, or a red one?"

D [10]He looked down at himself, at the colorless fabric of his clothing. [11]"But it's all the same, always."

E [12]Then he laughed a little. [13]"I know it's not important, what you wear. [14]It doesn't matter. [15]But—"

F [16]"It's the choosing that's important, isn't it?" The Giver asked him.

G [17]Jonas nodded. [18]"My little brother—" he began, and then corrected himself. [19]"No, that's inaccurate. [20]He's not my brother, not really. [21]But this new child that my family takes care of—his name's Gabriel."

H [22]"Yes, I know about Gabriel."

I [23]"Well, he's right at the age where he's learning so much. [24]He grabs toys when we hold them in front of him—my father says he's learning small-muscle control. [25]And he's really cute."

J [26]The Giver nodded.

K [27]"But now that I can see colors, at least sometimes, I was just thinking: what if we could hold up things that were bright red, or bright yellow, and he could *choose?* [28]Instead of the Sameness."

L [29]"He might make wrong choices."

M [30]"Oh." [31]Jonas was silent for a minute. [31]"Oh, I see what you mean. [33]It wouldn't matter for a new child's toy. [34]But later it does matter, doesn't it? [35]We don't dare to let people make choices of their own."

N [36]"Not safe?" The Giver suggested.

O [37]"Definitely not safe," Jonas said with certainty. [38]"What if they were allowed to choose their own mate? [39]And chose *wrong?*

P [40]"Or what if," he went on, almost laughing at the absurdity, "they chose their own *jobs?*"

Q [41]"Frightening, isn't it?" The Giver said.

R [42]Jonas chuckled. [43]"Very frightening. [44]I can't even imagine it. [45]We really have to protect people from wrong choices."

S [46]"It's safer."

T [47]"Yes," Jonas agreed. [48]"Much safer."

U [48]But when the conversation turned to other things, Jonas was left, still, with a feeling of frustration that he didn't understand.

DIRECTIONS: Choose or write the best answer to each of the following questions using the evidence provided in the passage. When required, list specific sentence numbers or paragraph letters from the story to support the answer.

1. What is the Sameness?

   _____

   _____

   List the letters of the 2 paragraphs that best support the answer. ____, ____

2. The Giver's role in this dialogue seems to be to:
   A. lecture Jonas about what is correct.
   B. advise Jonas on what he should do.
   C. listen to Jonas and question him.
   D. argue with Jonas.

3. What could be the result of people's making their own choices?

   _____

   _____

   _____

   Give the number of the sentence that best supports the answer. ____

4. You can infer that in Jonas's world:
   A. decisions are made for you.
   B. people make their own choices.
   C. people are allowed to vote.
   D. decisions are made by The Giver.

   List the letters of the 2 paragraphs that best support the answer. ____, ____

5. In sentence 40, what does the word *absurdity* most nearly mean?
   A. seriousness
   B. sadness
   C. silliness
   D. emptiness

6. Why is Jonas still frustrated at the end of the passage?

   _____

   _____

   _____

   _____

   Give the letter of the paragraph that best supports the answer. ____

7. Based on the passage, you could say that Jonas
   A. accepted his life without question.
   B. was questioning his society's rules.
   C. was ready to change his life completely.
   D. wanted The Giver to tell him what to do.

8. What is the primary conflict for Jonas?

   _____

   _____

   _____

   List the letters of the 2 paragraphs that best support the answer. ____, ____

9. What is the theme of the passage?
   A. Life is full of choices.
   B. Learning to think for yourself involves difficult choices.
   C. People need to make their own choices in life.
   D. Life is not always fair.

6. *Under the Blood-Red Sun* (Excerpt)
by Graham Salisbury

A [1]"I guess it's true that the government of Japan doesn't like us at the moment," Mr. Ramos said. [2]"But the real reason—the reason at the bottom of all the wars in the history of human life—is power. [3]It's like a drug. [4]Some men can't get enough of it. [5]They want your power and my power and everyone else's power. [6]They want it all for themselves. [7]Adolf Hitler, who started this thing, is one of those men."

B [8]I didn't understand. [9]What power?

C [10]Mr. Ramos looked us over a moment, then asked Rico, "If you wanted to get into someone else's class because you thought I was a lousy teacher...could you?"

D [11]"I guess so," Rico said, shrugging.

E [12]"You could. [13]You and your mom and dad could talk to the principal and get him to put you in Mrs. Collet's class, or Mrs. Elbert's class. [14]That's power. [15]Power to make a decision about yourself, then make a change if you want to. [16]If you wanted to read a book about Tarzan instead of reading your science book, could you?"

F [17]Rico smirked. [18]"Sure...I do it all the time."

G [19]Everyone laughed.

H [20]"That's power too," Mr. Ramos said passionately, reaching out his open hand and closing it into a fist. [21]"There are all kinds of small things that we never think about that give us a little power... and all those little powers add up to a pretty good amount."

I [22]"Yeah," Mose added. [23]"Like we could do whatever we want after school, even

forget about our homework, if we wanted to."

J [24]"That's right, Mose," Mr. Ramos said. [25]"And if you wanted, you could even do *more* homework, so you could go to college, and get a job that you like, one that you choose for yourself. [26]But think about this: What would it feel like if you *couldn't* do anything you wanted after school? [27]What if you were forced to keep your mouth shut and work in the cannery from the minute you got out of here until ten o'clock at night? [28]Even if you didn't want to?"

K [29]"I'd hate that."

L [30]"So would I," said Mr. Ramos. [31]"Not because of the work, but because it wasn't my *choice* to do that work. [32]So...what is power?"

M [33]There was another long period of silence.

N [34]"Freedom to make our own choices," Billy finally said.

DIRECTIONS: Choose or write the best answer to each of the following questions using the evidence provided in the passage. When required, list specific sentence numbers or paragraph letters from the story to support the answer.

1. What is the theme of the passage?
   A. Power is the reason people fight wars.
   B. Power is a quality admired in world leaders.
   C. Power is the ability to read whatever you want.
   D. Power is the freedom to make your own choices.

   Give the number of the sentence that best supports the answer. _____

2. What actual situation triggers the class discussion?
   A. a war
   B. a movie
   C. an argument
   D. an assignment

   List the numbers of the 3 sentences that best support the answer. _____, _____,

   _____

3. Describe what Mr. Ramos's relationship is to the other characters.

   _____

   _____

   _____

   Give the letter of the paragraph that best supports the answer. _____

4. Who is the narrator?

   _____

   _____

   Give the number of the sentence that best supports the answer. _____

5. Explain the difference between the two situations Mr. Ramos mentions in Paragraph J.

   _____

   _____

   _____

   _____

   _____

   _____

6. Name the two things being compared by the analogy in paragraph A.

   _____

   _____

   List the numbers of the 3 sentences that best support your answer.

   _____, _____, _____

7. Is sentence 21 a fact or an opinion? Explain the answer.

   _____

   _____

   _____

8. In sentence 20, Mr. Ramos reaches out his open hand and closes it into a fist. What does this gesture symbolize?

   _____

   _____

   _____

7. *The View From Saturday* (Excerpt) by E. L. Konigsburg

A [1]This first summer of their separation, Dad chose August for his visitation rights. [2]He picked us up early Friday evening. [3]Us means Ginger and me. [4]Ginger is my dog. [5]I do not know who was happier to see me at the airport—Dad or Ginger. [6]The worst part of the trip had been checking Ginger into the baggage compartment.

B [7]Dad always was a nervous person, but since the divorce he had become terminally so. [8]He was having a difficult time adjusting to being alone. [9]He had sold the house that we lived in when we were a family and had moved into a swinging* singles apartment complex, but my father could no more swing than a gate on rusty hinges.

C [10]For the first day and a half after I arrived, Dad hovered over me like the Goodyear blimp over the Orange Bowl. [11]He did not enjoy the hovering, and I did not enjoy being hovered, but he did not know what to do with me, and I did not know what to tell him, except to tell him to stop hovering, which seemed to be the only thing he knew how to do.

D [12]On Sunday, we went to see Grandpa Izzy and Margaret.

E [13]Grandpa Izzy was happy to see me. [14]Under those bushy eyebrows of his, Grandpa Izzy's eyes are bright blue like the sudden underside of a bird wing. [15]His eyes have always been the most alive part of him, but when Bubbe Frieda died, they seemed to die, too. [16]Since he married Margaret, though, they seem bright enough to give off light of their own. [17]He is sixty-nine years old, and he is in love.

*swinging: to be lively, trendy, exciting

DIRECTIONS: Choose or write the best answer to each of the following questions using the evidence provided in the passage. When required, list specific sentence numbers or paragraph letters from the story to support the answer.

1. What do you think the narrator means in sentence 9 when she says her dad can't swing?
   A. He is not a very good dancer.
   B. He is not good at home repairs.
   C. He has gotten too old.
   D. He doesn't fit the single life.

2. In sentence 10, what does the word *hovered* mean?
   A. flew past
   B. remained near
   C. disappeared
   D. lectured

3. In paragraph C, what is the main conflict between the narrator and her dad?
   A. They don't know what to do with each other.
   B. They are constantly fighting and arguing with each other.
   C. She doesn't want to visit him.
   D. They both like to talk a lot.

4. From paragraph E, you can infer that Grandpa Izzy's eyes
   A. see very poorly.
   B. look empty.
   C. reveal his feelings.
   D. are dark brown.

   List the numbers of the 2 sentences that best support the answer. _____, _____

5. From paragraph A, you can guess that the narrator lives with:

   _____

   Give the number of the sentence that best supports the answer. _____

6. In sentence 7, what does the narrator mean when she describes her dad as "terminally nervous?"

   _____

   _____

   _____

   _____

   _____

7. What has brightened Grandpa's eyes again?

   _____

   _____

   Give the number of the sentence that best supports the answer. _____

8. How would you describe the narrator's attitude towards her dad?
   A. adoring
   B. fearful
   C. annoyed
   D. scornful

8. *The Trolley to Yesterday* (Excerpt) by John Bellairs

[1]In single file they began to pick their way down the long, dark, echoing tunnel. [2]Brewster's bobbing pink light led the way, casting a faint pinkish sheen on the ancient barrel-vaulted ceiling and the mossy stones underfoot. [3]Now and then something would crunch under Johnny's foot, and he would look down and see that he had crushed the skeleton of a long-dead rat. [4]In one place the stones of the ceiling had fallen, and they had to wade through greenish stagnant water and pick their way over muddy granite blocks. [5]Finally, after what seemed like ages, they passed through a low arched doorway and found that they were standing at the bottom of a tall, circular stone shaft. [6]This was the dry well that Brewster had spoken of earlier. [7]They had reached the end of their underground journey. [8]Stone steps wedged into the wall spiraled toward the sky, and they climbed slowly. [9]Johnny was terrified. [10]If he missed his footing, he would go hurtling down the well shaft, and that would be the end of him. [11]But he knew that this was the only way out, and so he plodded doggedly on, with the professor in front of him and Fergie behind. [12]Finally, one by one, they clambered up over the worn lip of the well and stumbled out into a dark, rustling forest. [13]The professor wanted to search for Mr. Townsend, but he had not brought a compass with him, and there was no point in wandering aimlessly in the dark. [14]Besides, he was dead tired, and so were the others. [15]After a quick look around the professor threw himself down on the grass near the well, and the boys lay down near him. [16]In a very few seconds all three were asleep.

DIRECTIONS: Choose or write the best answer to each of the following questions using the evidence provided in the passage. When required, list specific sentence numbers or paragraph letters from the story to support the answer.

1. Which of these is a true statement about the tunnel?
   A. It is full of water.
   B. It is underground.
   C. It ends outside a forest.
   D. It is too small to walk through.

   Give the number of the sentence that best supports the answer. _____

2. What time of day is it at the end of the passage?
   A. morning
   B. noon
   C. afternoon
   D. evening

   List the numbers of the 2 sentences that best support the answer. _____, _____

3. What is the tunnel ceiling made of?
   A. dirt
   B. moss
   C. wood
   D. stone

   Give the number of the sentence that best supports the answer. _____

4. Which of these words is closest in meaning to *doggedly*, as used in sentence 11?
   A. easily
   B. stubbornly
   C. suddenly
   D. excitedly

5. What might cause Johnny to slip and fall while walking in the tunnel?

   _____

   _____

   _____

   _____

   Give the number of the sentence that best supports the answer. _____

6. Which of these is NOT a key event of the plot?
   A. They arrive in the forest.
   B. They walk through a tunnel.
   C. They climb up the well shaft.
   D. They wade through some water.

7. In sentence 9, why was Johnny terrified?

   _____

   _____

   _____

   _____

   Give the number of the sentence that best supports the answer. _____

8. Describe the change in mood from the beginning of the passage to the end.

   _____

   _____

   _____

   _____

9. **"How the Rhinoceros Got His Skin"**
   From *Just So Stories* (Excerpt)
   by Rudyard Kipling

A ¹The rhinoceros took off his skin and carried it over his shoulder as he came down to the beach to bathe. ²In those days it buttoned underneath with three buttons and looked like a waterproof.* ³He said nothing whatever about the Parsee's cake, because he had eaten it all; and he never had any manners, then, since, or henceforward. ⁴He waddled straight into the water and blew bubbles through his nose, leaving his skin on the beach.

B ⁵Presently the Parsee came by and found the skin, and he smiled one smile that ran all round his face two times. ⁶Then he danced three times round the skin and rubbed his hands. ⁷Then he went to his camp and filled his hat with cake-crumbs, for the Parsee never ate anything but cake, and never swept out his camp. ⁸He took that skin and he shook that skin, and he scrubbed that skin, and he rubbed that skin just as full of old, dry, stale, tickly cake-crumbs and some burned currants as ever it could *possibly* hold. ⁹Then he climbed to the top of his palm tree and waited for the rhinoceros to come out of the water and put it on.

C ¹⁰And the rhinoceros did. ¹¹He buttoned it up with the three buttons, and it tickled like cake-crumbs in bed. ¹²Then he wanted to scratch, but that made it worse; and then he lay down on the sands and rolled and rolled and rolled, and every time he rolled the cake-crumbs tickled him worse and worse and worse. ¹³Then he ran to the palm tree and rubbed and rubbed and rubbed himself against it. ¹⁴He rubbed so much and so hard that he rubbed his skin into a great fold over his shoulders, and another fold underneath, where the buttons used to be (but he rubbed the buttons off), and he rubbed some more folds over his legs. ¹⁵And it spoiled his temper, but it didn't make the least difference to the cake-crumbs. ¹⁶They were inside his skin and they tickled. ¹⁷So he went home, very angry indeed and horribly scratchy; and from that day to this every rhinoceros has great folds in his skin and a very bad temper, all on account of the cake-crumbs inside.

*waterproof: British word for raincoat

DIRECTIONS: Choose or write the best answer to each of the following questions using the evidence provided in the passage. When required, list specific sentence numbers or paragraph letters from the story to support the answer.

1. Which of the following is a form of literature that *best* describes the passage?
   A. science fiction
   B. fantasy
   C. biography
   D. nonfiction

2. Why did the Parsee put cake-crumbs in the rhinoceros's skin?

   _____

   _____

   _____

   Give the number of the sentence that best supports the example. ____

3. Which of these key events is NOT described in detail?
   A. the rhinoceros's taking off of his skin
   B. the rhinoceros's eating of the Parsee's cake
   C. the Parsee's putting cake-crumbs into the rhinoceros's skin
   D. the Parsee's finding of the rhinoceros's skin

4. Give two reasons why cake-crumbs were available for the Parsee to put in the rhinoceros's skin.

   _____

   _____

   _____

   _____

   Give the number of the sentence that best supports the answer. ____

5. Name one thing about the rhinoceros that changed in the story and describe the change.

   _____

   _____

   _____

   Give the number of the sentence that best supports the answer. ____

6. Which of these facts about rhinoceroses in general is NOT listed in the story?
   A. They have a single horn.
   B. They have bad tempers.
   C. They have great folds in their skin.
   D. They can blow bubbles through their nose.

7. Put the following events in the order in which they occurred in the passage.

   ____   rhinoceros takes off his skin.

   ____   Parsee puts cake-crumbs in rhinoceros's skin.

   ____   rhinoceros rubs against tree.

   ____   rhinoceros rolls in sand.

   ____   Parsee climbs to top of palm tree.

8. Which of these would be a good moral for the story?
   A. One good turn deserves another.
   B. Don't count your chickens till they're hatched.
   C. You get what you pay for.
   D. The punishment can be worse than the crime.

10. *Face to Face* (Excerpt)
by Marion Dane Bauer

A [1]In the mirror world, there was his bed, looking like a rumpled nest slept in by some stranger. [2]Also, his 4-H trophy and the ribbons, all of them won by his red Guernsey, Rilda. [3]They looked shinier, more brightly colored on the other side. [4]Even the reversed titles of the books on his shelf were mysterious and alluring, as if in that reflected world he might read them all again and find their stories new.

B [5]But most inviting of all was the place where the mirror image stopped, the unseen room beyond. [6]When he was younger he had believed, quite literally, that there was something hidden there, just beyond the inspection of his eye. [7]Something that didn't exist at all in the world he knew.

C [8]It was where he used to imagine his father had gone and was waiting to be found.

D [9]When Michael was told in science class that nothing was solid, that the entire world was composed of moving atoms, he had come home and tried to reach through the mirror with his hand. [10]He had thought that if he closed his eyes so that he wasn't aware of the non-solid atoms of his hand coming into contact with those of the mirror, he could find his way into that other world...like Alice.

E [11]He didn't care for the Alice stories, really. [12]Never had. [13]Reading them was like being caught in someone else's nightmare. [14]And he was too much of a farm boy to be fascinated by rabbit holes. [15]Rabbit holes held rabbits. [16]Nothing more.

F [17]But mirrors. [18]Mirrors were something else entirely.

DIRECTIONS: Choose or write the best answer to each of the following questions using the evidence provided in the passage. When required, list specific sentence numbers or paragraph letters from the story to support the answer.

1. In sentence 4, the word *alluring* means:
   A. unusual.
   B. shiny.
   C. dirty.
   D. attractive.

2. Based on paragraph A, his room in the mirror world seemed:
   A. different.
   B. frightening.
   C. annoying.
   D. drab.

   List the numbers of the 2 sentences that best support the answer. ____, ____

3. Why did Michael think he could reach through the mirror in his room?

   _____

   _____

   _____

   _____

   List the numbers of the 2 sentences that best support the answer. ____, ____

4. From paragraph E, the conclusion can be made that a farm boy is:
   A. independent.
   B. practical.
   C. silly.
   D. unrealistic.

5. The mood of the passage is:
   A. lighthearted.
   B. sad.
   C. angry.
   D. thoughtful.

6. In sentence 8, what can be inferred about Michael and his father?

   _____

   _____

   _____

7. In paragraph A, how did the images in the mirror differ from the real objects?

   _____

   _____

   _____

   _____

   _____

   List the numbers of the 2 sentences that best support the answer. ____, ____

8. When Michael was younger, the hidden place where the mirror image stopped had symbolized:
   A. his desire for a place to play.
   B. his fear of small spaces.
   C. his desire to see his father.
   D. his need for a place to hide.

   Give the letter of the paragraph that best supports the answer. ____

11. *The Bronze Bow* (Excerpt)
by Elizabeth George Speare

A [1]A boy stood on the path of the mountain overlooking the sea. [2]He was a tall boy, with little trace of youth in his lean, hard body. [3]At eighteen Daniel bar Jamin was unmistakably a Galilean, with the bold features of his countrymen, the sun-browned skin, and the brilliant dark eyes that could light with fierce patriotism and blacken with swift anger. [4]A proud race, the Galileans, violent and restless, unreconciled that Palestine was a conquered nation, refusing to acknowledge as their lord the Emperor Tiberius in far-off Rome.

B [5]Looking down into the valley, the boy could see the silver-gray terraces of olive trees splashed with burgeoning thickets of oleander. [6]He remembered that in the brown, mud-roofed town every clump of earth and every cranny in a stone wall would have burst into springtime flower. [7]Remembering, he scowled up against the hot noonday sun.

C [8]He was waiting for two figures to reappear among the boulders that tumbled on either side of the path just above him. [9]He was puzzled and uneasy, at odds with himself. [10]Who were these two who had been so foolhardy as to climb the mountain? [11]He was resentful that they had reminded him of the village, fearful that they might look back and discover him, yet unwilling to let them out of his sight. [12]Why was he so bent on following them, when all he wanted for five years was to forget that other world in the valley?

DIRECTIONS: Choose or write the best answer to each of the following questions using the evidence provided in the passage. When required, list specific sentence numbers or paragraph letters from the story to support the answer.

1. Which of the following best describes the setting?
   A. the valley
   B. a mountain path
   C. Rome
   D. another world

2. Which of these words best describes how Daniel is feeling?
   A. misunderstood
   B. fearless
   C. anxious
   D. forgetful

   Give the number of the sentence that best supports the answer. ____

3. Based on the information in paragraph A, which of the following can be said about Daniel?
   A. Daniel is no longer a boy.
   B. Daniel can be a fierce patriot.
   C. Daniel is angry.
   D. Daniel's people are unsettled.

   List the numbers of the 2 sentences that best support the answer. ____, ____

4. Based on the author's description of Daniel, what prediction can be made about how he might react to the two strangers if he is seen?
   A. He will stand his ground and confront them.
   B. He will cower and hope they do not harm him.
   C. He will ignore them.
   D. He will ask them about the people in the village.

5. The word *unreconciled* in sentence 4 means:
   A. unaccepting.
   B. disagreeing.
   C. unaware.
   D. recalling.

6. What is the author trying to convey about the history of Daniel's people?
   A. His people have been living in peace for the last five years.
   B. His people were once violent and restless.
   C. His people have been conquered by the Emperor Tiberius.
   D. His people are at war with Rome.

   Give the number of the sentence that best supports the answer. ____

7. During what season does the story take place?

   _____

   Give the number of the sentence that best supports the answer. ____

8. What inner conflict is Daniel dealing with in paragraph C?

   _____

   _____

   _____

   _____

   Give the number of the sentence that best supports your answer. ____

fiction _____

12. Head Chef at 14
by David White

A [1]"Rajiv, is the stove vent on?"

B [2]"Everything's under control, Mother. [3]You don't need to come in."

C [4]He appreciated his Indian heritage, but he wanted to cook American food. [5]He was 14 and had convinced his parents that he was old enough to cook the family dinner on his own. [6]They had agreed, on one condition—that he let his brother help. [7]Sanjay was 7. [8]Rajiv, groaning, had agreed.

D [9]"I'll make the dessert, and you cook the rest," his mother had said. [10]She had made apple pie. [11]She said she was ready to turn over the kitchen to her sons and eager to try their cooking.

E [12]His father was more direct: "I reserve the right to order pizza."

F [13]After checking the pork chops for the second time in the last minute, Rajiv turned to the potatoes. [14]He had forgotten to peel them before he sliced and boiled them, but most of the peels had come off anyway. [15]Carefully gripping the hot pot with pot holders, he dumped the contents into a colander in the sink. [16]"Sanjay , you're my helper, right? [17]Get the cheese ready."

G [18]Rajiv was following his mother's recipe, which called for the potatoes to be peeled, boiled, and then baked. [19]That way, you didn't have to bake them so long.

H [20]"OK, Sanjay , pour half of that bag of cheese over these potatoes I just put in the baking pan. [21]I'll check on the pork chops."

I [22]Sanjay was putting the empty bag in the trash when Rajiv turned back around.

J [23]"Where's the other half of the cheese?"

Pork Chops and Applesauce

Scalloped Potatoes with Cheese

Broccoli-Cauliflower Medley

Country Biscuits with Honey Butter

Apple Pie

K [24]"What other half?"

L [25]Rajiv hurriedly scooped as much cheese as he could out of the pan and back into the bag. [26]He opened the oven, put the potatoes in, and took out the broccoli-cauliflower medley. [27]He put that pan on the counter and put the saucepan with the butter sauce next to it. [28]It was time to take the biscuits out. [29]"Sanjay, pour that butter sauce over the vegetables."

M [30]Twenty minutes later, dinner was served.

N [31]"Rajiv, this meat is tender," his father said. [32]Rajiv beamed. [33]"And the potatoes are really cheesy." [34]Sanjay grinned.

O [35]"What kind of sauce did you put on the vegetables?" their mother wanted to know. [36]"It tastes sort of like honey."

P [37]Rajiv looked at Sanjay in surprise. [38]"I did what you told me to do," Sanjay said.

Q [39]"Rajiv, where's the honey butter for the biscuits?"

DIRECTIONS: Choose or write the best answer to each of the following questions using the evidence presented in the passage. When required, list specific sentence numbers or paragraph letters from the story to support the answer.

1. To be allowed to cook, what was the one thing that Rajiv *had* to do?

   _____

   _____

   _____

   Give the number of the sentence that best supports the answer. _____

2. How many times does Rajiv check the pork chops?
   A. one
   B. two
   C. three
   D. four

   List the numbers of the 2 sentences that best support the answer. _____, _____

3. What likely happened to the honey butter?

   _____

   _____

   _____

   _____

   List the letters of the 2 paragraphs that best support the answer. _____, _____

4. Put these steps in their proper order.

   _____ Bake potatoes

   _____ Boil potatoes

   _____ Put cheese on top of potatoes

   _____ Peel potatoes

5. Compare how Rajiv's parents viewed his cooking. His mother was eager to try it; his father was:

   _____

   _____

   _____

   Give the number of the sentence that best supports the answer. _____

6. Which of these statements can be made about Rajiv's mother?
   A. She is proud.
   B. She is trusting.
   C. She likes to cook.
   D. She likes dessert.

   Explain the answer.

   _____

   _____

   _____

   _____

7. In general, it can be said that Sanjay:
   A. likes to cook.
   B. likes his brother.
   C. doesn't follow directions well.
   D. doesn't know how to make apple pie.

   Explain the answer.

   _____

   _____

   _____

   _____

13. Love From Camp Gitchigoomi
by Cheryl Block

July 10, 1968

Dear Mom and Dad,

A ¹Life here at Camp Gitchigoomi is great! ²It's never boring; we're always on the go.

B ³We went hiking Monday. ⁴It was wonderful! ⁵I saw squirrels and deer. ⁶I got only a little bit of poison oak on my legs. ⁷It took awhile to get rid of the smell—my cabin mates and I had to eat and sleep outside. ⁸But I didn't know you shouldn't pet that cute little black and white animal.

C ⁹We had our Opening Campfire last night. ¹⁰We sang camp songs, did skits, and toasted marshmallows. ¹¹I accidentally got melted marshmallow in Jan Fujito's hair when I turned around to talk to Carlos. ¹²The counselors put the marshmallow out before her hair caught fire, and they just had to cut her hair a little to get out the melted marshmallow.

D ¹³The lake is beautiful, too. ¹⁴We went canoeing today, and it was really fun. ¹⁵Chad and I got our paddles stuck together. ¹⁶While we were trying to separate them, I pulled too hard on my paddle and hit Chad in the head. ¹⁷When I leaned over to help him, the canoes tipped over, and Chad and I fell in. ¹⁸It wouldn't have been a problem if Chad hadn't been unconscious. ¹⁹But the counselor got to him in plenty of time, and once they gave him mouth to mouth resuscitation, he was fine. ²⁰He was just a little waterlogged, although he did lose his glasses. ²¹I didn't need mouth

to mouth, but I was going to ask Mary Jensen to try it just in case. ²²However, I threw up on her while they were taking me to the infirmary. ²³I hope she won't hold it against me; she's awesome!

E ²⁴Tomorrow we go on an overnight hike. ²⁵We'll sleep under the stars and cook over a campfire. ²⁶I can't wait! ²⁷Everything we do is fun and exciting.

F ²⁸And guess what? ²⁹I think Mr. Purdy, the camp director, is impressed with my camping skills. ³⁰He says he's personally going to write to you. ³¹He says they've never had a camper like me!

Love,
Arthur

DIRECTIONS: Choose or write the best answer to each of the following questions using the evidence presented in the passage. When required, list specific sentence numbers or paragraph letters from the story to support the answer.

1. How does Arthur's point of view compare with the actual events?

   _____

   _____

   _____

   _____

2. In paragraph B, what kind of animal did Arthur try to pet?

   _____

   List the numbers of the 2 sentences that best support the answer. ____, ____

3. What caused the canoes to tip over?

   _____

   _____

   _____

   Give the number of the sentence that best supports the answer. ____

4. Based on events mentioned in the letter, what prediction can be made about what might happen at the cookout?

   _____

   _____

   _____

   List the letters of the 3 paragraphs that best support the answer.

   ____, ____, ____

5. Arthur could be characterized as:
   A. angry.
   B. unhappy.
   C. positive.
   D. disinterested.

   List the letters of the 2 paragraphs that best support the answer. ____, ____

6. Why is it important to Arthur that Mary not be mad at him?

   _____

   _____

   _____

   Give the number of the sentence that best supports the answer. ____

7. In sentence 2, what does "on the go" mean?

   _____

   _____

   _____

   _____

8. What is the best explanation for Mr. Purdy's writing to Arthur's parents?
   A. He writes to all the campers' parents.
   B. He wants them to know how much he likes Arthur.
   C. He wants them to know the problems Arthur is causing.
   D. He is going to ask if Arthur can stay an extra week.

   Give the letter of the paragraph that best supports the answer. ____

14. Race for Pepper
by Cheryl Block

A [1]Since the accident almost a year ago, Pepper had become her constant companion and confidant. [2]She shared her deepest feelings with him. [3]When Janelle felt down, Pepper was there to cheer her up, or just listen. [4]He seemed to sense Janelle's every need. [5]He could carry her pack and watch for traffic. [6]He could pick up things for Janelle when she dropped them. [7]Every night, Pepper slept at the foot of Janelle's bed, right beside the wheelchair.

B [8]Now Pepper needed *her*. [9]Janelle's mom first noticed Pepper's limp. [10]The vet said it was caused by hip dysplasia. [11]The cartilage in Pepper's hip had worn away. [12]She said Pepper was probably in constant pain when he walked, but Pepper never showed it. [13]The vet told them that the only solution for Pepper was a hip replacement. [14]But the surgery cost two thousand dollars, and Janelle's parents were still trying to pay off her medical bills. [15]It was up to Janelle to help Pepper.

C [16]She'd been giving it a lot of thought, and she had an idea. [17]The annual city fun run was coming up in a few weeks. [18]Janelle knew that runners collected donations based on how many miles they ran, and then donated the money to their favorite charity. [19]Janelle thought she could do the same thing, collecting the money for Pepper's surgery. [20]But would people want to donate money to a dog? [21]And would the city let her "run" the race in her wheelchair?

D [22]Janelle was determined to help Pepper any way she could. [23]She contacted City Hall and got permission to participate in the race. [24]She would have to start after the runners so she wouldn't create an obstacle. [25]That was fine. [26]Her goal was simply to finish the race, not win it. [27]She then started collecting the names of people who would sponsor her. [28]Every day after school, Janelle and Pepper would go from house to house in the neighborhood, asking people to sign up. [29]Not everyone was supportive, but most people were willing to pledge something.

E [30]Her friends at school found out about her cause and offered to help line up sponsors. [31]A local TV station interviewed her and put her story on the evening news. [32]Soon she had enough sponsors to pay for Pepper's operation!

F [33]On the day of the race, Janelle headed for the starting line, Pepper by her side. [34]Pepper couldn't run the race with her, but Janelle knew she'd finish—for Pepper's sake.

DIRECTIONS: Choose or write the best answer to each of the following questions using the evidence presented in the passage. When required, list specific sentence numbers or paragraph letters from the story to support the answer.

1. It can be inferred that the reason Janelle is in a wheelchair is that:
   A. she had an accident.
   B. she had a broken leg.
   C. she was born disabled.
   D. she was borrowing it.

   Give the number of the sentence that best supports the answer. _____

2. In sentence 1, the word *confidant* most likely means:
   A. an enemy.
   B. a nurse.
   C. a close friend.
   D. a neighbor.

3. Why did Janelle have to start the race after the runners?

   _____

   _____

   _____

   Give the number of the sentence that best supports the answer. _____

4. Why wasn't it important for Janelle to win the race?

   _____

   _____

   _____

   _____

   Give the number of the sentence that best supports the answer. _____

5. Which of these best describes Janelle?
   A. She was unsure of herself.
   B. She seemed shy and withdrawn.
   C. She didn't give up easily.
   D. She was friendly to everyone.

   Give the letter of the paragraph that best supports the answer. _____

6. Why did Janelle have to raise the money herself?

   _____

   _____

   _____

   _____

   Give the number of the sentence that best supports the answer. _____

7. What do you think will be the outcome of this story?

   _____

   _____

   _____

   _____

   Give the letter of the paragraph that best supports the answer. _____

8. Which of the following gives the theme of the story?
   A. Friendship is important.
   B. People are unreliable.
   C. Animals make good friends.
   D. Persistence pays off.

15. Sea Otter Attack
   by Carrie Beckwith

A [1]Five-year-old Wyatt Storm was rescued by his dog Friday afternoon from a sea otter attack. [2]The boy was swimming with his older sister about one quarter mile out from Guardian Beach.

B [3]Witness Karen Klaxir reported what happened next. [4]"I heard the cries of a small child, but I couldn't tell who or where exactly the cries were coming from. [5]There were so many people on the beach and in the water."

C [6]Family dog Kyra sprang into action. [7]The German shepherd mix ran into the ocean and swam straight to the children. [8]Witness John McCartney explained, "She knew exactly where to go, and she didn't waste any time getting there."

D [9]Wyatt's ten-year-old sister Janet, who was swimming with her brother, reported that the sea otter had grabbed him and then dragged him underwater. [10]The dog grabbed the boy's swim trunks with her teeth and pulled him away from the sea otter.

E [11]Abrahm Storm, the father, heard his daughter's screams and swam out to get his son from the dog. [12]Abrahm then carried Wyatt back to shore, his daughter Janet swimming just behind them.

F [13]Then Kyra was attacked by the sea otter. [14]"I couldn't tell who was winning the battle. [15]One just kept rolling over the other," an observer noted. [16]Kyra was taken under by the sea otter several times before finally managing to get away.

The Daily Express
Vol. XIX, No. 86   Saturday

Dog Saves Boy from Otter Attack

Five-year-old Wyatt Storm was rescued by his dog Friday afternoon from a seaotter attack. The boy was swimming with his older sister about one-quartermile out from Guardian Beach.

Witness Karen Klaxir reported what happened next. "I heard the cries of a small child, but I couldn't tell who or where exactlythe cries were coming from. There were so many people on the beach and in the water."

Family dog Kyra spranginto action. The German shepherd mix raninto the ocean and swam straight to the children.

Witness John McCartney explained, "She knew where to go and she didn't wasteany time getting there."

Wyatt's ten-yearold

Area of attack
Wyatt Storm was swimming 1/4 mile off shore when he was attacked by an otter. His dog, Kyra, saved his life.

X
1/4 mile

Guardian Beach

Kyra is doing fine after a trip to the animal hospital.

sister Janet, who was swimming with her brother, reported that the sea otter had grabbed him and dragged him underwater. The dog grabbed the boy's swimtrunkswith her teeth and pulled him away from the sea otter.

Abrahm Storm, the father, heard his daughter's screams and swam out to get hisson from the dog. Abrahm then carried Wyatt back to shore, his daughterJanet swimming just behind them.

See DOG, page 2

G [17]Five-year-old Wyatt suffered no serious injuries. [18]Kyra was rushed to the local animal hospital to treat several wounds to the head and is now recovering in the comfort of her owner's home.

H [19]In a televised interview last night, the boy's father said, "There is a special bond between those two. [20]I think Kyra considers Wyatt one of her own."

I [21]Biologist Steve Chan at Stanford Marine Station was perplexed about the attack. [22]"This type of aggressive behavior is unusual for the sea otter, although it is certainly capable of causing harm if it feels its young are being threatened. [23]That may have been the case with this situation. [24]The boy is lucky to be alive."

DIRECTIONS: Choose or write the best answer to each of the following questions using the evidence presented in the passage. When required, list specific sentence numbers or paragraph letters from the story to support the answer.

1. Number the following events in the order they actually occurred.

   _____ Kyra grabs the boy's swim trunks.

   _____ A sea otter grabs hold of Wyatt.

   _____ Kyra goes to the hospital.

   _____ Kyra swims out to get Wyatt.

   _____ Abrahm swims into the ocean.

2. Which of these traits best describes Kyra?
   A. playful
   B. protective
   C. unpredictable
   D. vicious

   List the numbers of the 4 sentences that best support the answer.

   _____, _____, _____, _____

3. Using paragraphs F–I, list three sentences that support the idea that sea otters can be aggressive.

   _____, _____, _____

4. Mark the following statements F for fact or O for opinion.

   _____ The otter attacked the boy because it was protecting its young.

   _____ Kyra was attacked by the sea otter.

   _____ Kyra considers Wyatt one of her own.

   _____ The boy was swimming about 1/4 mile out from the beach.

5. Why do you think one of the witnesses didn't get to the children before the dog?

   _____

   _____

   _____

   _____

   List the numbers of the 2 sentences that best support the answer. _____, _____

6. How might Kyra respond if she detected a burglar trying to crawl into Wyatt's room?

   _____

   _____

   _____

7. Describe the time and place of the attack.

   _____

   _____

   _____

   Give the letter of the paragraph that best supports the answer. _____

8. What is the best explanation for what might have caused the sea otter to attack the boy?
   A. It was provoked by the dog.
   B. It was protecting its young.
   C. It was hungry.
   D. It was sick and wounded.

   List the numbers of the 2 sentences that best support the answer.

   _____, _____

16. He Said, She Said
by Carrie Beckwith

A [1]"Promise me Jose will not be allowed in the same room with us," Luisa pleaded with her mother.

B [2]"Jose is your brother, not a contagious disease. [3]Besides, I don't know why he would want to spend his evening with a room full of girls."

C [4]"Momm…puh-leeze…," she whimpered.

D [5]"Okay, Jose will stay in his room, but I am not putting him in the doghouse."

E [6]"Yes! [7]Thank you!" [8]Luisa hugged her mom and bounced around the narrow kitchen, clapping her hands in victory.

F [9]Within minutes the doorbell rang.

G [10]"We brought chocolate-covered chewy bears!" Dolores and Monica chimed in unison. [11]"A pound and a half!"

H [12]Soon the small living room was filled with the talk and tattle of nine 12- and 13-year-old girls.

I [13]"Let's play Rumor," Keesha offered. [14]"Everyone get in a circle." [15]The girls moved to the center of the floor and sat cross-legged. [16]"You start the game by thinking of something really juicy. [17]Then you whisper it into the ear of the person sitting next to you, who whispers it into the ear of the person sitting next to her. [18]You can whisper the secret only once. [19]Then, when the last person has heard the secret, she has to say what she thinks it is out loud. [20]Just wait till you see what happens! [21]I'll go first." [22]Keesha paused for a second then leaned over to Moesha: "Irene kissed John on the cheek, and she said he's fallen for her like a puppy dog!" [23]Moesha whispered the secret into

Veronica's ear, who whispered it into Luisa's ear, who whispered into Monica's ear.

J [24]"Irene kissed John on the cheek, and she said he felt like a frog?"

K [25]"Monica, shhh! [26]Keep it to yourself!" Keesha cried as the girls burst into laughter.

L [27]Meanwhile, a mysterious green blanket had sneaked out of its room, crawled down the hallway, and made itself quite comfortable near the entryway to the living room.

M [28]"What! [29]You think I look like a Greek god?" Jose kidded as he peeked his head out from underneath the blanket.

N [30]"Jose!" Luisa screeched.

O [31]"Stop right there, brother!" Moesha shouted as nine squealing girls chased after him.

P [32]With lightning quick reflexes, Jose made a mad dash to his room. [33]"I always knew you loved me!" he called out, as a storm of pillows came crashing over his head.

DIRECTIONS: Choose or write the best answer to each of the following questions using the evidence presented in the passage. When required, list specific sentence numbers or paragraph letters from the story to support the answer.

1. Which of the following statements best summarizes the story?
   A. Luisa has a party and her brother interrupts it.
   B. Luisa has a party with her mother's permission.
   C. Jose eavesdrops on the girls and then gets chased out.
   D. The girls play Rumor and discover Keesha's secret.

2. List the following events in the order in which they occurred.

   ____ The doorbell rang.

   ____ Jose ran to his room.

   ____ Moesha whispered the secret.

   ____ The girls hit Jose with pillows.

3. How did the blanket and the entryway to the living room affect the events of the story?

   _____

   _____

4. Which of the following inferences is best supported by the passage?
   A. Jose is Luisa's little brother.
   B. The girls are having a good time.
   C. Luisa's mom is in her bedroom.
   D. The girls are in love with Jose.

   Give the letter of the paragraph that best supports the answer. ____

5. List the paragraph from the passage that supports the idea that the secret Keesha began with in paragraph I got misinterpreted. ____

6. Luisa's mom probably decided to keep Jose out of the living room because:
   A. she knew he was contagious.
   B. there wasn't enough room for him.
   C. her daughter pleaded with her.
   D. she knew he wouldn't want to be there anyway.

   Give the letter of the paragraph that best supports the answer. ____

7. What probably caused Jose to peek his head out from under the blanket and make himself known?

   _____

   _____

   _____

   Give the letter of the paragraph that best supports the answer. ____

8. In general, Jose could be described as:
   A. shy.
   B. mischievous.
   C. loud.
   D. serious.

   List the letters of the 3 paragraphs that best support the answer.

   ____, ____, ____

9. In sentence 32, two things are being compared using figurative language. What is that comparison and what does it mean?

   _____

   _____

   _____

17. My Most Embarrassing Day
by Carrie Beckwith

A [1]The thought of Mom dropping me off in front of the theater was more embarrassing than having to walk with my little brother to school every day. [2]How could she do this to me? [3]Didn't she understand that Bret Michaels was the most popular boy in school? [4]"Mom, just try to remember what it was like to be 14 years old. [5]Didn't you want to do things on your own?"

B [6]"I am not going to let you walk to the theater by yourself in the dark, Meagan."

C [7]"But there is nothing to worry about, Mom. [8]I'm old enough to…"

D [9]"That's enough, Meagan." [10]Mom turned up the radio. [11]She was tuning me out. [12]Now every car within a mile of us could hear Willie Nelson belting out "To All the Girls I've Loved Before." [13]I slunk down in the seat and pulled my turtleneck sweater up to my nose.

E [14]Mom turned the radio down again and then turned into the back parking lot. [15]"I'll watch you until you get in." [16]I smiled, filled with gratitude. [17]

"Thanks, Mom. [18]I'll meet you at 8:30 right here—*in back*."

F [19]"Have a good time, sweetie. [20]Do you have enough money?"

G [21]"Yes, I'm fine," I reassured her. [22]My hands were sweating. [23]I hoped he wouldn't

try to hold them. [24]But if he didn't, would that be a bad sign? [25]Stop worrying and just relax, I told myself over and over again as I walked up to the ticket box. [26]And then I saw something that I never would have expected. [27]The most popular boy at school pulled up to the front of the theater in an old station wagon. [28]Bret's baby sister was in a car seat in back. [29]He kissed his mom on the cheek and patted his little sister on the head. [30]Then he waved when he saw me and said, "Meagan, come here. [31]I want you to meet my mom and my little sis."

H [32]In that brief moment, I realized that it wasn't my mother that embarrassed me anymore; it was that silly girl with the turtleneck sweater pulled up to her nose.

DIRECTIONS: Choose or write the best answer to each of the following questions using the evidence presented in the passage. When required, list specific sentence numbers or paragraph letters from the story to support the answer.

1. At about what time does the story take place?
   A. 3:00 p.m.
   B. 6:30 p.m.
   C. 8:30 p.m.
   D. 7:30 p.m.

   List the numbers of the 2 sentences that best support the answer. ____, ____

2. What caused Meagan's mother to turn up the radio and tune Meagan out?

   _____

   _____

   Give the number of the sentence that best supports the answer. ____

3. How do you predict Meagan will act the next time her mother drops her off where her friends will be?

   _____

   _____

   _____

   Give the number of the sentence that best supports the answer. ____

4. Who is the girl Meagan refers to in sentence 32?

   _____

   Give the number of the sentence that best supports the answer. ____

5. List the numbers of the three sentences within the passage that support the idea that Meagan's mom is concerned about her. ____, ____, ____

6. How did Meagan's point of view change by the end of the story?

   _____

   _____

   _____

   Give the number of the sentence that best supports the answer. ____

7. What is the main reason Meagan wanted to walk to the theater alone?
   A. She wanted to go in the back entrance.
   B. She saw Bret in the back parking lot with his mom.
   C. She didn't want Bret to see her with her mom.
   D. The music coming from the car was embarrassingly loud.

   Give the letter of the paragraph that best supports the answer. ____

8. Compare Meagan's treatment of her mother to Bret's treatment of his mother.

   _____

   _____

   _____

   _____

18. The Game Winner
by David White

A [1]The count was 1 and 2—one ball and two strikes. [2]There were two outs, and the Eagles, behind 4–2, were looking at their last chance to score. [3]The runners on first and second were ready to run like the wind at the sound of contact.

B [4]Maria stepped back into the batter's box, digging a hole in the dirt for her front foot. [5]She settled in, waved the bat over her head, and stared down the pitcher.

C [6]Was that fear in his eyes? [7]He was the second pitcher of the day for the Bearcats, the first pitcher having moved to right field after the Eagles scored their first run. [8]The new pitcher had worn a smug smile after getting two quick outs, but the Eagles had stormed back, getting three straight singles and scoring their second run. [9]A home run now would win the game. [10]An out would end it.

D [11]The pitch came suddenly. [12]Maria swung. [13]Contact! [14]With the crack of the bat, the baserunners were off, sprinting around the bases, hoping to cross home plate. [15]The crowd roared as their eyes followed the flight of the ball. [16]The pitcher turned his head and watched, helpless.

E [17]Maria put her head down and sped

toward first base, intending to make a wide turn and zoom toward second. [18]The infielders hoped for a catch but were ready to throw the ball if it hit the ground. [19]The ball sailed high and deep—right into the right fielder's glove and right out again. [20]The ball rolled to the wall as the right fielder ran after it. [21]Uma and Emeko, the two baserunners, scored. [22]Maria tore around third base and steamed home. [23]The right fielder heaved a desperate throw to the infield. [24]The second baseman's relay throw to home plate thumped into the catcher's mitt too late, and Maria scored the winning run.

DIRECTIONS: Choose or write the best answer to each of the following questions using the evidence presented in the passage. When required, list specific sentence numbers or paragraph letters from the story to support the answer.

1. List three words the author uses to suggest that the three baserunners ran fast.

    _____

    _____

    List the numbers of the 3 sentences that best support the answer.

    ____, ____, ____

2. What does paragraph B suggest about how Maria felt?
    A. She was tense.
    B. She was scared.
    C. She was confident.
    D. She was inexperienced.

    What event in the story supports the answer?

    _____

3. What had the Eagles done between the first two outs and Maria's turn at bat?

    _____

    _____

    _____

    Give the number of the sentence that best supports the answer. ____

4. One of the sentences in paragraph A contains a simile. Write that sentence below and then underline the simile.

    _____

    _____

    _____

5. Give three examples from paragraphs D and E of how the author describes the sounds of the game.

    _____

    _____

    _____

    Give the number of the sentence that best supports each answer.

    ____, ____, ____

6. Why did the infielders hope for a catch, as described in sentence 18?

    _____

    _____

    _____

    Give the number of the sentence that best supports the answer. ____

7. What was the score when the new pitcher took over for the Bearcats?

    _____

    List the numbers of the 2 sentences that support the answer. ____, ____

8. Why was the pitcher "helpless," as described in sentence 16?

    _____

    _____

9. Which of these was NOT a key event in the story?
    A. Maria's base hit
    B. the roar of the crowd
    C. the arrival of a new pitcher
    D. the scoring of the winning run

19. A Test of Friendship
by Cheryl Block

A ¹The big game was less than two weeks away. ²John knew he had to hand in his history paper by tomorrow and get a passing grade this time in order to play in the game next week. ³As the team's best running back, he had to play. ⁴Without him, they could lose. ⁵Yet no matter how hard he tried, he just couldn't come up with a good idea for his paper—any idea. ⁶Time was running out!

B ⁷He and his best friend, Ed, were working on their papers at the library. ⁸Ed was done with his paper. ⁹He'd been trying to help John, but John's mind was still as blank as his notepad. ¹⁰John was starting to panic.

C ¹¹Ed went to the reference aisle to look up information for his bibliography. ¹²John glanced over at Ed's place and saw Ed's neatly typed paper sitting on top of his book. ¹³John started to read it. ¹⁴It was going to be another A paper for Ed. ¹⁵John still had nothing new on his paper. ¹⁶He glanced around. ¹⁷Ed was still in the stacks, and no one else was around. ¹⁸John took Ed's paper to the copy machine. ¹⁹He just needed an idea to get him started. ²⁰He'd reword the paper so his teacher wouldn't recognize it.

D ²¹John put Ed's paper back on the book and started editing his copy.

E ²²"I'm glad to see you finally working, John," Ed said as he came back to the table. ²³"Do you need any help?"

F ²⁴"No, thanks, I've finally got a good idea. ²⁵I think I'll take my paper home and do some research on the Internet. ²⁶See you tomorrow, Ed." ²⁷John hurriedly got his things together and left.

G ²⁸He did his best to rewrite Ed's paper so the teacher wouldn't see the similarities. ²⁹It wasn't *really* cheating, he kept telling

himself. ³⁰He'd just used Ed's ideas to get himself started. ³¹He'd even added some information he'd found on the Internet. ³²Besides, Ed probably wouldn't mind. ³³Ed knew how important this game was to him and to the school. ³⁴But he still felt uneasy about what he'd done as he headed for school.

H ³⁵Mr. Fessler handed back the papers on Monday. ³⁶John couldn't wait to see his grade. ³⁷He just knew he'd passed. ³⁸But Mr. Fessler didn't give John his paper. ³⁹He didn't return Ed's either. ⁴⁰Instead he told John and Ed that he wanted to see both of them after class. ⁴¹Ed looked surprised; John felt queasy. ⁴²Mr. Fessler knew!

I ⁴³"Well, it seems that someone got help with his history paper. ⁴⁴I have to assume it was you, John. ⁴⁵However, it is not appropriate, Ed, for you to write someone else's paper. ⁴⁶Therefore, I am giving you both F's."

J ⁴⁷Ed's face went white. ⁴⁸John felt like crawling into a hole. ⁴⁹He realized what he had to do to make things right.

DIRECTIONS: Choose or write the best answer to each of the following questions using the evidence presented in the passage. When required, list specific sentence numbers or paragraph letters from the story to support the answer.

1. Based on paragraphs A and B, there is NO evidence to support the idea that John:
   A. is a top player.
   B. is friends with Ed.
   C. is good at history.
   D. likes to win.

2. In paragraph B, what kind of figurative language does the writer use? Write the sentence.

   _____

   _____

3. Why did Mr. Fessler assume it was John who got help with the paper?

   _____

   _____

   List the numbers of the 2 sentences that best support the answer. ____, ____

4. Which of the following was a key event in the plot?
   A. John and Ed went to the library.
   B. John copied Ed's paper.
   C. John read Ed's paper.
   D. Mr. Fessler handed back the papers.

5. Why is it ironic that John got an F on his paper?

   _____

   _____

   List the numbers of the 2 sentences that best support the answer. ____, ____

6. What was the primary conflict in the story?

   _____

   _____

   _____

   _____

   Give the letter of the paragraph that best supports the answer. ____

7. Which of the following best states the theme of the story?
   A. Winning is important, no matter what the cost.
   B. It pays to be honest.
   C. Cheating can have painful consequences.
   D. It is important to rely on our friends.

8. Based on paragraphs A and B, John could be described as:
   A. organized.
   B. relaxed.
   C. worried.
   D. bored.

9. Why do you think John felt queasy in sentence 41?

   _____

   _____

10. What will John do to help his friend Ed?

    _____

    _____

    _____

20. Old Woman of the Oak
by Margaret Hockett

A [1]I crossed the stream, wound my way through the bushes, and came to a clearing. [2]The oak sprawled before me.

B [3]I pressed a dark knot on the pale gray trunk. [4]A rope ladder immediately snaked its way down through rustling red leaves. [5]A note had been tacked to the third rung: CAREFUL, JUDE. ROPE WET. [6]That was Old Meg, never one to waste words.

C [7]Soon, I was swinging my legs into the entrance. [8]Meg sat in her "living room" in the old oak she called home. [9]She was as gnarled as the tree, but her eyes usually crackled with fire. [10]Today they were flat.

D [11]"Won't be much longer," she said. [12]"They're going to bulldoze the field for the new road."

E [13]"No way!" I said in disbelief. [14]"We'll stop them—" [15]She held up her hand.

F [16]"But where will you go…?" I started.

G [17]She was moving her rocker back, baack, baaack—until it was on the edge of the runner and you thought she was going all the way over!—and then forward. [18]She'd do that when she was making up her mind.

H [19]"Been here 'bout long enough. [20]Seen the sun set nine thousand times, and ain't none of them been the same as the one before." [21]I followed her gaze past dewy leaves, a patch of meadow, and jutting rocks of the coast. [22]An inky line was forming a boundary between sea and sky. [23]Suddenly, it spread, as if an artist were washing the scene with a dark tint. [24]My mood darkened with it as Meg's meaning came home to me.

I [25]"I'm leaving you my Oak Log," she announced. [26]Her precious journal! [27]Meg thought the road project was a sign that her time had come, that her life was over! [28]I couldn't accept that.

J [29]As I walked back to town, I ignored the slapping branches, the wet stream, and the cold night. [30]I was making a plan.

DIRECTIONS: Choose or write the best answer to each of the following questions using the evidence presented in the passage. When required, list specific sentence numbers or paragraph letters from the story to support the answer.

1. What resulted from pressing the tree knot in paragraph B?

   _____

2. Paragraph B suggests that Meg's speech is:
   A. brief.
   B. lengthy.
   C. mean.
   D. descriptive.

   Give the number of the sentence that best supports the answer. _____

3. In sentence 9, *gnarled* most likely means:
   A. green.
   B. twisted.
   C. tall.
   D. flat.

4. Why did Jude need to be careful in climbing to Meg's home?

   _____
   _____

5. In sentence 24, "came home to me" means:
   A. became clear to me.
   B. entered my house.
   C. confused me.
   D. made me sad.

6. Jude is most likely to make a plan to:
   A. force Meg to move.
   B. move in with Meg.
   C. get the Oak Log.
   D. stop the bulldozing.

   List the numbers of the 2 sentences that best support the answer. _____, _____

7. Which of the following is probably NOT a conflict implied in the passage?
   A. Jude wanted to stop the bulldozing, but Meg was against stopping it.
   B. Meg loved her home but also thought it was time to let go.
   C. Jude wanted to help Meg but felt that he could do nothing.
   D. Jude respected the journal, but felt bad about Meg's giving it to him.

8. Describe where the oak tree was located.

   _____
   _____
   _____

   List the numbers of the 3 sentences that best support the answer.
   _____, _____, _____

9. In sentence 23, what is the darkening of the sky used to symbolize?

   _____
   _____

   Give the number of the sentence that best supports the answer. _____

10. In sentence 24, what does Jude infer from Meg's comments?

   _____
   _____
   _____

   Give the number of the sentence that best supports the answer. _____

21. Middle School: First Day Survival
by Carrie Beckwith

A [1]Adam Jackson greeted the new students who filled the auditorium: "Welcome to Chipman Middle School. [2]I'm the school's student body president, and I'm here today to help ease any fears you might have about middle school. [3]And believe me," he chuckled, "I feel overly qualified to help you in this area.

B [4]"I couldn't sleep the night before my first day of school. [5]Would I be able to find all my classes? [6]Would I have enough time to get from the English building to the math building? [7]Who would I eat lunch with? [8]Would 8th graders point me in the wrong direction if I asked where the art building was? [9]I taped my schedule and a map of the school to my binder and studied it for over an hour the night before.

C [10]"I begged my mom to drop me off at school an hour early so I could find my first class. [11]Luckily, it was the first building I saw when she dropped me off. [12]Since I had some extra time, I decided to try to find my other classes. [13]After advisory, I would go northeast to the peach colored bungalow. [14]Then I would have to run to the opposite side of campus for math class—Ahhh! [15]I panicked. [16]Ten minutes between classes didn't seem like enough time. [17]I managed to get to all but two of my classrooms before the first bell of the day rang. [18]I had never seen so many kids in one place. [19]They were crawling out of the cracks in the walls!

D [20]"Mrs. Jelica's class was the best, and I'm not just saying that because she's standing in the doorway over there." [21]Mrs. Jelica smirked as the students softly chuckled at the remark. [22]"I had enjoyed reading in elementary school, but this class was different. [23]We were going to be reading

Fall Schedule
Jackson, Adam

Period	Class	Teacher	Time
1	Advisory	Raghavan	8:30
2	English	Jelica	9:00
3	PreAlgebra	Won	10:00
4	Soc Studies	Littleton	11:00
	Lunch		12:00
5	Art	Smitz	1:00
6	Home Econ.	Johnson	2:00

Hemingway and Steinbeck.

E [24]"Well, I made it to math class on time and even found a few friends from my old school. [25]The cafeteria was pretty easy to locate—at least it was once I asked one of the cheerleaders how to get there. [26]Don't be afraid to do this, guys. [27]If I can do it, anybody can.

F [28]"At lunch, I sat next to someone I didn't know. [29]I had never done that before. [30]I just smiled and said, 'I'm Adam.' [31]We ended up talking for the rest of the lunch hour. [32]Then I knew middle school was going to be all right.

G [33]"The rest of the afternoon flew by. [34]Before I knew it, school was over and I had to drag myself back to the bus stop.

H [35]"Today, I'm an after-school English tutor, a journalist for the school newspaper, and your very humble president. [36]Now, I'm going to let you get to your first class. [37]And, by the way, the art building is on the north side of campus." [38]Adam smiled and the rest of the kids laughed, a little less anxious now than they were before.

DIRECTIONS: Choose or write the best answer to each of the following questions using the evidence presented in the passage. When required, list specific sentence numbers or paragraph letters from the story to support the answer.

1. What is the main purpose of Adam's speech?
   A. to show new students how to get around campus
   B. to tell new students how nervous he was about his first day of school
   C. to minimize the fear new students might have about middle school
   D. to let new students know how different middle school is going to be

   Give the number of the sentence that best supports the answer. _____

2. Compared to Adam's middle school, his elementary school:
   A. had fewer students.
   B. had more buildings.
   C. had more students.
   D. had fewer buildings.

   Give the number of the sentence that best supports the answer. _____

3. Which of the following character traits best describes Adam now?
   A. shy and insecure
   B. confident and outgoing
   C. mistrustful and secretive
   D. slow and cautious

   List the letters of the 2 paragraphs that best support the answer. _____ , _____

4. Compare Adam's attitude in the beginning of his first day of school to his attitude by the end of the first day.

   _____

   _____

   _____

5. What type of figurative language is used in sentence 19?

   _____

6. List two things Adam did to help ease his transition into middle school.

   _____

   _____

   _____

7. Which direction is the English building from the art building?
   A. northwest
   B. southeast
   C. southwest
   D. northeast

8. The "X" on the map represents Adam on his first day. Third period has just ended, and Adam is lost. Give him accurate directions to his next class.

   _____

   _____

   _____

9. How do you predict Adam will feel about his first day of high school?

   _____

   _____

10. What probably caused Mrs. Jelica to smirk?

    _____

    _____

22. A Dramatic Plea
by Margaret Hockett

Now Is the Time to Act! by Jason Irving

A [1]Hi! [2]As president of the "Two Face Drama Club," I extend a hearty invitation to you and your friends to join us now. [3]The club offers great benefits, and as a member, you'll get to do the following.

- [4]Help decide which two plays will be performed during the school year. ([5]Last year we did *Lizzard of Oz* and *Grease Monkeys*.)
- [6]Have first chance to audition for your favorite roles.
- [7]Take free acting classes! ([8]Last year's guest instructors taught Speaking Sincerely and Crying on Cue.)

B [9]Club membership will also help you develop organizational and leadership skills. [10]You will participate in meetings twice monthly. [11]You will work at fundraisers three times a year. [12]And you will recruit new members.

C [13]As president of the club, I offer a free movie ticket to each of the first five new members. [14]So don't miss out—sign up today! [15]Just come to room 509 after 2:30, put your name on the list, and submit your $15 membership dues. [16]I'll send you a meeting schedule—and a movie ticket if you're quick. [17]See you soon!

D [18]P.S.: Over 50% of our members have moved or graduated since last spring, leaving us with twenty-five members. [19]We will lose our school funding (and cancel all plays!) unless membership increases to thirty before October 1. [20]So it's important that you join us now!

The masks of comedy and tragedy are often used as symbols for drama.

DIRECTIONS: Choose or write the best answer to each of the following questions using the evidence presented in the passage. When required, list specific sentence numbers or paragraph letters from the story to support the answer.

1. How many members have left the club since last spring? Choose the one best answer.
   A. twenty-five
   B. nearly fifty
   C. more than twenty-five
   D. about a third

   Give the number of the sentence that best supports the answer. ____

2. Explain why the name of the club includes the words "Two Face."

   _____

   _____

3. The title of Jason's news article (Now is the Time to Act!) really has two meanings. Explain them.

   _____

   _____

   _____

4. Give an example of how the writer applies each of the following techniques to persuade others to join the club.

   Grabbing attention: _____

   _____

   Listing benefits: _____

   _____

   Giving gifts: _____

   _____

   Giving a warning: _____

   _____

5. How is Jason setting an example for one of the members' responsibilities?

   _____

   _____

   Give the number of the sentence that mentions that responsibility. ____

6. If you join, you can definitely
   A. get a part in a play.
   B. receive free lessons.
   C. get free movie tickets.
   D. be elected to an office.

   Give the number of the sentence that best supports the answer. ____

7. Label each of the following as F for fact or O for opinion.

   ____   The club offers great benefits.

   ____   The first 5 new members will get free tickets.

   ____   It's important to join now.

   ____   *Grease Monkeys* was performed.

8. What threatens the functions of the drama club?

   _____

   _____

   Give the number of the sentence that best supports the answer. ____

9. Describe both the cause and the effect implied in sentence 19.

   _____

   _____

23. The Way of the Wild
   by Carrie Beckwith

A ¹Grass-covered plains and the yellow-trunked acacia trees extended as far as the eyes could see. ²The hot African sun was beginning to set, turning the sky a pinkish orange at its horizon. ³From the tree house, they could see in every direction. ⁴To their left and behind the bushes, two male impalas stood watch. ⁵Skirting the watering hole just below them was a giraffe. ⁶Back and forth it paced, unwilling to stop and take a drink. ⁷The quiet was eerie. ⁸Only the wind seemed bold enough to make a sound as it whistled through the branches of the tree house. ⁹Then a roar sounded, like an old, rusty hinge.

B ¹⁰"What was that?" Emily whispered with excitement. ¹¹

"It's coming from over there," the native pointed, then focused his binoculars in the direction of a distant tree. ¹²"Ahh…yes," he calmly replied. ¹³"You've just discovered the reason for all the hesitation at the watering hole."

C ¹⁴"You mean it's a—?"

D ¹⁵"Yes, that it is."

E ¹⁶Nearly twenty minutes passed. ¹⁷The impalas moved in closer to the giraffe at the watering hole. ¹⁸Still, not one dared dip his head to drink. ¹⁹The fear of capture was too much for the thirsty animals.

F ²⁰The clouds were closing in on the last of the day's light. ²¹"I won't be able to see anything now," Emily sulked.

G ²²"Don't worry, *Mzungu*. ²³You will not be disappointed," Juma smiled.

H ²⁴"What?"

I ²⁵"Shhh…just wait."

J ²⁶Just then the large yellow beast jumped down from the tree. ²⁷Very quietly, it stalked its prey.

K ²⁸"It's going for the giraffe!" Emily cried. ²⁹"Doesn't the giraffe see it, Juma? ³⁰It's coming straight at him!"

L ³¹The nervous impalas scattered at the sound of breaking twigs. ³²Sensing the disturbance, the giraffe bolted from the watering hole. ³³But his long limbs were not fast enough. ³⁴The great cat pounced.

M ³⁵"He's going to kill him, Juma! ³⁶Are we just supposed to watch?"

N ³⁷"There is nothing we can do, and there is nothing we should do, Emily. ³⁸This is the way of the wild. ³⁹It all takes care of itself," Juma said as he rested his binoculars on the ledge. ⁴⁰Emily turned away, unable to watch the final moments.

DIRECTIONS: Choose or write the best answer to each of the following questions using the evidence presented in the passage. When required, list specific sentence numbers or paragraph letters from the story to support the answer.

1. List the numbers of the four sentences from the story that give clues to the ending. ____, ____, ____, ____

2. Contrast Emily's attitude about the attack with Juma's attitude.

   _____

   _____

   _____

   List the letters of the 2 paragraphs that best show this contrast. ____, ____

3. Write the simile that is used in paragraph A.

   _____

4. Give the letter of the paragraph that best describes where the story takes place. ____

5. What caused the impalas to run?

   _____

   _____

   Give the number of the sentence that best supports the answer. ____

6. List three examples of how the author uses sound to build tension in the story.

   _____

   _____

   _____

7. Why were the animals unwilling to drink at the watering hole?

   _____

   _____

   _____

   Give the number of the sentence that best supports the answer. ____

8. What do Juma's words and actions reveal about his character?
   A. He is unfamiliar with wild animals.
   B. He worries about helpless animals.
   C. He understands wild animals.
   D. He is unsure of himself.

   List the letters of the 4 paragraphs that best support the answer.

   ____, ____, ____, ____

9. What most likely happened to the giraffe?

   _____

   _____

   List the numbers of the 3 sentences that best support the answer.

   ____, ____, ____

10. How do Emily's feelings about watching the animals change?

    _____

    _____

    _____

    _____

    _____

24. Amazon Adventure
by Cheryl Block

A [1]Sirah Patel was caught up in another round of Amazon Adventure, the hot new video game. [2]The primary goal of the game was to find the ancient treasure of the Moche while surviving the perils of the Peruvian jungle. [3]Sirah had just crossed the river, narrowly escaping an attack by man-eating piranhas. [4]He had reached the second level of play and was climbing the slopes of an old volcano.

B [5]As he reached the mouth of the crater, the volcano started to erupt. [6]The effects were so realistic, the room started to shake. [7]Suddenly, Sirah felt an intense pull towards the screen. [8]He was being sucked inside the game! [9]He threw down the controller, but it was too late. [10]He was caught in a swirling vortex, and there was no escape. [11]He was spinning down a dark hole, deeper and deeper until he found himself at the bottom of the crater. [12]He was no longer playing the game, he was in it!

C [13]From the jungle above, he could hear the distant throbbing of native drums. [14]He didn't know if the tribe was friendly or not, but he wasn't sure he wanted to find out. [15]Long ago, the natives had worshipped the volcano, throwing gold and jewels into its yawning mouth in hopes of appeasing its angry outbursts. [16]It was very likely that their treasure was still somewhere within the bowels of this ancient mountain. [17]But how to find it?

D [18]The smell of rotten eggs from the sulfuric fumes was overpowering, and the heat from the bubbling pools of molten lava was intense. [19]Huge black snakes slithered in and out of crevices in the walls. [20]But as he considered climbing back up to the top, the cries of the approaching tribesmen convinced him otherwise. [21]Better to remain in the hot, acrid depths of the volcano than face a band of angry natives armed with spears.

E [22]He now knew that he would have to play this game for real if he hoped to return home!

DIRECTIONS: Choose or write the best answer to each of the following questions using the evidence presented in the passage. When required, list specific sentence numbers or paragraph letters from the story to support the answer.

1. In sentence 15, how does the author use personification to describe the volcano?

   _____

   _____

   _____

   _____

2. In sentence 10, what does the word *vortex* most likely mean?
   A. a landslide
   B. a whirlpool
   C. a crater
   D. a river

3. In sentence 9, why did Sirah throw down the game controller?
   A. He was hoping to stop the game.
   B. He got tired of playing.
   C. He was angry for losing.
   D. He couldn't hold on to it.

4. Which of the following is NOT a reason the natives might be angry?
   A. They did not like strangers.
   B. They thought he was stealing the treasure.
   C. They considered him to be trespassing.
   D. They were eager to share the treasure.

5. Sirah's attitude at the end of the passage can be described as:
   A. unhappy.
   B. enthusiastic.
   C. realistic.
   D. amused.

6. Why was there treasure inside the volcano?

   _____

   _____

   _____

   _____

   Give the number of the sentence that best supports the answer. _____

7. The mood of the story could be described as:
   A. peaceful.
   B. hilarious.
   C. exciting.
   D. tragic.

8. What event was linked to Sirah's being pulled into the game?

   _____

   _____

   _____

   Give the number of the sentence that best supports the answer. _____

9. What literary form is this story?
   A. comedy
   B. mystery
   C. science fiction
   D. fable

25. Sketches of Summer
by Margaret Hockett

A [1]His eyes scanned the charcoal curve of the horizon. [2]It would be hard to see the sail…he would see it only if the winds were strong and fair, and he could catch the gleam of the white sheet billowing off the mast. [3]He knew it was a vain hope.

B [4]Even if he saw the ship, he would not see her, perhaps not ever again. [5]The sea had taken his father away when he was a child and his parents had divorced. [6]And now it was taking her. [7]Against her wishes, she was going to live with her mother.

C [8]He had never meant to care for a girl. [9]Girls giggled and told lies and made silly faces. [10]They were always in groups, always talking about boys. [11]He didn't want them to talk about him.

D [12]He kept to himself, sketching with his favorite pen, drawing the characters that were in his head or doodling the symbols and shapes that became a language of his own. [13]Then one day when the tide was in, she was there, looking over his shoulder. [14]Not saying or asking anything, she watched him fill the pages of his notebook. [15]He came to expect her as he went to the same place on the pier each day. [16]He knew that unlike the others, the silly girls, she really *saw* his drawings and could decipher their hidden meanings. [17]It was a language he could share for the first time.

E [18]One day she wasn't there. [19]He tried to draw, but nothing on the page came out with the right shape. [20]When she came back, they talked—about his father and about her

parents and their separation.

F [21]Now the tide was going out, and she was going with it.

G [22]His life would be as it was last spring, but not the same, not ever the same.

H [23]He opened his sketch pad. [24]A folded piece of paper dropped out. [25]Opening it, he saw his own face, a cartoon likeness of him smiling as he never did unless he smiled at her. [26]Behind him on the page, she had drawn a boat. [27]A cartoon wind was in the sails, pushing it in on a big wave to the shore, pushing it toward him.

I [28]On the hull of the boat was a name: NEXT SUMMER. [29]Under the picture she had written, "See you!" [30]As the sun dropped below the horizon, he looked out at the water. [31]No sail caught the fading light, but he saw her. [32]And he smiled.

DIRECTIONS: Choose or write the best answer to each of the following questions using the evidence presented in the passage. When required, list specific sentence numbers or paragraph letters from the story to support the answer.

1. At what time of day does the story take place?

    _____

    _____

    Give the paragraph that best supports the answer. ____

2. Give two examples of how this girl compares to his idea of girls in general.

    _____

    _____

    _____

    List the letters of the 2 paragraphs that best support the answer. ____, ____

3. In telling a story, an author sometimes describes events out of the actual order of occurrence. (The author may use *flashback* to tell of a previous event). Number the following paragraphs according to the actual sequence of their events within the characters' lives.

    ____ A and B

    ____ D and E

    ____ F and G

    ____ H and I

4. Who drew the picture the boy found in his sketch pad?

    _____

    Give the number of the sentence that best supports the answer. ____

5. In sentence 17, what was meant by "language he could share"?

    _____

    _____

    _____

    List the numbers of the 2 sentences that best support the answer. ____, ____

6. What message do you think the boy understood from the cartoon, and why?

    _____

    _____

    _____

    _____

    _____

    _____

7. Why does it say "he saw her" in sentence 31?
    A. He actually saw her on the boat, though he couldn't see the sail.
    B. She was on the shore because she had decided not to go after all.
    C. He was looking at a picture of her that he had drawn.
    D. He was able to imagine her after getting her message.

8. How is the plot resolved?
    A. She finally leaves on a ship.
    B. He decides to let her go.
    C. He learns of her plan to return.
    D. He learns to like girls.

26. 15 Minutes of Fame
by Margaret Hockett

A [1]Buzzing saxophones swung in unison. [2]Lights swept the stage and then merged at the figure of a female, head bowed. [3]The head came up slowly while the lights pulsed to the rhythm of the drums. [4]The figure gained energy as the flashing lights outlined her movements. [5]Her sequins sparkled as she swayed and gestured. [6]Her powerful voice roared through the driving beat. [7]The audience screamed and swayed. [8]Young girls cried with joy, and grown men fainted. [9]The air was charged with excitement throughout the performance. [10]Finally, she bowed with a flourish to thunderous applause as blackness filled the room.

B [11]Overhead lights came on. [12]An empty room met her eyes as she breathed heavily and blinked. [13]Dazed, she rose slowly. [14]Dustballs danced over hardwood boards that creaked as she walked, hesitantly, to the office. [15]She paid her fee and left.

C [16]Walking home, she reviewed the brochure. [17]"Yes," she allowed, "it was a thrill while it lasted." [18]But the place in her mind where esteem would live remained, like that room, unfurnished.

HOLO FAME—Thrill Of A Lifetime!

[19]Holo Fame gives you realistic sets and audiences using holograms* and sound effects. [20]Your "audience" will laugh at your jokes and sway to your music. [21]No need for talent—no real people need see you!

[22]Tell us what kind of audience you prefer—anywhere between the extremes of *reserved* and *boisterous*. [23]Choose your accompaniment, costumes, and costars. [24]Use our free makeup artists.

[25]It's safe! [26]Even though the "stage" seems to revolve twenty feet in the air, it's at ground level, so you can't fall off.

[27]The only lasting effects will be your new glow of confidence and your memory of the thrill of a lifetime!

*hologram: 3-dimensional projected image

Brochure text appears above.

DIRECTIONS: Choose or write the best answer to each of the following questions using the evidence presented in the passage. When required, list specific sentence numbers or paragraph letters from the story to support the answer.

1. Who was the "she" of paragraph B?
   A. the performer
   B. an audience member
   C. a dreamer
   D. an office worker

2. The audience consisted of:
   A. regular people.
   B. famous people.
   C. projected images.
   D. dummies.

   Give the number of the sentence that best supports the answer. _____

3. The word *boisterous*, as used in sentence 22, most likely means:
   A. reserved.
   B. polite.
   C. rude.
   D. noisy.

4. Much of the first paragraph describes:
   A. a performance by a real superstar.
   B. an illusion created by special effects.
   C. a vivid and detailed dream.
   D. a rock concert at a large arena.

5. By paragraph B, the room where the performance had taken place was:
   A. empty.
   B. clean.
   C. crowded.
   D. enormous.

6. Describe the setting of the story.

   _____

   _____

   _____

7. Two lasting things were promised at the end of the brochure. Explain whether or not they were fulfilled.

   _____

   _____

   _____

   _____

   _____

   _____

8. Describe the use of personification in paragraph B.

   _____

   _____

   _____

   _____

   _____

9. Describe the metaphor used in sentence 18, and explain what is meant by "unfurnished."

   _____

   _____

   _____

   _____

   _____

   _____

27. A Flood of Help
by David White

A [1]The rain continued to fall, the people were soaked, but their determination did not falter. [2]The houses needed saving, and so the houses would be saved.

B [3]Rain had drenched the town for nine hours straight, and the river had been overflowing its banks for the last 15 minutes. [4]One by one, the families had secured the inside of their homes and piled sandbags around the outside. [5]By the thousands, the raindrops fell.

C [6]"Mom, can we take a break?" Pam Mathis said, her arms limp at her sides.

D [7]"Is the rain taking a break?" her mother replied wearily. [8]"Our neighbors need our help. [9]They'd do the same for us."

E [10]"You're right," Pam said, sighing as she and her brother and sister resumed filling the sturdy bags with sand.

F [11]Many of the rest of the 80 residents of Carruth quickly but carefully tied the tops of the bags and heaved them onto the Jordans' and the Chows' trucks for transport across town to the danger zones.

G [12]The only houses still in danger were the Miller house and the Mendes cottage, both farmhouses whose surrounding land was washing away. [13]The Millers had lost their entire crop in the last flood, five years ago. [14]They faced a similar fate now.

H [15]The sandbags arrived and were stacked around the threatened houses as people offered up silent and spoken prayers for dry skies. [16]It wasn't just the Millers and the Mendeses who would suffer if the houses and farms were lost. [17]The community depended on those farms for their vegetables. [18]The Mendeses also had two large apple orchards, in which squashed apples now slumped in the mud.

I [19]For one thrilling moment, the clouds parted, the sky lightened, and the rain stopped. [20]"Our prayers have been answered!" Sally Smith cried. [21]Desperate eyes turned skyward. [22]Just as suddenly, the rain returned. [23]Grim looks replaced hopeful smiles, and the work continued.

J [24]Word of the rising floodwaters brought help: 60 people from nearby Lewiston arrived to lend their hands and strong backs to the daunting task at hand. [25]With renewed vigor, the Mathises, Millers, Mendeses, and all the rest of the people of Carruth shoveled, tied, and stacked. [26]Hoping against hope and bolstered by the arrival of fresh troops, they were determined to triumph.

K [27]An hour later, all was quiet. [28]The torrent had become a drizzle and then disappeared. [29]Dark clouds dotted the sky, but an easterly wind was blowing them away. [30]The houses were not flooded. [31]The Millers thought some of their vegetable crop had a chance of recovering. [32]The Mendeses said their grain would probably survive. [33]The apple trees had taken a beating but were still standing. [34]The people of Lewiston took home with them the eternal gratitude of their neighbors.

L [35]As the sun brightened and the day lengthened, the people of Carruth slept.

DIRECTIONS: Choose or write the best answer to each of the following questions using the evidence presented in the passage. When required, list specific sentence numbers or paragraph letters from the story to support the answer.

1. Which of these statements best captures the main idea?
   A. Rain threatens a town.
   B. A river overflows its banks.
   C. People from a neighboring town help out.
   D. Neighbors work together to save two houses and farms.

2. How would the loss of the farms affect the rest of the community?

   _____

   _____

   _____

   _____

   Give the number of the sentence that best supports the answer. _____

3. The mood of the people of Carruth is:
   A. hopeless.
   B. thoughtful.
   C. determined.
   D. overwhelmed.

   List the numbers of the 2 sentences that best support your answer. _____, _____

4. Why were the Miller house and the Mendes cottage threatened?

   _____

   _____

   _____

   Give the number of the sentence that best supports the answer. _____

5. The author suggests that the people aren't sure they will save the houses. Give two phrases from paragraph I to support that idea.

   _____

   _____

   _____

6. What does *torrent* mean, as used in sentence 28?
   A. windstorm
   B. thunderstorm
   C. heavy rain
   D. heavy flooding

7. What is the condition of the houses other than those belonging to Mendes and Miller?
   A. They have been washed away.
   B. They have been abandoned.
   C. They have been secured.
   D. They have been demolished.

   List the numbers of the 2 sentences that best support the answer. _____, _____

8. Based on information in the passage, it can be said that in general, the people of Carruth are:
   A. helpful.
   B. unfriendly.
   C. secretive.
   D. unprepared.

9. Explain how the people of Carruth are like the apple trees.

   _____

   _____

   Give the number of the sentence that best supports the answer. _____

28. Diving In
by Margaret Hockett

A [1]I was standing before the lifelike painting of Phineus McGee fighting his battle at Pirate Cove. [2]I could almost smell the sea and hear the cry of seagulls as I ran my finger over the white of his billowing sleeve. [3]Out of that sleeve grew a sword, its edge gleaming in the sunlight. [4]The opponent had a toothless grin and was about to plunge his sword into Phineus. [5]My sense of justice (not to mention adventure) demanded that I join the battle! [6]I would dive into the scene and fight as Phineus.

B [7]Here's the thing about picture diving (a little-known art from the West Indies): you have to be confident. [8]You stand back, focus on your target, and run. [9]Diving into a specific *character* requires precision. [10]I stood back, took aim, and ran.

C [11]"Arrrgh!" Red Rooster grunted in surprise. [12]I had blocked his thrust so that his sword clattered to the deck. [13]His hair matted with sweat as he dodged my own thrust and wrestled me for my sword.

[14]I summoned Phineus' strength as I cried, "I'll rip ya limb from limb, scurvy dog!" [15]The stench of Rooster's fetid breath gave me extra willpower, and I shook him off. [16]I staggered back and started thinking maybe this wouldn't be so easy. [17]Now he was coming back at me with his sword! [18]It was inches from my nose when I remembered. [19]Phineus *died* in this fight! [20]If I didn't leave the picture now, I'd be killed.

D [21]I panicked and searched my memory.

[22]How could I dive *out*? [23]I was backed against portside as the ship swayed; the sea sloshed over the rail. [24]Water. [25]I got a flashback from my picture-diving instruction: "To return from your adventure, soak yourself in water."

E [26]If I could only buy some time! [27]But Rooster was about to bury his sword in me, and I closed my eyes for the worst. [28]The ship lurched. [29]Rooster lost his balance. [30]As I slid through the rails, my own sword snapped up just in time to scratch Rooster's cheek as he regained balance. [31]"Me face, me face…!" was the last thing I heard.

F [32]Still feeling soaked, but thoroughly relieved, I stand again before the framed battle scene. [33]The oil painting looks much the same as before—or does it? [34]I look closely at Phineus' challenger. [35]Is it my imagination, or is that a new scar under his left eye?

DIRECTIONS: Choose or write the best answer to each of the following questions using the evidence presented in the passage. When required, list specific sentence numbers or paragraph letters from the story to support the answer.

1. How does sentence 2 give the reader a clue as to what might happen later?

   _____

   _____

   _____

2. Explain what is meant by the figurative language used in sentence 3.

   _____

   _____

   _____

3. In general, picture diving requires all of the following EXCEPT:
   A. confidence.
   B. focus.
   C. running.
   D. precision.

   List the numbers of the 3 sentences that best support the answer. ____, ____,

   ____

4. Match each point of view to the character to whom it most likely belongs. Use each letter only once.

   ___ 1. Phineus is a foe to be conquered.

   ___ 2. I'm an outside observer.

   ___ 3. I'm defending the captain's honor.

   ___ 4. I must defend my ship.

   A. Narrator before picture diving
   B. Red Rooster
   C. Captain Phineus
   D. Narrator in the picture

5. The word *fetid*, as used in sentence 15, most likely means:
   A. foul.
   B. sweet.
   C. encouraging.
   D. inspiring.

6. Why did a new scar appear on Rooster's face in the picture (sentence 35)?

   _____

   _____

   _____

   Give the number of the sentence that best supports the answer. ____

7. The main conflict in the story is between:
   A. Rooster and himself.
   B. the narrator and himself.
   C. Phineus and the narrator.
   D. Rooster and the narrator.

8. The story could be classified as any of the following EXCEPT:
   A. fantasy.
   B. nonfiction.
   C. mythical.
   D. adventure.

9. Why was the narrator panicked in paragraph D?

   _____

   _____

   _____

   Give the number of the sentences that best support the answer. ____, ____

29. The Comeback Can
by Carrie Beckwith

A [1]Alexander began his science demonstration with a question: "If I push this coffee can forward on a perfectly flat tabletop, which direction do you predict it will go?"

B [2]"It can only go forward, if that's the direction you push it," Ramon offered.

C [3]"That's a good guess, but this coffee can is going to do more than that." [4]Alexander held his coffee can up for the class to observe. [5]"This can is going to roll forward and then roll backwards. [6]It's a little trick I taught it the other night," he teased his audience.

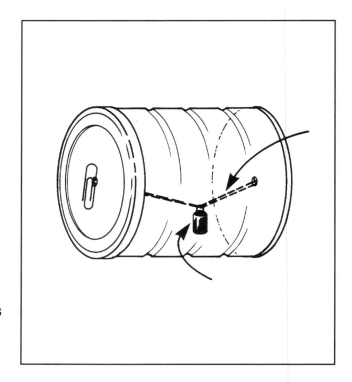

D [7]Alexander's classmates watched with anticipation as he pushed the coffee can forward on the table. [8]"Look, it's going backwards now!"

[9]Immediately, a flood of questions came pouring in. [10]"How did you do that, Alexander?"

[11]"Do you have a little trained mouse in there?" they questioned.

E [12]"No, there's some kind of instrument that's causing it to roll backward," another student guessed.

F [13]"Right you are, Ali," Alexander answered. [14]"Now, let me explain." [15]Alexander opened the lid of the coffee can and revealed the mechanism inside. [16]"I punched a small hole in the center of the bottom of the can and another small hole in the center of the plastic lid. [17]Then I slipped a rubber band through the hole in the bottom of the can and secured it with a paper clip to the outside of the can to keep it from slipping back into the can. [18]I fastened a small weight to the center of the rubber band and then pulled the rubber band through to the other side and secured it with another paper clip. [19]When I rolled the can across the tabletop, the rubber band twisted in a forward direction. [20]The twisting increased the tension in the rubber band, which then caused the can to stop and roll back in the opposite direction when the rubber band was taut. [21]That's it. [22]It's a simple experiment using Newton's First Law of Motion—an object at rest tends to stay at rest unless it is acted on by a force. [23]And, an object moving at a constant velocity continues at that velocity unless it is acted on by a force. [24]In this case, the can moved forward when I pushed it with my hand, creating a force. [25]The can continued moving forward until another force acted upon it—the twisted rubber band. [26]I've made copies of the diagram I used to construct the can. [27]If anyone would like to try this at home, please take a copy."

G [28]The class applauded Alexander's science demonstration.

H [29]"Thank you," he said with a smile and then whispered into his can, "Good job, Mickey. [30]We'd better get an A for this."

DIRECTIONS: Choose or write the best answer to each of the following questions using the evidence presented in the passage. When required, list specific sentence numbers or paragraph letters from the story to support the answer.

1. It can be inferred from his presentation that Alexander:
    A. is easily confused.
    B. has a sense of humor.
    C. is very shy.
    D. acts stuck-up.

    List the numbers of the 3 sentences that best support the answer. ____, ____,
    ____

2. Number the following steps in the order they should occur.

    ____ Fasten the rubber band to the plastic top with a paper clip.

    ____ Pierce two holes in the can: one on top, one on bottom.

    ____ Tie a weight to the rubber band.

    ____ Pull a rubber band through the hole in the bottom of the can.

    ____ Get a coffee can, rubber band, and weight.

3. Explain why Alexander whispered into his can, "Good job, Mickey."

    _____

    _____

    _____

4. The main purpose of Alexander's science project was most likely to:
    A. demonstrate a scientific principle.
    B. joke about the mouse trick.
    C. get the class involved.
    D. answer questions from the class.

    List the numbers of the 3 sentences that best support the answer.

    ____, ____, ____

5. What caused the can to roll backwards?

    _____

    _____

6. What do you predict would happen if Alexander placed the can at the bottom of a slightly elevated ramp and then twisted the lid away from the ramp? Explain the answer.

    _____

    _____

    _____

7. What type of figurative language does the author use in sentence 9? Explain your answer.
    A. simile
    B. metaphor
    C. idiom
    D. irony

    _____

    _____

8. Label each of these statements either F for fact or O for opinion.

    ____ "That's a good guess…"

    ____ "The can moved forward when I pushed it with my hand."

    ____ "When I rolled the can across the tabletop, the rubber band twisted in a forward direction."

    ____ The class applauded Alexander's science demonstration.

30. The Prime Suspect
by David White

A [1]When he thought about it later, Detective Pinkerton concluded that the woman *must* have known about the stolen papers. [2]Yet for all the questions he asked, Courteney Baker revealed nothing but what she wanted him to know.

B [3]*He* wanted to know about the people who would show up suddenly at her mansion in the dead of night and leave a few hours later. [4]*He* wanted to know why she had so many Southern sympathizers as maids and stablehands. [5]*She* wanted to know why he didn't just leave her alone. [6]*She* wasn't a spy, she continued to say, even though he believed otherwise.

C [7]The latest group of stolen papers contained troop placement reports and reinforcement schedules for the Army of the Potomac and were supposed to be delivered to the front lines, to the Union commander, General George McClellan. [8]Yet somehow (and Pinkerton had found this out only after the fact), those papers were stolen, copied, and returned, all without the messenger's being the wiser.

D [9]Who took them? [10]How did they get all the way to Robert E. Lee, the Confederate commander? [11]What part did Courteney Baker play in the scheme? [12]Pinkerton was under great pressure to stop these thefts because the war was going badly for the North. [13]He didn't have answers to any of these questions, but he thought he knew where to get them.

E [14]"Tell me, Miss Baker," he had said in yet another visit to her Louisville estate, "why do you think I keep calling on you?"

F [15]"I haven't the faintest idea, Mr. Pinkerton," she had replied airily. [16]"I do know that I cannot leave my house, since you issued the order to keep me under house

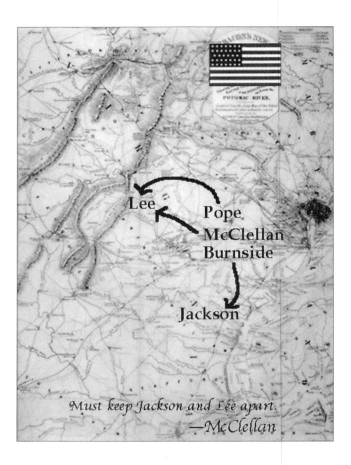

Must keep Jackson and Lee apart.
—*McClellan*

arrest." [17]Her smile was sweet.

G [18]"I have the president's full authority," Pinkerton had said forcefully. [19]"Tell me what you know about those plans!"

H [20]But it was always the same. [21]He tried to reason with her, to threaten her with imprisonment. [22]She was steadfast. [23]She knew nothing, had seen nothing, would venture nothing. [24]None of her friends knew anything, had seen anything, or cared to speculate on why so many "mysterious" visitors found their way to and from Baker Hill at odd hours.

I [25]As for McClellan, he was badly beaten by Lee, in large part because the Southern troops continued to know exactly where to strike.

J [26]If Courteney Baker permitted herself a private smile at this result, Pinkerton never knew it.

DIRECTIONS: Choose or write the best answer to each of the following questions using the evidence presented in the passage. When required, list specific sentence numbers or paragraph letters from the story to support the answer.

1. What famous event in American history is the background for the story?

   _____

   List the numbers of the 4 sentences that best support the answer. ____, ____, ____, ____

2. Which of these words best describes Courteney Baker?
   A. unkind
   B. unpatriotic
   C. secretive
   D. cooperative

   List the numbers of the 2 sentences that best support the answer. ____, ____

3. Why do you think "the Southern troops continued to know exactly where to strike," as described in sentence 25?

   _____

   _____

   _____

   List the numbers of the 3 sentences that best support the answer. ____, ____, ____

4. Which of these paragraphs gives the strongest evidence for why Pinkerton thought Courteney Baker was a spy?
   A. Paragraph F
   B. Paragraph B
   C. Paragraph J
   D. Paragraph D

5. Identify the idiom used in Paragraph B.

   _____

6. Describe the difference in attitudes of Courteney Baker and Detective Pinkerton in paragraphs F and G.

   _____

   _____

   _____

7. What is the primary mystery of the story?
   A. what was in the stolen plans
   B. where the plans were stolen
   C. what Pinkerton knew about the stolen plans
   D. what Courteney Baker knew about the stolen plans

   List the numbers of the 3 sentences that best support the answer. ____, ____, ____

8. If, as a result of the battle, Detective Pinkerton decided to question Courteney Baker again, what would be the probable outcome?

   _____

   _____

   _____

   List the numbers of the 4 sentences from paragraphs A and H that best support the answer. ____, ____, ____, ____

31. A Week in Ancient Greece
by David White

MONDAY: [1]Today, we began learning about ancient Greek culture. [2]The Greeks valued individual freedom and the exchange of ideas, which led to a stable and representative government; the development of a great philosophical tradition, inventions, and artistic marvels. [3]They also fought many wars, but in those times who didn't?

TUESDAY: [4]The Greek exchange of ideas had its basis in democracy, which began in Athens about 600 B.C. [5]Every male citizen could serve in the assembly and vote on laws and policies. [6]Women couldn't vote. [7]My Aunt Joan wouldn't like that. [8]Unlike Americans, who elect their leaders, the Greeks chose their officials by lot. [9]In other words, they drew a number from a pot and the people who got the right numbers got to serve in government—for one year!

WEDNESDAY: [10]Today's topic was philosophy, which featured truths and ideas applied logically to the world around us. [11]Philosophers like Socrates, Plato, and Aristotle had spirited debates about what things really were and whether all like things were the same. [12]Again, we saw the importance of the exchange of ideas: without the freedom to argue these points, the Greeks wouldn't have made their famous theories. [13]Socrates was free to question others about how well they thought they knew something. [14]Aristotle gave us a logical proof called the syllogism: Mr. van Noord gives all his students tests; I am one of his students; therefore, Mr. van Noord will give me a test. [15]Speaking of tests, I should study tonight. [16]Good thing I'm writing all these things down!

THURSDAY: [17]Another thing the Greeks did because they had the freedom to do so was invent different kinds of theater. [18]Previously, performances had been simple songs and dances

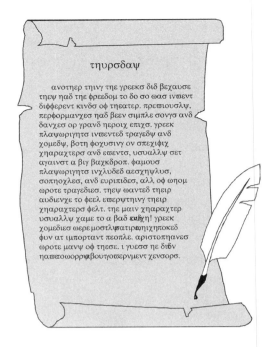

or grand heroic epics. [19]Greek playwrights invented tragedy and comedy, both focusing on specific characters and events, usually set against a big backdrop. [20]Famous playwrights included Aeschylus, Sophocles, and Euripides, all of whom wrote tragedies. [21]They wanted their audience to feel everything their characters felt. [22]The main character usually came to a bad end—ouch! [23]Greek comedies were mostly satire, which poked fun at important people. [24]Aristophanes wrote many of these. [25]I guess he didn't have to worry about government censors!

FRIDAY: [26]Greek people believed that strongly developed individual talent would bring a city-state its greatest glory, even more so than conquest. [27]Mr. van Noord also gave us a preview of next week: we'll study Greek math and science and then pottery, sculpture, and architecture. [28]Ancient Greece must have been a fascinating place to live. [29]All those ideas floating around might have been too much for me, though—I like physical exercise. [30]I'm glad they also gave us the Olympics.

DIRECTIONS: Choose or write the best answer to each of the following questions using the evidence presented in the passage. When required, list specific sentence numbers or paragraph letters from the story to support the answer.

1. Which phrase best describes what most influenced ancient Greek society in the story?
   A. cultural masterpieces
   B. philosophical arguments
   C. the birth of democracy
   D. the exchange of ideas

   List the numbers of the 2 sentences that best support the answer.

   ____, ____

2. *Antigone* is a famous Greek play about a woman who speaks out against the government and is sentenced to death because of it. Which of these people probably wrote *Antigone*?
   A. Aristotle
   B. Aristophanes
   C. Socrates
   D. Sophocles

   List the numbers of the 2 sentences that best support the answer.

   ____, ____

3. In general, the Greeks placed the highest value on
   A. individual enlightenment.
   B. cultural enrichment.
   C. collective achievement.
   D. democratic government.

   List the numbers of the 2 sentences that best support the answer. ____, ____

4. How could an ancient Greek stay in government for more than one year?

   _____

   _____

   _____

   Give the number of the sentence that best supports the answer. ____

5. Which of these sentences from the passage contains BOTH a fact and an opinion?
   A. Every male citizen could serve in the assembly and vote on laws and policies.
   B. Ancient Greece must have been a fascinating place to live.
   C. I'm glad they also gave us the Olympics.
   D. They also fought many wars, but in those times who didn't?

6. Explain the difference between Greek comedy and Greek tragedy.

   _____

   _____

   _____

   _____

   _____

   _____

   List the numbers of the 3 sentences that best support the answer.

   ____, ____, ____

7. Which of these sets of statements is a syllogism?
   A. All mice have families. Stuart is a mouse. Therefore, Stuart has a sister.
   B. All mice wear shoes. Stuart is a mouse. Therefore, Stuart wears shoes.
   C. All dogs run. Simon runs. Therefore, Simon is a dog.
   D. All dogs have tails. Simon is a dog. Therefore, Simon eats dog food.

nonfiction _____

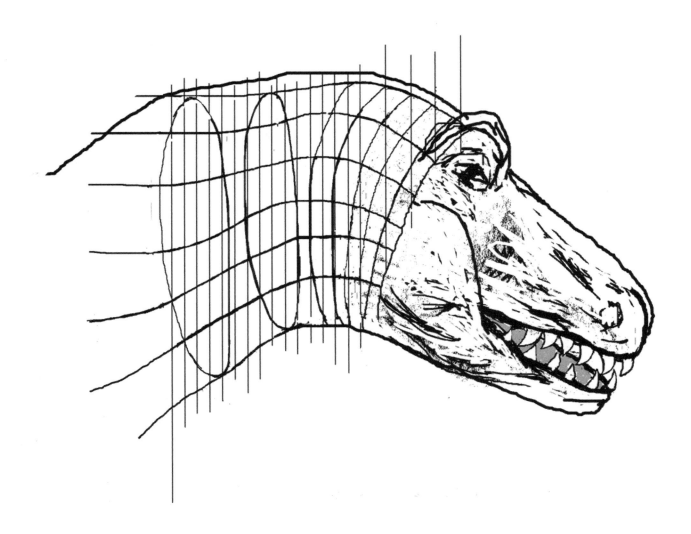

32. Put Your Heart Into It
by David White

A [1]You ran three miles and your friend lifted weights for an hour. [2]Who got the most exercise? [3]It depends.

B [4]Exercise can be divided into three categories: aerobic, strength, and flexibility, all of which improve your blood flow, a necessity for living longer.

C [5]Aerobic exercises like running, biking, and swimming strengthen your heart, enabling it to do more work with less effort. [6]These exercises also create a more regular flow of oxygen into the blood and accelerate the removal of carbon dioxide from the blood. [7]In other words, these exercises fine-tune your respiratory system.

D [8]Strength exercises like weightlifting build your overall muscle mass and endurance, making you less prone to injury. [9]The larger your muscles, the more blood flows to them. [10]And, having more blood flowing to the muscles means having more oxygen, which helps keep your bones strong, too.

E [11]Flexibility exercises like stretching help get your blood flowing in the areas you want to exercise. [12]If you're planning on lifting weights to build up your arms and chest, then you should stretch your upper body before lifting those weights. [13]Muscles at rest are cold and tight and can tear easily if asked to work too hard. [14]A stretched muscle is warm and fluid and more receptive to weight resistance. [15]Again you can see the importance of blood flow: warming up a muscle increases the blood (and oxygen)

TO YOUR HEALTH

flowing around that muscle. [16]Such oxygen-rich blood makes you stronger. [17]Stretching is also important after doing aerobic or strength exercises to relax the muscles you've worked. [18]Just like muscles at rest, muscles that have been recently worked are tight and need to be stretched out.

F [19]So what can all this exercise do for you? [20]It can lower your blood pressure, your cholesterol, your body fat and weight and, in turn, your risk of heart disease, the number one killer in America. [21]A healthy body means a healthy heart. [22]Exercise can increase your level of fitness so you don't get winded walking up the stairs. [23]It can reduce tension and stress and help you sleep better at night. [24]Plus, people who exercise say they just plain feel better. [25]It can happen to you.

DIRECTIONS: Choose or write the best answer to each of the following questions using the evidence presented in the passage. When required, list specific sentence numbers or paragraph letters from the story to support the answer.

1. The main idea of the story is that exercise can:
   A. build your overall muscle mass.
   B. lower your blood pressure.
   C. keep your body healthy.
   D. increase oxygen in your blood.

   Give the number of the sentence that best supports the answer. _____

2. Using examples from the passage, list how each of the three categories of exercise affects your blood flow.
   Aerobic _____

   _____

   Strength _____

   _____

   Flexibility _____

   _____

   Give the number of the sentence that best supports each answer.

   _____, _____, _____

3. Muscles at rest:
   A. are usually the body's larger muscles.
   B. require a large amount of weight resistance to work them properly.
   C. need more exercise than muscles in use.
   D. have less blood flowing around them than the same muscles in use.

   List the numbers of the 2 sentences that best support the answer. _____, _____

4. Which of these best sums up the benefit of exercise described in sentence 23?
   A. improved respiration
   B. rest and relaxation
   C. strength and endurance
   D. improved fitness

5. What happens when you do not stretch your legs after running?

   _____

   _____

   _____

   _____

   List the numbers of the 2 sentences that best support the answer. _____, _____

6. Which of these functions of a plant is the direct opposite of what the human body does?
   A. It absorbs sunlight and converts it to energy.
   B. It serves as a producer in the food chain.
   C. It makes its own food through photosynthesis.
   D. It takes in carbon dioxide and gives off oxygen.

   Give the number of the sentence that best supports the answer. _____

7. How is the article organized?
   A. by topic
   B. by time order
   C. as an argument
   D. as a comparison

33. Galileo's Vision
by David White

A [1]It was a clear night in 1610 when Galileo Galilei looked through his telescope and saw the four closest moons of Jupiter. [2]They were only dots in the sky, but they were there.

B [3]It was quite a discovery. [4]In fact, the moons Galileo saw were the first moons other than our own moon that anyone had ever seen.

C [5]Now, Galileo didn't invent the telescope. [6]Hans Lippershey of Holland did in 1608. [7]He designed it so people could look at things far away. [8]But Galileo was the first to use a telescope to look at stars and planets.

D [9]Using the telescope, Galileo also discovered that our moon was not the perfect, mysterious sphere everyone thought it was. [10]He proved that the moon was filled with craters. [11]He also proved that the light that seemed to be coming from the moon was actually a reflection of light coming from the sun.

E [12]Galileo was also the first scientist to prove a theory by testing it and recording results. [13]Until that time, scientists would prove their theories by making arguments without giving evidence.

F [14]Galileo was the first to provide visual evidence in support of the theory that Earth revolves around the sun. [15]A man named Copernicus of Poland had written in 1543 that Earth was not the center of the universe. [16]He had said that the sun was the center of what we call the solar system and that Earth circled the sun. [17]Not many people believed

him. [18]Teachings until that time had placed Earth firmly at the center of the universe, with everything else revolving around it. [19]Galileo, night after night, saw the moons of Jupiter at different points in the sky. [20]It was clear that they were circling Jupiter, not Earth. [21]What Galileo saw helped prove Copernicus's theory.

G [22]Astronomy has come a long way since 1610. [23]We now know that Jupiter has at least 16 moons. [24]We know that our own solar system has eight planets. [25]We know that six of those planets have moons. [26]We know that the universe contains other solar systems like ours. [27]We have telescopes searching the night sky for signs of life. [28]Thousands of people now do what one man started on a hill in Italy almost 400 years ago.

DIRECTIONS: Choose or write the best answer to each of the following questions using the evidence presented in the passage. When required, list specific sentence numbers or paragraph letters from the story to support the answer.

1. Which of these best explains why people before Galileo hadn't seen moons around Jupiter?
   A. They hadn't looked in the right place.
   B. They hadn't turned the telescope toward the night sky.
   C. They thought Jupiter didn't have moons.
   D. They thought Earth was the center of the universe.

   Give the number of the sentence that best supports the answer. _____

2. Which of these words best describes the process that Galileo introduced to scientific theory?
   A. visualization
   B. determination
   C. argumentation
   D. experimentation

   Give the number of the sentence that best supports the answer. _____

3. The author's purpose in writing this passage was probably:
   A. to discuss modern astronomy.
   B. to show how to use a telescope.
   C. to prove Galileo's theories about the universe.
   D. to show Galileo's contributions to science.

4. Scientists before Galileo proved theories by making arguments. This kind of proof can best be described as:
   A. theoretical.
   B. historical.
   C. natural.
   D. technical.

5. Compare the two scientific theories described in paragraph F.

   _____

   _____

   _____

   _____

   _____

6. Explain one way that Galileo changed the way people thought about the moon.

   _____

   _____

   _____

   _____

   _____

   Give the letter of the paragraph that best supports the answer. _____

7. Which of these statements about the passage is an opinion?
   A. The moon is filled with craters.
   B. Galileo put the telescope to good use.
   C. Galileo discovered four moons of Jupiter.
   D. People didn't believe Copernicus's theory at first.

34. Goalsetting
by Margaret Hockett

A [1]Jan used to do her homework quickly then go home, eat supper, and watch TV until bedtime. [2]When she failed algebra, she said, "I guess I'm just no good at math." [3]When she was passed over for basketball, she said, "I'm just not tall enough!" [4]In fact, Jan was convinced that her fate lay outside her own control.

B [5]That was before she took a "Do It Yourself" course.

C [6]Now she sets goals for herself. [7]She plans how to achieve those goals. [8]And she takes the steps to accomplish those goals. [9]You, too, can take charge of your life by setting goals and believing in yourself.

D [10]First, decide what you *really* want to achieve, and set a goal. [11]Put your goal into words.

E [12]Next, break that goal into major steps. [13]For example, if you dream of drumming in a band, do the following:

   [14]1) Get a set of drums to practice on.

   [15]2) Set up a schedule for practicing.

   [16]3) Find a group of musicians with a similar goal.

   [17]4) Practice on a regular schedule.

   [18]5) Volunteer to play for events.

F [19]When you have identified the major steps to reach your goal, break them into smaller ones that you can begin taking now. [20]For example, how could you get some drums? [21]Look in the newspaper ads for used sets, call the owners, and check out sets until you find one you like. [22]Then find a way to earn extra cash to pay for it (or make a trade).

G [23]The most important ingredient for success is to *believe* you can do it! [24]"Okay," you say, "how can I strengthen my belief?" [25]Do the first step and don't worry about the next. [26]Once you have identified some owners of percussion equipment, you will feel more like going ahead with the next step. [27]"It won't hurt to call them," you'll say. [28]Once you have called, your belief that you will reach your goal will be even stronger. [29]By the time you have acquired a drum set of your own, you will be emboldened to take even more difficult steps. [30]Gradually, you will build the confidence to achieve your dream.

H [31]By the way… remember Jan? [32]She has advanced so far in math that she is now tutoring others in algebra. [33]That is, when she's not too busy practicing basketball with her new teammates!

DIRECTIONS: Choose or write the best answer to each of the following questions using the evidence presented in the passage. When required, list specific sentence numbers or paragraph letters from the story to support the answer.

1. Compare how Jan's evenings were spent at the start of the article and how they were probably spent at the end.

   _____

   _____

   _____

   List the numbers of the 3 sentences that best support the answer. ____, ____,

   ____

2. Which set of steps is most important to the main idea of the passage?
   A. getting drums, practicing, finding musicians
   B. setting a goal, identifying steps, breaking them down
   C. looking in the paper, checking drums, earning cash
   D. taking a "Do It Yourself" course, practicing, being responsible

   List the letters of the 3 paragraphs that best support the answer. ____, ____,

   ____

3. According to the passage, which of the following is *most* important for success?
   A. setting goals to do what you enjoy
   B. listing the obstacles to the goal
   C. having faith you can reach the goal
   D. moving toward your goal every day

   Give the number of the sentence that best supports the answer. ____

4. The word *emboldened*, as used in sentence 29, means:
   A. encouraged.
   B. foolish.
   C. too bold.
   D. loud.

5. Which of the following is most likely the author's point of view?
   A. Anyone can be successful.
   B. You get only one chance to believe in yourself.
   C. Success is a matter of chance.
   D. Belief in yourself comes only after taking steps toward the goal.

   Give the number of the sentence that best supports the answer. ____

6. Jan's newfound success is a result of her
   A. getting sick of being in a rut.
   B. being told she has to pass math.
   C. wanting to be a tutor.
   D. being inspired by taking a course.

   Give the number of the sentence that best supports the answer. ____

7. Number the following steps to become a writer in the order the author would suggest.

   ____ Identify publishers of the type of writing you choose to do.

   ____ Buy a reference book of publishers.

   ____ Decide what kind of writer you want to be.

   ____ Request writing guidelines from appropriate publishers.

8. Write a one- or two-sentence summary of the information in the passage.

   _____

   _____

   _____

   _____

35. The Long and Short of Color
by Margaret Hockett

A [1]Is a Ferrari *really* red—or is it just an illusion? [2]Where do the colors come from, and why do objects appear to have color?

B [3]It all starts with white light. [4]White light is made of waves of different lengths corresponding to different colors. [5]If the white light goes through a special glass called a prism, the light is bent, or *refracted* (its direction is changed). [6]The fact that short and long waves are bent by differing amounts enables the light to separate into the colors that we see.

C [7]The band of colors resulting from the separation of white light is called the color *spectrum*. [8]There are seven basic colors in the spectrum. [9]They include red, which has the longest wavelength. [10]In descending order of wavelength, the rest are orange, yellow, green, blue, indigo, and violet.

D [11]You may wonder why an object appears to be a particular color. [12]Colored objects reflect some colors of light and absorb others. [13]An object seems to *be* a particular color based on how it reflects light. [14]Why is a blue chair *blue*? [15]The chair is hit by all the colors in the light. [16]Of all the colors of light hitting the chair, many are allowed to pass into the chair, or become "absorbed." [17]It is the light that is bounced off the chair, not the chair itself, that is blue.

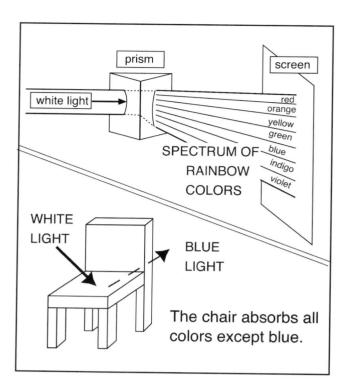

SPECTRUM OF RAINBOW COLORS

red
orange
yellow
green
blue
indigo
violet

WHITE LIGHT

BLUE LIGHT

The chair absorbs all colors except blue.

[18]This reflected blue light is what our eyes receive, though we say that the *chair* is blue.

E [19]What if an object were made of a material that absorbed *all* colors? [20]From such an object, none of the white light could escape, and the object would appear to be black.

F [21]What about an object that absorbs none of the colors but reflects them all? [22]Since all parts of the white light are reflected, that object will appear white.

G [23]The magic of color makes the world a fascinating place. [24]And maybe it just doesn't matter whether or not it's an illusion.

DIRECTIONS: Choose or write the best answer to each of the following questions using the evidence presented in the passage. When required, list specific sentence numbers or paragraph letters from the story to support the answer.

1. In white light, if a book appears to be red, which of these are true about the book? (Choose all that apply.)
   A. It is absorbing red light.
   B. It is absorbing all colors of light except red.
   C. It is reflecting the shortest wavelengths of visible light.
   D. It is reflecting the longest wavelengths of visible light.

   Give the letters of the paragraphs that best support the answer. ____, ____

2. Which of the following best describes the *sequence* of events as portrayed in the passage?
   A. Light strikes an object, the object reflects light, the viewer sees the object's reflected light as its color.
   B. A viewer sees a colored object, the object reflects light, light strikes the object.
   C. Light strikes an object, the viewer sees the object's color, the object reflects the color.
   D. The object reflects colored light, a viewer sees the light, the light strikes the object.

   Give the letter of the paragraph that best supports the answer. ____

3. How does the prism affect the yellow light differently from how it affects the blue light? Use the passage and the illustration to answer.

   _____

   _____

   List the numbers of the 2 sentences that best support the answer.

   ____, ____

4. How is violet light different from orange light?
   A. It is closer to yellow.
   B. Its wavelength is greater.
   C. Its wavelength is shorter.
   D. It is not absorbed.

5. Let's say we start with light that has no blue in its spectrum. We shine the light on an object that can reflect only blue. What color will the object appear to be?
   A. blue
   B. black
   C. white
   D. red

   Give the letter of the paragraph that best supports the answer. ____

6. As used in sentence 18, the word *reflected* most nearly means:
   A. bent around.
   B. allowed through.
   C. bounced back.
   D. absorbed.

7. Which of these is a generalization that can be made from the information given in the passage?
   A. Without light, there is no color.
   B. White light contains the eight basic colors.
   C. A chair that reflects blue absorbs the other colors.
   D. The number of wavelengths has no limit.

8. The author's purpose is to:
   A. describe the wavelengths of light.
   B. show how light is bent with a prism.
   C. convince you the world is magic.
   D. explain why things appear colored.

36. Making Apple Pie
by David White

[1]LaTonya set out to make an apple pie.
[2]Here is the recipe her mother gave her:

Crust

2 $\frac{1}{2}$ cups all purpose flour
1 tablespoon sugar
1 teaspoon salt
$\frac{1}{2}$ cup (1 stick) chilled unsalted butter,
    cut into small pieces
$\frac{1}{2}$ cup chilled solid vegetable shortening,
    cut into small pieces
5 tablespoons (about) ice water

Filling

7 apples of several cooking varieties,
    peeled, cut into $\frac{1}{4}$-inch-thick slices
$\frac{1}{2}$ cup plus 2 tablespoons sugar
$\frac{1}{2}$ cup packed golden brown sugar
$\frac{1}{4}$ cup all purpose flour
1 tablespoon fresh lemon juice
$\frac{1}{2}$ teaspoon fresh lime juice
1 teaspoon ground cinnamon
$\frac{1}{2}$ teaspoon ground nutmeg
$\frac{1}{4}$ teaspoon ground cloves
$\frac{1}{4}$ teaspoon ground allspice
1 teaspoon vanilla

For crust:

[3]Combine flour, sugar, and salt in food processor. [4]Alternately turning the processor on and off, add the pieces of chilled butter and vegetable shortening until mixture resembles coarse meal. [5]Gradually blend in enough water by tablespoonfuls to form moist clumps. [6]Gather dough into ball. [7]Divide dough into two pieces and flatten into disks. [8]Wrap in plastic and refrigerate 1 hour.

For filling:

[9]Position rack in lowest third of oven

COMMON MEASUREMENTS
1 pint = 2 cups
1 cup = 16 tablespoons, or 8 ounces
1 tablespoon = 3 teaspoons

and preheat to 400°F. [10]In a large bowl, toss apples with $\frac{1}{2}$ cup sugar, brown sugar, flour, lemon juice, lime juice, cinnamon, nutmeg, cloves, allspice, and vanilla.

For pie:

[11]Roll out one dough disk on lightly floured surface to 12-inch-diameter round. [12]Transfer to 9-inch-diameter deep dish glass pie plate. [13]Trim dough hanging over the edges to $\frac{1}{2}$ inch. [14]Brush edge of crust lightly with water. [15]Sprinkle remaining sugar onto crust. [16]Put apple mixture inside crust, mounding in center. [17]Roll out second dough disk to 12-inch-diameter round. [18]Place atop apple mixture. [19]Trim dough overhang to 1 inch. [20]Fold top crust edge under bottom crust edge. [21]With your fingers, crimp the edges decoratively to seal.

[22]Cut several slits in crust to allow steam to escape. [23]Place pie on baking sheet. [24]Bake until crust is golden brown and juices bubble (covering crust edges with aluminum foil if browning too quickly) about 1 hour 10 minutes. [25]Place pie on a rack to cool.

DIRECTIONS: Choose or write the best answer to each of the following questions using the evidence presented in the passage. When required, list specific sentence numbers or paragraph letters from the story to support the answer.

1. Why does the dough get divided into two pieces?

   _____

   _____

   Give the number of the sentence that best supports the answer. _____

2. Contrast the use of water in preparing the crust and in preparing the unbaked pie.

   _____

   _____

   _____

   List the numbers of the 2 sentences that best support the answer. _____, _____

3. What is the reason for cutting slits in the pie crust?
   A. so the juices can bubble
   B. so the steam can escape
   C. so the crusts won't burn
   D. so the pie can cool more quickly

   Give the number of the sentence that best supports the answer. _____

4. Put the following steps in order.

   _____ Add butter to dry mixture

   _____ Cut slits in crust

   _____ Refrigerate dough

   _____ Bake pie

   _____ Put filling into pie plate

   _____ Divide dough into two pieces

5. Why shouldn't all the sugar go into the filling mixture?

   _____

   _____

   _____

   Give the number of the sentence that best supports the answer. _____

6. What does the word *crimp* mean, as used in sentence 21?
   A. press together
   B. cut off
   C. add sugar to
   D. remove top from

7. If LaTonya lost her measuring tablespoon, about how many teaspoons of ice water would she use to make the crust?

   _____

   _____

8. What is the purpose of separating the crust directions from the filling directions?

   _____

   _____

   _____

9. How many ounces of sugar will you use to prepare the crust?

   _____

37. Making Mountains
by Cheryl Block

A [1]Where do mountains come from? [2]All mountains are formed by movement in the earth's crust. [3]The earth's crust, looking like a giant jigsaw puzzle, is made up of several large pieces, or plates. [4]These plates are constantly moving as a result of currents and pressures in the earth's mantle, so the earth's surface is always changing. [5]These changes, however, occur very slowly. [6]It can take hundreds of years for a mountain to develop. [7]By definition, a mountain must rise at least 2,000 feet above sea level.

B [8]There are four ways that mountains are formed by movement within the earth. [9]*Volcanoes* are formed when magma, molten rock from inside the earth's crust, rises through vents and erupts as lava. [10]As the lava and ash pile up, they form a mountain. [11]Most single mountain peaks, such as Mt. St. Helens in Washington, are the result of volcanic activity. [12]However, volcanic mountains can also form long chains, such as the Hawaiian Islands.

C [13]*Dome mountains* are also formed by magma. [14]However, molten rock beneath the earth's surface moves up under the crust but does not erupt. [15]Instead, the rising crust forms a dome. [16]An example of dome mountains is the Black Hills of South Dakota.

D [17]When the earth's crust breaks into large blocks of rock, it creates *block mountains*. [18]These blocks usually split along fault* lines and slide in opposite

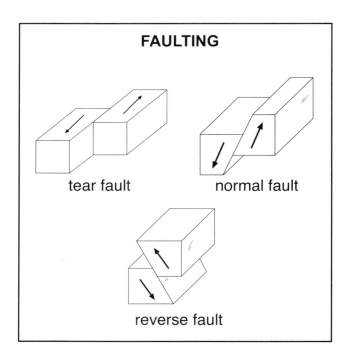

FAULTING

tear fault

normal fault

reverse fault

directions, some moving upward and some moving downward. [19]The Sierra Nevada Mountains in California are block mountains created by faulting.

E [20]The most common formations are *fold mountains*. [21]These occur when the large plates of the earth's crust move against each other, pushing and squeezing the crust into folds. [22]As the plates collide, one plate is forced below another. [23]Because the great pressure of the plates pushing together is exerted over a long period of time, the pressure causes the crustal rock between these plates to gradually bend and fold over. [24]The slow-moving crust is crushed and tilted, thrusting upward along the point of collision to form young mountains. [25]Some of the world's greatest mountain ranges, such as the Himalayas, the Rockies, and the Alps, have been formed by folding.

*fault: a break in the earth's surface caused by movement of the earth's crust

DIRECTIONS: Choose or write the best answer to each of the following questions using the evidence presented in the passage. When required, list specific sentence numbers or paragraph letters from the story to support the answer.

1. What are the similarities and differences between a volcano and a dome mountain?

    _____

    _____

    _____

    _____

    List the letters of the 2 paragraphs that best support the answer. ____, ____

2. The Black Hills are an example of:
    A. dome mountains.
    B. volcanic mountains.
    C. fold mountains.
    D. block mountains.

    Give the number of the sentence that best supports the answer. ____

3. The main idea of the article is:

    _____

    _____

    Give the letter of the paragraph that best supports the answer. ____

4. From the article, it can be inferred that:
    A. mountains can begin forming undersea.
    B. mountains form only on land.
    C. mountains are formed all at once.
    D. mountains occur only in warm climates.

    Give the number of the sentence that best supports the answer. ____

5. A mountain is the result of:

    _____

    Give the number of the sentence that best supports the answer. ____

6. A volcano is built from:
    A. crust.
    B. lava and ash.
    C. rock and ash.
    D. magma.

    Give the number of the sentence that best supports the answer. ____

7. When blocks of rock move diagonally towards each other, it is called:
    A. a tear fault.
    B. a normal fault.
    C. a reverse fault.
    D. a block fault.

8. The folding of rocks is caused by two plates:
    A. sliding in opposite directions.
    B. pulling apart from each other.
    C. thrusting downward.
    D. pushing together.

    Give the letter of the paragraph that best supports the answer. ____

9. From the article, the conclusion can be made that mountains:
    A. stop growing once they are formed.
    B. continue to grow and change.
    C. change only after an earthquake.
    D. grow a specific amount every year.

    Give the letter of the paragraph that best supports the answer. ____

38. Researching the Renaissance
by David White

[1]Ling searched the Internet for information about Italy's great Renaissance artists. [2]She found this web page:

Leonardo

[3]Leonardo Da Vinci was a famous painter, architect, sculptor, engineer, and scientist. [4]He first made a name for himself painting religious images, including *The Last Supper.* [5]He also created <u>notebooks</u> of scientific drawings, many of the human body. [6]Included in these notebooks were plans for such modern inventions as the tank, the car, and the parachute. [7]He was fascinated with the idea of flying like a bird. [8]He also painted the *Mona Lisa* (right), still one of the most recognizable paintings in the world. [9]His paintings and notebooks influence artists and engineers today.

[10]**More About Leonardo (links)**
<u>From Vinci to Florence: Leonardo's Artistic Journey</u>
<u>Leonardo's Inventions and Their Modern Equivalents</u>
<u>The Renaissance in Italy</u>

Michelangelo

[11]Michelangelo, like Leonardo, was a leader of the Italian Renaissance. [12]He was a master painter, architect, and sculptor. [13]He is most famous for painting the ceiling of the <u>Sistine Chapel</u> in Rome and for sculpting a giant statue of the Hebrew King <u>David</u> (left). [14]Also, he designed the dome of <u>St. Peter's Church</u> in Rome. [15]This dome is still the largest of any church in the world. [16]Like Leonardo, Michelangelo painted many religious paintings, including *The Last Judgment.* [17]His works of art are still admired and copied today.

[18]**More About Michelangelo (links)**
<u>The Sistine Chapel: Beauty on a Breathtaking Scale</u>
<u>Michelangelo's Influence on Modern Sculpture</u>

Raphael

[19]Raphael, too, is famous for sculpture and for religious paintings, including the *Sistine Madonna.* [20]However, his most famous painting is *School of Athens* (snapshot left), which portrays a meeting between <u>Plato</u> and <u>Aristotle</u> amid the intellectual activities at the famous <u>Academy</u>. [21]Like Leonardo and Michelangelo before him, Raphael painted his people as realistic, a change from the abstract images of medieval artists. [22]This is the artists' legacy: they showed things as they were, not as the artist wished them to be.

[23]**More About Raphael (links)**
School of Athens: Renaissance High-Water Mark
<u>Raphael and the High Renaissance in Italy</u>

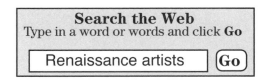
Search the Web
Type in a word or words and click **Go**

| Renaissance artists | **Go** |

DIRECTIONS: Choose or write the best answer to each of the following questions using the evidence presented in the passage. When required, list specific sentence numbers or paragraph letters from the story to support the answer.

1. The passage about Michelangelo supplies evidence that he did all of the following EXCEPT:
   A. sculpt a statue.
   B. design a church dome.
   C. paint a religious painting.
   D. keep a scientific notebook.

   List the numbers of the 3 sentences that best support the answer. ____, ____, ____

2. Which of these did Leonardo probably also study?
   A. history
   B. politics
   C. anatomy
   D. languages

   Give the number of the sentence that best supports the answer. ____

3. The word *Renaissance* means "rebirth." The Renaissance was a rebirth of interest in the early civilizations of Greece, Rome, and Israel. Name two examples of art listed in the story that support this idea.

   _____

   _____

   _____

4. Is the underlined part of the following sentence a cause or an effect? "He is also famous for painting the *Mona Lisa*."

   _____

   _____

5. Based on sentences 9 and 17, which of the following general statements could be made about all 3 men?
   A. Their work survives them.
   B. Their peers admired them.
   C. Their reputation preceded them.
   D. Their work still inspires people.

6. Name three things that all three men had in common.

   _____

   _____

   _____

   _____

   _____

7. Which of these sentences is the best summary of the article?
   A. The Renaissance was a time of great artists, long wars, and political unrest.
   B. During the Renaissance, great artists produced beautiful paintings, sculptures, and buildings.
   C. Artists of the Renaissance focused on religion and realism above all else.
   D. The Renaissance featured famous men who were masters in the fields of art, architecture, and science.

39. Soccer's Deadly Weapon: Mia Hamm
by Cheryl Block

A [1]She's been called "the most dangerous forward on the field." [2]Mia Hamm, high-scoring forward for the U.S. team, has been one of soccer's brightest stars. [3]Her foundation, the Mia Hamm Foundation, is dedicated to funding research for bone marrow diseases and to developing sports programs for young women.

B [4]Mia was born March 17, 1972, in Selma, Alabama. [5]Since her father was a fighter pilot with the Air Force, her family moved often when she was growing up. [6]Her dad coached and refereed soccer games. [7]Mia started her soccer career playing with her two older brothers and three older sisters. [8]With six children in the family, she learned early how to hold her own.

C [9]By the time she reached her teens, Mia was an experienced soccer player. [10]At age 15, she was recruited as the youngest player ever on the U.S. Soccer Federation women's national team.

D [11]Mia attended the University of North Carolina, graduating with a degree in political science. [12]During the five years she attended the University before graduating, she led the school to four NCAA soccer championships. [13]In her third year of college, however, she took a year off from the college soccer season to play in the first FIFA (Federation Internationale de Football Association) Women's World Cup Championships in China in 1991. [14]Mia scored the game-winning goal in their first match, and the U.S. team went on to win the Cup.

E [15]In 1994, Mia was named U.S. Soccer Female Athlete of the Year. [16]As Mia says, though, "My motivation is not awards but just to get better every year."

F [17]Mia won her first gold medal at the Atlanta Olympics in 1996, even though she played with a severely sprained ankle after injuring it in the first match. [18]In the final match against China, more than 75,000 fans packed the stadium to watch the United States win the gold medal. [19]In 1999, the United States women's national team won the Women's World Cup for a second time, hosting the world's best attended women's sporting event with nearly 100,000 spectators. [20]This was a significant change from the 500 or so spectators who had watched the U.S. team play when Mia first joined them as a teenager. [21]Little did those early soccer fans know that they were watching an athlete who would become the U.S. team's all-time leading scorer with 107 goals so far, and one of the soccer world's greatest players.

DIRECTIONS: Choose or write the best answer to each of the following questions using the evidence presented in the passage. When required, list specific sentence numbers or paragraph letters from the story to support the answer.

1. Based on paragraph B, how did Mia's family help to develop her interest in soccer?

   _____

   _____

   _____

   _____

2. Mia won her first Olympic medal:
   A. while still in college.
   B. after she graduated from college.
   C. while still in high school.
   D. before she joined the U.S. women's national team.

   List the numbers of the 3 sentences that best support the answer.

   _____, _____, _____

3. Mia's personal goal for playing soccer is to:
   A. win as many awards as possible.
   B. always strive to improve.
   C. play to be recognized.
   D. do only what's necessary.

   Give the number of the sentence that best supports the answer. _____

4. Sentence 17 suggests that Mia is a person who:
   A. puts herself first.
   B. is easily discouraged.
   C. craves attention.
   D. does not quit.

5. Why is Mia considered the U.S. team's all-time leading scorer?

   _____

   _____

   Give the number of the sentence that best supports the answer. _____

6. Why was the attendance at the 1999 Women's World Cup significant?

   _____

   _____

   Give the number of the sentence that best supports the answer. _____

7. Based on this passage, you could conclude that Mia:
   A. has contributed to the growth of women's soccer.
   B. is best at playing goalie.
   C. is determined to win as many awards as possible.
   D. has a desire to one day coach soccer.

8. Based on paragraph F, the conclusion can be made that interest in women's soccer has:
   A. decreased.
   B. stayed the same.
   C. increased.
   D. varied.

40. Measuring Time
   by Cheryl Block

A [1]Could you tell time if you didn't have a watch or a clock? [2]The clock as we know it wasn't invented until the late 1200s. [3]So how did ancient man keep track of time?

B [4]Early man measured time by observing the movements of the sun. [5]He learned to watch the shadows cast by the sun as it moved across the sky. [6]At sunrise, the sun's shadow was long, by midday it was shorter, and by sunset it had lengthened again.

C [7]The first sundials were developed more than 4,000 years ago to measure the sun's shadow. [8]The sun's shadow moves across the dial and points to the "hours" marked on it. [9]Early Babylonian astronomers divided the imaginary circular path of the sun into 12 equal parts. [10]Then they divided the periods of daylight and darkness into 12 parts each, resulting in a 24-hour day. [11]However, the Babylonian *hour* was not the same as what we call an hour. [12]Their hour varied in length from day to day because the Babylonians counted twelve hours of sunshine every day, no matter how long or short the day was. [13]Therefore, in the summer, each daylight hour was longer and in the winter, each daylight hour was shorter.

D [14]A sundial measured only daylight hours and worked only if the day was clear. [15]So other devices, such as the water clock and the candle clock, were invented to keep time at night and on cloudy days. [16]The candle clock was simply a candle that had marks on it for each hour; time was kept by burning the candle. [17]The earliest Egyptian water clock was a container from which water drained at a steady rate. [18]Marks inside the pot measured the water level and showed how much time had passed.

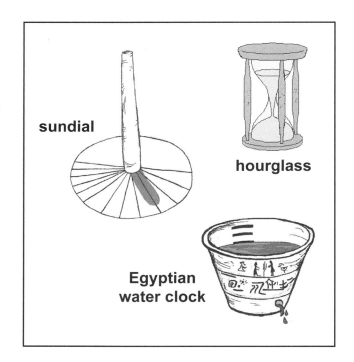

sundial

hourglass

Egyptian water clock

E [19]Greek and Roman water clocks were more intricate than Egyptian water clocks. [20]Sometimes several bowls were connected, and water ran from one to the next. [21]Some of the clocks even had dials and hands to mark the hours. [22]In these clocks, the hands were attached to little wooden ducks that floated on the surface. [23]As the water ran out, the ducks were lowered, pulling the hands down.

F [24]Water clocks, however, could get clogged or freeze, and flames on candle clocks blew out. [25]So the Romans invented the sand clock, or hourglass. [26]Sand didn't freeze and, since the container was sealed, it didn't get clogged as easily. [27]It was also portable. [28]Hourglasses are even used today.

G [29]None of these early clocks were very reliable, and none of them told you exactly what time of day it was. [30]They simply kept track of how much time had passed since the bowl was filled with water or the candle was lit. [31]It would take the development of the mechanical clock in the late Middle Ages to begin a more accurate measurement of time.

DIRECTIONS: Choose or write the best answer to each of the following questions using the evidence presented in the passage. When required, list specific sentence numbers or paragraph letters from the story to support the answer.

1. How does our hour contrast with that of the Babylonians?

   _____

   _____

   _____

   List the numbers of the 2 sentences that best support the answer. ____, ____

2. Why are there 13 lines marked on the sundial?

   _____

   _____

   Give the number of the sentence that best supports the answer. ____

3. What caused the hands of a water clock to turn?

   _____

   _____

   _____

   _____

   List the numbers of the 2 sentences that best support the answer. ____, ____

4. How did the early Egyptian water clock measure time?

   _____

   _____

   _____

5. How might a water clock get clogged?

   _____

   _____

6. What were the advantages of using sand in a clock?
   A. Sand didn't freeze or clog as easily.
   B. Sand passed more quickly than water.
   C. Sand was easier to find than water.
   D. Sand clocks were sturdier.

7. How did the design of the hourglass make it portable?

   _____

   _____

   _____

8. In general, NONE of the early clocks indicated:
   A. how many hours had passed.
   B. the length of the sun's shadow.
   C. how many minutes had passed.
   D. the number of daylight hours.

   List the numbers of the 2 sentences that best support the answer. ____, ____

9. What is the main idea of the article?
   A. Man relied on the sun to keep track of time.
   B. Time was unimportant to early man.
   C. Early clocks measured only daylight.
   D. Man invented different ways to measure time.

41. ElectroMagic
by Margaret Hockett

A [1]Imagine sound waves flowing through speakers. [2]Giant cranes lifting tons of scrap metal. [3]Wheels and turbines spinning. [4]All of these events can be enabled by the electromagnetic motor. [5]But what is electromagnetism, and how can it be used to make a motor?

B [6]The difference between the regular, or permanent, magnet and the electromagnet is that an electromagnet depends on a flow of electricity to create a magnetic field. [7]Any magnetic force has direction. [8]That is why magnets have south and north poles. [9](The north pole is attracted to the earth's North Pole.) [10]If you put two magnets together, the north end of one will attract the south end of the other and repel its north end. [11]We can put this fact to use when making an electromagnet.

C [12]Electricity itself creates a magnetic force. [13](When electric current flows through a wire, a magnetic field is created.) [14]So if you take a bar of iron, wrap it with a wire, and connect the wire ends to a battery, the bar becomes an electromagnet. [15]Which end of this electromagnet is north and which is south? [16]It depends on the direction of the electric current. [17]If you changed the direction of the electricity, the end that was south would become north and the end that was north would become south.

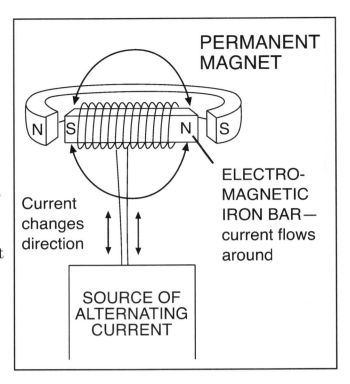

PERMANENT MAGNET

N S   N S

Current changes direction

ELECTRO-MAGNETIC IRON BAR— current flows around

SOURCE OF ALTERNATING CURRENT

D [18]Now, let's place our electromagnet between the poles of a curved permanent magnet that is fixed in place. [19]Of course, each pole of the electromagnet will be attracted to the opposite pole of the permanent magnet. [20]We'll also attach our electromagnet to a source of alternating current so the poles of the electromagnet change back and forth. [21]This reversing of poles makes each pole of the electromagnet attract one and then the other of the two poles of the permanent magnet. [22]The result? [23]The electromagnet spins and we now have a basic electromagnetic motor!

DIRECTIONS: Choose or write the best answer to each of the following questions using the evidence presented in the passage. When required, list specific sentence numbers or paragraph letters from the story to support the answer.

1. What is the author's main purpose?

   _____

   _____

   Give the number of the sentence that best supports the answer. _____

2. Which of the following are necessary to make the electromagnet spin in an electromagnetic motor? (Choose all that apply.)
   A. the reversal of the flow of current
   B. the continuous switching of the poles of the permanent magnet
   C. the attraction of opposite magnetic poles
   D. the disconnection of the current source

   Give the letter of the paragraph that best supports the answer._____

3. What is the first step in building an electromagnet?
   A. Send current through a wire.
   B. Place an electromagnet between poles of a permanent magnet.
   C. Coil wire around an iron bar.
   D. Connect both ends of a wire.

   Give the number of the sentence that best illustrates that step. _____

4. Let's say you set up the magnet as described in the passage, but you place the electromagnet between the south poles of two different permanent magnets. Predict the results.

   _____

   _____

5. What generalization can be made from the information given?
   A. Magnetism requires the flow of electric current.
   B. Electromagnetic motors are used to perform different types of work.
   C. No work can get done without alternating current.
   D. All electromagnets must be spinning electromagnetic motors.

   Give the letter of the paragraph that best supports the answer. _____

6. What is the main difference between a permanent magnet and an electromagnet?
   A. Permanent magnets do not need electricity to produce a magnetic field.
   B. Electromagnets need alternating current.
   C. In permanent magnets, poles are attractive to opposite poles of another magnet.
   D. Electromagnets attract best without current.

   Give the number of the sentence that best supports the answer. _____

7. It can be inferred that alternating current:
   A. changes direction only once.
   B. keeps reversing its direction of flow.
   C. runs both directions at the same time.
   D. flows without changing direction.

   List the numbers of the 2 sentences from paragraph D that best support the answer. _____, _____

42. Sports Stats
by David White

A [1]Think you don't need math to play sports? [2]You couldn't keep score or total statistics without it.

B [3]Take basketball, for example. [4]You use addition to figure points, rebounds, and assists. [5]You use subtraction to determine how many minutes are left in the half or in the game. [6]But most of all, you use division to compile statistics. [7]Coaches and fans can compare the performances of players by using statistics. [8]For instance, you could say that NBA player Kobe Bryant was 3-for-4 in the first quarter. [9]This means that he attempted four shots and made three of them. [10]But how did he compare to fellow NBA player Kevin Garnett, who was 4-for-6? [11]To get the answer, you use division to determine the percentage of shots each player made.

C [12]To find percentage, you divide the smaller number by the larger number. [13]Bryant's percentage is 3 divided by 4, or .75, which is 75 percent. [14]So we say Bryant made 75 percent of his shots. [15]Garnett's percentage is 4 divided by 6, or .67, which is 67 percent. [16]Garnett made 67 percent of his shots. [17]Even though Garnett made one more shot than Bryant, he attempted two more, so his percentage is lower.

D [18]This percentage comparison is especially helpful with larger numbers. [19]If all you know is that Bryant's shooting statistics are 150-for-200 and Garnett's shooting statistics are 225-for-300, then you might have a difficult time comparing their performances. [20]But calculate their percentages and you'll find that they're the same: 75 percent.

E [21]You can also figure a player's percentage over time to see if he or she is maintaining a high (or low) level of performance. [22]If Bryant has made 65 of 100 shots, then he is shooting 65 percent

NBA Team Statistics

Team	Shooting %	Opponents' Shooting %
Blazers	.47	.42
Hornets	.44	.45
Jazz	.46	.45
Knicks	.45	.41
Lakers	.45	.41
Magic	.45	.45
Pacers	.46	.45
Spurs	.46	.42

for the season. [23]If he is 10-for-20 in his next game, then his overall shooting percentage goes down because that game's percentage is only 50, which is lower than his season percentage. [24]The adjusted seasonal figures are 75-for-120 (65+10=75 and 100+20=120), or about 63 percent.

F [25]One way coaches and players use this percentage information is to estimate probability. [26]Let's say that Kobe Bryant's free throw percentage was 80 percent. [27]His teammate, Shaquille O'Neal, had a much lower free throw percentage—56 percent. [28]If their team was depending on one player to make two free throws, whom did they want to shoot those free throws? [29]Kobe Bryant. [30]Why? [31]His free throw percentage was higher because he made more of the free throws he attempted. [32]Therefore, he had a *higher probability* of making the shots than O'Neal did.

G [33]Now, the only way to find out whether Bryant will make those shots is to let him shoot. [34]But playing the percentages is a key part of game strategy. [35]You want to use your knowledge to your team's advantage.

DIRECTIONS: Choose or write the best answer to each of the following questions using the evidence presented in the passage. When required, list specific sentence numbers or paragraph letters from the story to support the answer.

1. According to the passage, which basic math task is NOT used in computing statistics?
   A. addition
   B. subtraction
   C. multiplication
   D. division

   List the numbers of the 3 sentences that best support the answer.

   _____, _____, _____

2. Name two ways coaches use statistics.

   _____

   _____

   _____

   _____

   List the numbers of the 2 sentences that best support the answer. _____, _____

3. In the first 10 games, a player made 50 of 100 shots. In his latest game, he was 15-for-20. What was his shooting percentage before the latest game, and what is it now?

   _____

   _____

4. Rank these players according to their shooting percentages. Use 1 for the highest and 4 for the lowest.

   _____ Kidd   9-for-12

   _____ Jamison   11-for-22

   _____ Iverson   7-for-10

   _____ Webber   9-for-10

5. Kobe Bryant's shooting percentage suddenly dropped from 63 to 59 percent. What probably caused this?

   _____

   Give the letter of the paragraph that best supports the answer. _____

6. If Shaquille O'Neal improved his free throw shooting, which of these would most likely be true of his teammates?
   A. They would want to pass him the ball more.
   B. They would want to improve their own free throw shooting.
   C. They would want him to play better defense.
   D. They would want to know their probability of making free throws.

   List the numbers of the 4 sentences that best support the answer.

   _____, _____, _____, _____

7. Which of these statements best describes the main idea?
   A. to teach the value of probability
   B. to teach the calculation of percentages
   C. to show how math is used in sports
   D. to show how much math athletes need to know

   Give the letter of the paragraph that best supports the answer. _____

8. According to the diagram, the Blazers
   A. are first on the list in defense.
   B. are last on the list in shooting.
   C. have made more shots than their opponents.
   D. have made more shots than they have missed.

43. Secrets of Special Effects
by Cheryl Block

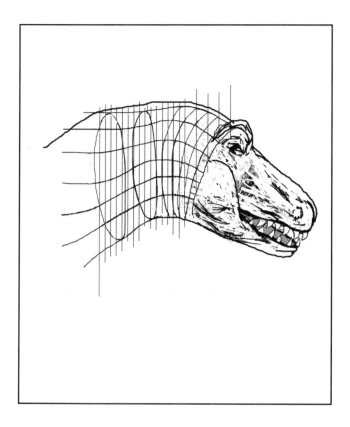

A [1]The attack by a *Tyrannosaurus rex* in the movie *Jurassic Park* (1993), one of the greatest action scenes in modern film, was actually done with a computer generated image of a dinosaur. [2]Using the computer to create special effects has revolutionized modern filmmaking. [3]Computer animation combines the creativity of art with the technical skills of math and science. [4]Instead of building actual models of dinosaurs or space creatures, special effects technicians can bring to life three-dimensional images created on the computer.

B [5]It takes an intense effort to create a computer generated image (CGI). [6]The work is very detailed and is done in stages. [7]An artist may start with a two-dimensional pencil sketch of a creature. [8]Then a three-dimensional image called a "wire-frame" is created on the computer. [9]The wire-frame is created by connecting specific digital lines to key parts of the body to form a digital framework, or "skeleton," of the animal. [10]This framework must be measured exactly and to scale with the intended size of the creature. [11]The wire-frame is usually built in stages to connect each part of the creature's body. [12]If the animal has wings, for instance, separate wire frames must be made to show the wings in different positions.

C [13]Next, a special software program is used to mold "muscles" around the skeleton. [14]These muscles are used to make the creature appear to move realistically. [15]Each movement is created frame by frame. [16]A creature's features can be digitally animated to show large body movements and even facial expressions. [17]Special software is then used to paint realistic skin textures, shadows, spines, etc. on the three-dimensional model.

D [18]The use of CGI has given filmmakers the ability to combine these realistic animated creatures with live-action footage of real actors in actual settings. [19]A computer generated image can be programmed to move and "interact" with the actors onscreen. [20]In *Jurassic Park*, the wire-frame model of the T-Rex was blended into the action frame by frame, creating the illusion that a full-size dinosaur was on the rampage.

E [21]The animated film *Toy Story* (1995) was the first full-length film done completely by computer animation. [22]More than 100 computers were used to create the 110,000 frames of Buzz's and Woody's animated adventures. [23]Who knows where computer animation will take films next?

DIRECTIONS: Choose or write the best answer to each of the following questions using the evidence presented in the passage. When required, list specific sentence numbers or paragraph letters from the story to support the answer.

1. What is the main idea of this article?
   A. Computer-generated special effects have significantly changed film animation.
   B. Computers are being used in many aspects of filmmaking.
   C. Computer-generated images can now be blended with live-action footage in films.
   D. Computers can be used to create three-dimensional images.

2. After the wire-frame is built, the next step is to:
   A. add facial expressions.
   B. mold the muscles.
   C. paint the skin texture.
   D. move the muscles.

   Give the number of the sentence that best supports the answer. _____

3. A "wire-frame" is composed of

   _____

   _____

   Give the number of the sentence that best supports the answer. _____

4. What was the author's purpose in writing this article?
   A. to explain how cartoons are made
   B. to describe how a film uses special effects
   C. to compare different kinds of special effects
   D. to explain how computer images are used in special effects

5. What effect can a filmmaker hope to achieve by blending the computer image with the live-action footage?

   _____

   _____

   _____

   Give the number of the sentence that best supports the answer. _____

6. A wire-frame is a kind of
   A. outline.
   B. body cast.
   C. grid.
   D. sculpture.

7. In contrast to early cartoon figures, computer images appear to be:
   A. three-dimensional.
   B. able to move.
   C. two-dimensional.
   D. in full color.

   Give the number of the sentence that best supports the answer. _____

8. Why was the film *Toy Story* important in filmmaking history?

   _____

   _____

   _____

   Give the number of the sentence that best supports the answer. _____

44. Emperor Kublai Khan
by Carrie Beckwith

A [1]Kublai Khan, grandson of Genghis Khan, was the first Mongol to conquer and rule over China. [2]He declared himself emperor in 1271 and adopted the Chinese tradition of dynastic rule.* [3]He named his dynasty "Yuan," meaning the origin of the universe.

B [4]Khan realized that in order to rule China successfully, he would have to follow Chinese ways. [5]His people, the Mongols, were excellent fighters and conquered China by sheer force. [6]However, Khan did not want the Chinese to view him as a barbarian. [7]Unlike his grandfather, Kublai did not kill large numbers of people once they had been conquered. [8]Instead, he chose to work with them to rebuild what was lost during war. [9]He wanted the Chinese to believe his rule had been given the Mandate of Heaven.** [10]To help accomplish this goal, Khan appointed Confucians, or Chinese philosophers, as his government advisors.

C [11]Khan knew the economic stability of China depended on agriculture. [12]If the farmers were ignored, the whole empire would suffer. [13]So the villages that had been destroyed by the Mongol invasion were rebuilt and the farmlands were restored. [14]Khan also redistributed the land and gave farmers larger plots. [15]He gave them seeds and established grain reserves in case of drought or floods.

D [16]Art, science, and religion flourished during Khan's dynasty. [17]Artists were given new artistic freedom. [18]The ceramics, or "china," were exported worldwide. [19]Scientists were given new respect and made many advances in astronomy and map making. [20]Religious beliefs of all kinds were allowed. ([21]Khan wanted to be accepted by people of all religious backgrounds, so Taoists, Buddhists, Muslims, and Christians were all welcome in his court.) [22]As Khan had hoped, these accomplishments in art, science, and religion proved to many that he did have the Mandate of Heaven.

E [23]In 1294, Khan died and was buried in his homeland of Mongolia. [24]His soldiers laid him to rest and covered his body with dirt. [25]Then they rode over his burial site with their horses to mark out all trace of the site. [26]To this day, no one knows where Kublai Khan was buried.

F [27]His son ruled successfully for a period of time. [28]But the emperors that followed Khan's son were ineffective. [29]In 1368, after less than 100 years, the Yuan Dynasty was brought down by a peasant rebellion.

*dynastic rule: rule by a family or group, usually for a long period of time

**Mandate of Heaven: the approval, or authorization, of rule by Heaven

DIRECTIONS: Choose or write the best answer to each of the following questions using the evidence presented in the passage. When required, list specific sentence numbers or paragraph letters from the story to support the answer.

1. From the passage, the conclusion can be made that the emperors who ruled after Khan and his son:
   A. upheld the dynasty.
   B. strengthened the dynasty.
   C. bankrupted the dynasty.
   D. weakened the dynasty.

   List the numbers of the 2 sentences that best support the answer. ____ ,

   ____

2. The main purpose of the passage is to:
   A. explain how the Yuan Dynasty fell.
   B. present the artistic achievements of the Yuan Dynasty.
   C. explain how Kublai Khan ruled China.
   D. compare Mongol rule of China to Chinese rule.

3. We can infer that Khan wanted to be accepted by the:
   A. peasants.
   B. Chinese.
   C. Mongols.
   D. soldiers.

   Give the letter of the paragraph that best supports the answer. ____

4. Number the following events in their correct order.

   ____ Khan's son rules.

   ____ Khan declares himself emperor.

   ____ The Yuan Dynasty ends.

   ____ Khan is buried.

   ____ Some people come to believe Khan has received the Mandate of Heaven.

5. What caused some people to believe that Khan had received the Mandate of Heaven?

   _____

   _____

   _____

   _____

   Give the number of the sentence that best supports the answer. ____

6. What four things did Khan do to help farmers?

   _____

   _____

   _____

   _____

   _____

   _____

   List the numbers of the 3 sentences that best support the answer.

   ____ , ____ , ____

7. What do Kublai Khan's actions tell you about his character?
   A. He was artistic.
   B. He was tolerant.
   C. He was merciless.
   D. He was unsure of himself.

   List the letters of the 2 paragraphs that best support the answer. ____ , ____

45. Is the Earth Heating Up?
by Cheryl Block

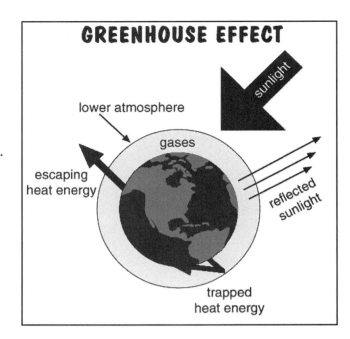

GREENHOUSE EFFECT

sunlight

lower atmosphere

gases

escaping heat energy

reflected sunlight

trapped heat energy

A [1]Global warming could affect the future of our earth's environment. [2]Humans are warming the earth's atmosphere by burning fossil fuels and cutting down forests. [3]In turn, this warming is affecting Earth's climate and atmosphere.

B [4]One cause of global warming is what is called the "Greenhouse Effect." [5]The atmosphere surrounding Earth is made up mainly of oxygen and nitrogen, with a trace of carbon dioxide and other gases. [6]Sunlight striking the earth changes to heat energy. [7]Some of this energy is absorbed by soils, plants, and water. [8]Gases in the atmosphere, such as carbon dioxide (CO_2), methane, and water vapor, also absorb some of this heat energy, thus warming the atmosphere. [9]The rest is normally reflected back from Earth's surface. [10]The glass or plastic walls in a greenhouse let in sunlight and then trap its heat. [11]The gases in the atmosphere act in the same way as the greenhouse walls, letting the sunlight pass through the atmosphere, but then keeping some heat energy from escaping. [12]If, however, the amount of these gases in the atmosphere increases, the amount of heat energy absorbed by them also increases. [13]This extra heat trapped in the atmosphere causes global warming, a warming of the atmosphere and an increase in Earth's temperature.

C [14]An increase in the carbon dioxide levels in the atmosphere has been significant in increasing global warming. [15]CO_2 is formed when fossil fuels such as coal and oil are burned. [16]The amount of CO_2 in the atmosphere started increasing in the 19th century, especially after the start of the Industrial Revolution and the development of large factories. [17]Cutting down forests has also increased the amount of CO_2 in

the atmosphere because the trees normally would have absorbed some of the carbon dioxide.

D [18]The amount of other gases in the atmosphere is also increasing. [19]Methane is released during coal mining and from garbage in landfills. [20]Since the 1980s, methane levels have been rising each year. [21]Methane is even more effective than CO_2 at trapping heat.

E [22]Scientists theorize two major effects of global warming. [23]The first, which may already be occurring, is a change in weather patterns which will cause changes in temperature, the amount and pattern of rainfall, and the frequency and intensity of storms. [24]Environmental scientists are concerned that continued global warming could cause Earth's surface to warm up to a dangerous level, altering natural and agricultural ecosystems, and endangering life. [25]This increased temperature could lead to the second major effect of global warming: a partial melting of the polar icecaps and a rise in sea level which could drastically affect coastal environments.

DIRECTIONS: Choose or write the best answer to each of the following questions using the evidence presented in the passage. When required, list specific sentence numbers or paragraph letters from the story to support the answer.

1. How does cutting down forests increase CO_2 in the atmosphere?

   _____

   _____

   _____

   Give the number of the sentence that best supports the answer. _____

2. What is the main idea of the article?
   A. Global warming is good for the earth's environment.
   B. The Greenhouse Effect is a factor in global warming.
   C. The Greenhouse Effect is caused by increasing carbon dioxide.
   D. Global warming is caused by cutting down forests.

3. What causes higher levels of methane in the atmosphere?

   _____

   _____

   _____

   Give the number of the sentence that best supports the answer. _____

4. How does gas in the atmosphere function similarly to the glass or plastic in a greenhouse?

   _____

   _____

   _____

   List the numbers of the 2 sentences that best support the answer.

   _____, _____

5. Why are increasing methane levels in the atmosphere a concern?

   _____

   _____

   _____

   Give the number of the sentence that best supports the answer. _____

6. How does the amount of the gases in the atmosphere affect the amount of heat energy in the atmosphere?

   _____

   _____

   Give the number of the sentence that best supports the answer. _____

7. Why might levels of carbon dioxide have begun to increase during the Industrial Revolution, as indicated in sentence 16?

   _____

   _____

   _____

   Give the number of the sentence that best supports the answer. _____

8. According to the diagram, both heat energy and sunlight are:
   A. reflected into space.
   B. trapped in the atmosphere.
   C. reflected back to Earth.
   D. absorbed by gases.

46. Gimme Some Latitude! (and a little longitude wouldn't hurt)
by Margaret Hockett

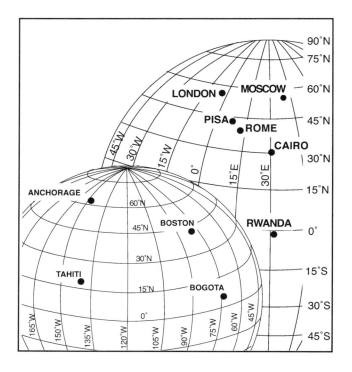

A [1]Latitude and longitude lines are very useful for pinpointing locations. [2]For instance, let's say your "friends" run off to explore the world without you. [3]So you set a private investigator on their trail and the P.I. gets the goods from an informant: the pair were last seen at 44° N, 10° E. [4]So you know right where to go to give them a "Pisa" your mind.

B [5]Here's how it works: the lines divvy up the whole world into a grid. [6]Latitude lines are parallel and run east and west. [7]The first line is at 0° latitude, which is the equator. [8](Your P.I. could *really* be hot on the trail there!) [9]The rest of the latitude lines are numbered from the equator and are labelled N or S according to which side of it they are on. [10]The last latitude lines are really just points at the poles (90° S and 90° N). [11]Longitude lines, or meridians, run north and south. [12]The first, at 0° longitude, is called the Prime Meridian. [13]The rest of the longitude lines are numbered from the Prime Meridian and are labelled E or W, according to the side of it on which they lie. [14]At 180° longitude, on the side of the world opposite the Prime Meridian, is the International Dateline. [15]When you cross this one, you are suddenly catapulted into a new hemisphere and a whole new day. [16](Hmm…if you can't find your friends, at least you could get a new "date" here!)

C [17]Back to our example. [18]When you hear that your disloyal friends are at a winter tea party at 42° N 71° W, will you know to pack your warm clothes and head to Boston? [19]Suppose they are spotted eating tropical fruits at 17° N 139° W; will you go bananas or go to Tahiti? [20]What if they're rumored to be in a large city with fertile soil at 30° N 31° E? [21]Will you be in de "nile" as you head for Cairo?

D [22]I think you get the hang of it. [23]Now, with all this information, you can make up a really cool game to entertain your friends when they realize the error of their ways and come groveling back. [24]In fact, they'll never want to [city name]* again!

*city located at 42° N, 12° E

DIRECTIONS: Choose or write the best answer to each of the following questions using the evidence presented in the passage. When required, list specific sentence numbers or paragraph letters from the story to support the answer.

1. The main purpose of the passage is to:
   A. show the usefulness of latitude and longitude.
   B. show how to track someone down.
   C. describe the positions of geographical locations.
   D. convince you to solve problems.

   Give the number of the sentence that best supports the answer. _____

2. If someone were to walk along the Prime Meridian to the North Pole and beyond, that longitude line would become:
   (Choose all that apply.)
   A. the International Dateline.
   B. the equator.
   C. 0° longitude.
   D. 180° longitude.

   Give the number of the sentence that best supports the answer. _____

3. Which of the following is NOT reasonable to conclude?
   A. The eastern and western hemispheres have different days.
   B. The day changes as you cross the International Dateline.
   C. It is a day earlier in the western hemisphere than in the eastern.
   D. The day changes as you cross the Prime Meridian.

4. Label the following as T for true or F for false.
   _____ 0° longitude is the equator.

   _____ 90° N is the North Pole.

   _____ 0°, 0° is where the equator crosses the International Dateline.

   _____ 30° N, 75° W is in Asia.

5. Explain why coordinates are given in place of the verb in sentence 24.

   _____

   _____

6. Label each of the following F for fact or O for opinion.
   _____ Tahiti is located at 17° N, 139° W.

   _____ The International Dateline and Prime Meridian separate the world into halves.

   _____ Latitude/longitude is the best system for locating people or things.

   _____ Cairo is on the Nile River.

7. Describe one way in which the lines of latitude and longitude are different and one way in which they are alike.

   Difference:_____

   _____

   Similarity:_____

   _____

8. The word *groveling*, as used in sentence 23, most likely means:
   A. dancing.
   B. acting snobby.
   C. knowledgeably.
   D. acting humble.

9. The phrase "gets the goods," as used in sentence 3, most likely means:
   A. retrieves the couple.
   B. finds information.
   C. picks up packages.
   D. extracts a confession.

47. Finding the Career for You
by Carrie Beckwith

A [1]Have you given time to consider what you want to do with your life once you've completed your education? [2]If not, then now is a good time to start!

B [3]To begin with, you should know a little bit about yourself. [4]For example, are you practical, intellectual, creative, persuasive, or social? [5]You probably consider yourself a combination of these traits, but, most likely, you will identify more closely with two or three of them.

C [6]Next, brainstorm the things that interest you. [7]For example, if you are creative, you might enjoy a career in music, drama, or the arts. [8]If you have trouble identifying what interests you, talk with a friend or family member who is a good listener, or write about your values and principles and what you want to accomplish in life.

D [9]Your abilities are another important factor to consider. [10]If you're strong in math, then you'd probably be a good engineer or accountant. [11]If you would rather be working with people than numbers, then you'd probably be a good social worker, office manager, or salesperson.

E [12]Aptitude or interest inventory tests are a great way to help you discover your personality type, interests, and abilities. [13]There are several of these types of tests on the Internet. [14]Search under the key words "personality test" and "career assessment." [15]Your school may also be able to provide such tests.

F [16]Once you have an idea about which careers might interest you, begin to explore them! [17]Talk to people who have jobs that interest you. [18]Volunteer your time. [19]Go to the library's reference section and research the specific careers you are considering.

G [20]If you feel you have too many options and unknowns, then make a list of your possible career options. [21]One by one, study each career and list its pros and cons. [22]Next, decide how important each pro and con is (not very important, important, or very important). [23]For example, you may list three cons and one pro, but decide that the cons are not very important and that the pro is very important. [24]Therefore, although the option would seem to be a bad choice (more cons than pros), it is actually a good choice because the pro is *more important* than the cons.

H [25]Getting started on a career path can save you time in the future. [26]You will know which classes to take in high school and college and which types of internships, volunteer work, or paid jobs you will be interested in. [27]Don't worry if you have a change of heart and suddenly decide that you don't want to be a teacher or a lawyer. [28]Researching a career is all about self-discovery. [29]You may change your mind several times. [30]In fact, you may change your career several times in your life. [31]The important thing is to think about these things and test the waters a little before braving the working world. [32]Good luck and get going!

DIRECTIONS: Choose or write the best answer to each of the following questions using the evidence presented in the passage. When required, list specific sentence numbers or paragraph letters from the story to support the answer.

1. What is the author's viewpoint on how to choose a career?
   A. Take whatever job you're offered.
   B. Research a career path based on interests and abilities.
   C. Evaluate your options to make the best career choice.
   D. Try out several careers and then choose the best one.

2. Number the steps that Ali should take in the order in which the author of the article would advise.

   _____ Ali talks to a family member.

   _____ Ali makes a list and rates each option.

   _____ Ali volunteers at a local elementary school.

   _____ Ali brainstorms different career options.

   _____ Ali takes an aptitude test and discovers she's creative.

3. In sentence 31, what does the author mean when she suggests that you "test the waters"?

   _____

   _____

4. Label the following statements F for fact or O for opinion.

   _____ It's perfectly acceptable to change your mind about a career.

   _____ The public library's reference section has information on careers.

   _____ Now is a good time to start researching a career.

5. What two things does the article mention might happen if you successfully research a career before you have to find a job?

   _____

   _____

   _____

   _____

   Give the number of the sentence that best supports the answer. _____

6. Pablo can't decide if he wants to become a veterinarian, a writer, a pharmacist, or a horse trainer. According to the passage, what should he do?

   _____

   _____

   _____

   Give the letter of the paragraph that best supports the answer. _____

7. You are trying to decide if you want to become a social worker. There are two very important cons and two important pros. According to the passage, should you still consider becoming a social worker? Explain your answer.

   _____

   _____

   _____

   Give the letter of the paragraph that best supports the answer. _____

48. Training for the Ballet
by Carrie Beckwith

A [1]Professional ballet dancers have perfected the art of making the most extraordinary movements of the body look graceful and easy. [2]However, this grace and ease takes years of hard work and dedication.

B [3]Training begins very early in life, usually when dancers are between the ages of six and ten. [4]Ballet class is held daily and begins with *barre* work, which is a series of warm-up exercises using the five basic positions of ballet. [5]During *barre* work, students work on placement, or the relationship of one part of the body to another, and turnout, the outward position of the feet. [6]Once the muscles have been warmed up, students move to the center of the floor and begin center practice, or *exercises au milieu*. [7]During center practice, dancers work on slow, sustained movements like the *ports de brau* and the *arabesque*. [8]These exercises build strength and balance. [9]Jumps, turns, and quick combinations of movements are practiced last.

C [10]Once a firm base in *barre* and center work is established, a dancer must learn the *pas de deux*, or double work, which is done with a partner. [11]In the *pas de deux*, the role of the male dancer is to lift and support the female dancer. [12]Male dancers must be very strong and often do weight lifting exercises during ballet class.

D [13]After almost a decade of training, dancers may decide to join a professional ballet company. [14]However, because the field is so competitive, few dancers actually make the transition from student to professional.

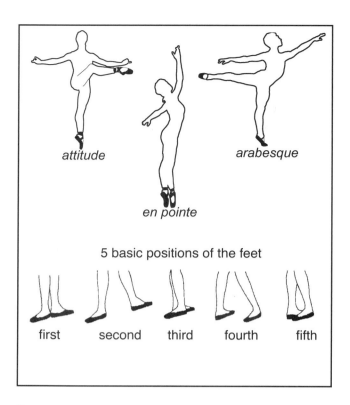

attitude   *arabesque*

en pointe

5 basic positions of the feet

first   second   third   fourth   fifth

[15]A dancer must not only be exceptionally skilled with the standard steps; he or she must also fit a physical ideal. [16]She must be of medium height, very slim, with long neck, arms, and legs. [17]He must be of medium height or tall, extremely strong, but not bulky. [18]Those dancers who do make it into a ballet company usually begin in the *corps de ballet*, which is the company's largest group of male and female dancers who always dance as a group. [19]A *corps* dancer may one day become a soloist, who has the privilege of dancing alone, but can also be included in groups of up to four. [20]At the very top of the hierarchy is the principal dancer, who is often the main attraction of a performance.

E [21]To the observer, the life of a professional ballet dancer may seem very glamorous. [22]In reality, it is a lot of hard work and determination. [23]Most ballet dancers, however, will tell you that the ballet is their life, and they wouldn't have it any other way.

DIRECTIONS: Choose or write the best answer to each of the following questions using the evidence presented in the passage. When required, list specific sentence numbers or paragraph letters from the story to support the answer.

1. The main idea is to describe:
   A. what is done during *barre* and *exercises au milieu.*
   B. how difficult it is to become a professional dancer.
   C. the training of a ballet dancer.
   D. the structure of a ballet company.

2. What type of work must be done before center work?

   _____

   List the numbers of the 2 sentences that best support the answer. ____, ____

3. Label the following statements F for fact or O for opinion.

   ____ Male ballet dancers do weight lifting exercises.

   ____ The professional ballet dancer learns the *pas de deux.*

   ____ The life of a dancer is fascinating.

   ____ The principal dancer has the most desirable position within the ballet company.

4. Which of the following inferences is supported in the passage?
   A. There are fewer principal dancers than *corps* dancers.
   B. There are fewer *corps* dancers than soloists.
   C. There are more principal dancers than soloists.
   D. There are fewer male dancers than female dancers.

   Give the number of the sentence that best supports the answer. ____

5. If the dancer shown *en pointe* were to lower her heels directly onto the floor, which position would her feet be in?
   A. first
   B. second
   C. fourth
   D. fifth

6. What is the *pas de deux?*

   _____

   _____

   List the numbers of the 2 sentences that best support the answer. ____, ____

7. List the different levels of dancers and the order in which the levels progress.

   _____

   _____

   _____

   List the numbers of the 3 sentences that best support the answer.

   ____, ____, ____

8. In the illustration, which movement shows the dancer standing on one leg with the other leg elevated behind?

   _____

9. In general, the training of someone who wants to be a dancer requires
   A. a demanding instructor.
   B. an education in music and fine arts.
   C. a long-term commitment.
   D. a large financial strain.

   List the numbers of the 3 sentences that best support the answer.

   ____, ____, ____

49. From Superman to X-Men
by Carrie Beckwith

A [1]In 1897, a collection of old newspaper cartoon strips were bound together and sold for a nickel apiece. [2]The comic book was called "Yellow Kid," and it was the first successful comic book ever published. [3]The public loved it and soon similar comic books, like "Mutt and Jeff" and "Buster Brown," began to appear.

B [4]The next big boost for comic books came with the invention of the first comic book superhero—"Superman"! [5]The visitor from another planet could leap tall buildings and go faster than a speeding bullet. [6]Superhero comics, in general, became very popular, and new superheroes like "Wonder Woman," "Batman," and "Captain Marvel" were created.

C [7]In 1941, America went to war and so, too, did the comics. [8]The new heroes were American soldiers and spies. [9]They fought Nazis, piloted war planes, and investigated underground resistance movements. [10]When WWII ended, so did the popularity of the war hero.

D [11]A short time after WWII, comic book sales were revived with the creation of crime comic books, like "True Crime," "Women Outlaws," and "War Against Crime." [12]Horror comic books also began to flourish. [13]Suddenly, comic book buyers couldn't get enough of them.

E [14]It didn't take long before parents and lawmakers started questioning how these horror and crime comics were affecting people, especially children. [15]By the early 1950s, a Senate subcommittee was organized to review the content of comic books. [16]The committee issued the Comic Code Authority, which placed firm regulations on the types of stories and art that could be published. [17]By the mid '50s, many comic book publishers were once again going out of business.

F [18]In the 1960s, a new science fiction superhero saved the day. [19]His name was Flash, and he was the fastest man alive. [20]"Spider Man" and the "Incredible Hulk" were created soon after. [21]Unlike some of the original superheroes, these new superheroes had human problems and didn't always enjoy their superhero abilities. [22]Bruce Banner didn't want to change into the Incredible Hulk and Spider Man was a teenage nerd who climbed walls and spun webs, but often wished he were just an ordinary teenager.

G [23]Within the last three decades of the 20th century, many successful comic book superheroes have been teenagers. [24]The revised "X-Men" comic book is about a group of teenage mutants with very human problems, like dating and "fitting in." [25]Another hit comic book with teenage superheroes is "Teenage Mutant Ninja Turtles." [26]In fact, the comic book was so popular, a television miniseries and a movie spun off from it in the late '80s.

H [27]Who knows who or what the next big craze in comic books will be? [28]If the future of comic books is anything like its past, it will be full of twists and turns.

DIRECTIONS: Choose or write the best answer to each of the following questions using the evidence presented in the passage. When required, list specific sentence numbers or paragraph letters from the story to support the answer.

1. How is the story organized?
   A. in order of importance
   B. in time order
   C. by type of comic book
   D. by type of superhero

2. Based on the article, the conclusion can be made that the business of publishing comic books has been:
   A. a great success.
   B. inconsistent.
   C. a great failure.
   D. steady.

3. Sequence the following events in the order in which they occurred.

   _____ Superhero comic books become a big hit.

   _____ "Teenage Mutant Ninja Turtles" are the big rage.

   _____ "Yellow Kid" makes its first appearance.

   _____ WWII ignites the popularity of soldier and spy heroes.

   _____ Science fiction superheroes revive the comic book industry.

   _____ Crime and horror comics gain popularity.

4. What do the words "spun off," as used in sentence 26, most likely mean?
   A. resulted
   B. halted
   C. picked out
   D. combined

5. What caused people in the early '50s to take a closer look at comic books?

   _____

   _____

   _____

   Give the number of the sentence that best supports the answer. _____

6. What is the major change from the superhero of the past to the superhero of today?

   _____

   _____

   _____

   Give the number of the sentence that best supports the answer. _____

7. In general, the image of the superhero is:
   A. unpopular.
   B. realistic.
   C. unchanging.
   D. changing.

   List the numbers of the 3 sentences that best support the answer.
   _____, _____, _____

8. It can be inferred that comic books are:
   A. usually about war and crime.
   B. very short stories.
   C. influenced by politics.
   D. read and enjoyed by everyone.

   List the letters of the 2 paragraphs that best support the answer. _____, _____

50. Secret Codes
by Margaret Hockett

A [1]Have you ever sent a secret message? [2]If so, you may have used one of these three types of secret codes: *camouflage*, *substitution*, or *repositioning*.

B [3]A camouflage code conceals your writing. [4]It can include marks disguised as part of a picture, or invisible ink penned between the lines of a decoy message.

C [5]In a substitution code, the letters are replaced. [6]Using a very simple code, you would find each letter of your message in the regular alphabet then replace it with the letter that is one position away:

A B C D E F G H I J K L M N O P Q R S T U V W X Y Z

B C D E F G H I J K L M N O P Q R S T U V W X Y Z A

D [7]The message COME AT ONCE would be coded as DPNFBUPODF. [8]This code is easy to break if it is intercepted, so use several alphabets. [9]Under the regular alphabet below is one that is offset by 2 letters and then one that is offset by 5:

A B C D E F G H I J K L M N O P Q R S T U V W X Y Z

C D E F G H I J K L M N O P Q R S T U V W X Y Z A B

F G H I J K L M N O P Q R S T U V W X Y Z A B C D E

E [10]To make decoding difficult, alternate, letter by letter, between the alphabets. [11]Of course, you must give your friend a "key" so he can unlock the message—"25" would mean 2 letters up then 5 letters up, then 2 then 5, etc. [12]Then he'll know that NJVXIT means LET'S GO.

F [13]Another example of substitution is shown at top left within the illustration. [14]Replace each letter with row and column numbers to write or even "tap" a message.

G [15]A third type of secret coding is based on letter repositioning. [16]In such codes, you might write the message in a different direction or mix up the letters. [17]The message in the lower left of the illustration reads diagonally. [18]Of course, your friend needs to

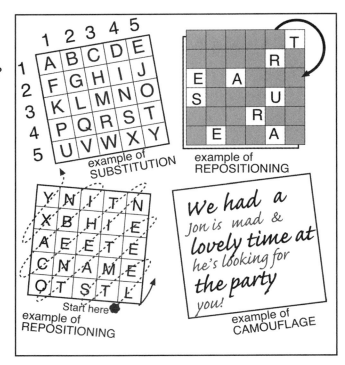

example of SUBSTITUTION

example of REPOSITIONING

example of REPOSITIONING

We had a
Jon is mad &
lovely time at
he's looking for
the party
you!

example of CAMOUFLAGE

Top left: "HI" is 2324. Top right: cutout is rotated to write "Treasure at…." Bottom right, invisible ink is revealed between lines of a friendly letter.

know where to start and what direction to follow. [19]You and your friend must agree on a codeword to use for the key—like "<u>Do</u>ll<u>ar</u>" for <u>diagonal</u>, <u>lower</u> <u>right</u>.

H [20]Another repositioning variation is to use a cardboard cutout to arrange your message on a grid. [21]First, you lay the cardboard template on a blank grid and write only in the squares revealed by the holes. [22]When you run out of holes, turn the template right by 90° and continue filling in your message. [23]Rotate and write until the grid is filled. [24](Use dummy letters in unfilled boxes.) [25]To read your message, your friend lays an identical template on the grid and reads the revealed letters, rotating as you did and continuing until the entire message is revealed.

I [26]We have looked at only three types of codes and have seen but a few examples of each. [27]There are many more codes to be conquered. [28]Who knows? [29]Perhaps you'll even create one of your own!

DIRECTIONS: Choose or write the best answer to each of the following questions using the evidence presented in the passage. When required, list specific sentence numbers or paragraph letters from the story to support the answer.

1. What is the author's purpose?

_____

_____

2. As used in sentence 21, the word *template* most likely means:
  A. grid.
  B. cardboard.
  C. holes.
  D. guide.

3. Which of the following provides the best summary of the article?
  A. Secret codes include camouflage (letter hiding), substitution (letter replacing), and repositioning (letter rearranging), among others.
  B. Someone had to make up all those codes, including camouflage and repositioning, and substitution, and yours may be just as good as those.
  C. Everyone from children to adults finds it useful to know how to use secret codes at one time or another.
  D. The best known secret code involves an alphabet substitution, though there are also two other main types.

4. Suppose you are given the message FAILNEDX and the key of 2 (meaning to take the first letter then every second letter) to get FIND ALEX. What type of code would that be?
  A. camouflage
  B. substitution
  C. repositioning
  D. none of the above

List the numbers of the 2 sentences that best support the answer.

_____ , _____

5. As used in sentence 10, what does the word *decoding* mean?

_____

_____

_____

6. Write the word CAT using the substitution code in paragraph C but with letters that are offset by two places, not one.

_____

_____

7. Using the substitution code at the top left in the illustration, translate the following message: 223511531155

_____

_____

8. What is the message given in the repositioning code at the lower left in the illustration?

_____

_____

9. From sentences 11, 19, and 25, you can generalize that in order to interpret a message, the receiver needs:
  A. a tool to decode the message.
  B. information on where to start.
  C. a template.
  D. a code word.

51. The Making of the Constitution
by Carrie Beckwith

A [1]The Constitutional Convention began on May 25, 1787, and lasted for four months. [2]However, the words *Constitutional Convention* were never used to describe the gathering. [3]The original intent of the meeting was to rewrite the Articles of Confederation, not to create a new form of government. [4]Most people during this time feared a single (national) government, having only recently won their freedom from Great Britain. [5]They preferred to have independent, separate state governments because this gave them more control. [6]So, when representative Edmund Randolph of Virginia presented his plan for a strong national government that would rule over the states, many of the representatives were furious, especially those from the smaller states.

B [7]Eventually, the representatives did agree to a national government (although they didn't use the word *national*), which would include a Congress that had two parts (called houses) and a president and vice president. [8]Now the concern was representation in the new Congress. [9]Small states feared they would be at a disadvantage. [10]The Articles of Confederation had given equal representation to each state. [11]Under the new plan, Congress would be represented according to state population. [12]After many heated debates, the men finally made a compromise. [13]In one house of Congress (the House of Representatives), the states would be represented based on population. [14]In the other house (the Senate), the states would be represented equally.

C [15]Some representatives also felt the Constitution needed a bill of rights.* [16]They feared the new president would become like a king and that the rights of individuals would be in danger. [17]In response

to this concern, James Madison and other nationalists agreed to add a bill of rights once the Constitution was approved.

D [18]Not all states agreed with these compromises. [19]However, the Constitution needed approval from only 9 of the 13 states in order to be accepted. [20]In a series of letters to newspapers, Alexander Hamilton, James Madison, and John Jay did their best to convince the people that the Constitution for the new government would not be abused. [21]The men explained how every bill passed in the House of Representatives would have to be voted on and approved by the Senate. [22]If approved by the Senate, the bill would go to the president, who could decide to reject the bill. [23]If this happened, the bill would go back to Congress, and if 2/3 of Congress decided to approve the bill, it would pass regardless of the president's rejection. [24]In addition, a Supreme Court would make sure that laws were constitutional. [25]The nationalists argued that this system of "checks and balances" would keep the government from becoming a tyranny (where one ruler had complete control) because each of the three branches of government could "check," or balance, the power of the other two.

E [26]On June 21, 1788, the Constitution of the United States of America went into effect after the 9th state voted in its favor. [27]It was a great victory for the nation and the beginning of a new united American people.

*bill of rights: a list of the rights the government should provide and protect

DIRECTIONS: Choose or write the best answer to each of the following questions using the evidence presented in the passage. When required, list specific sentence numbers or paragraph letters from the story to support the answer.

1. Why were many of the delegates surprised when they first heard Edmund Randolph's plan for a new government?
   A. They were expecting something more drastic.
   B. They were not expecting to change the current system of government.
   C. They didn't realize Randolph was a nationalist.
   D. They thought the current system of government was working well.

   List the numbers of the 2 sentences that best support the answer. ____, ____

2. Why did the delegates agree to a national government but avoid describing it as "national"?

   _____

   _____

   _____

   Give the number of the sentence that best supports the answer. ____

3. Why was a bill of rights added to the Constitution?

   _____

   _____

   Give the number of the sentence that best supports the answer. ____

4. If 60 of the 100 members of the Senate voted to override the president's rejection, what would happen to the bill?

   _____

5. When first approved, the Constitution had a bill of rights. True or False?

   Give the number of the sentence that best supports the answer. ____

6. Why would small states have been at a disadvantage according to Randolph's plan?

   _____

   _____

   _____

   List the numbers of the 2 sentences that best support the answer. ____, ____

7. Give one view of the nationalists that differed from the view of the people who were unsure of the Constitution.

   _____

   _____

   _____

   List the numbers of the 2 sentences that best support the answer. ____, ____

8. Which of the following statements are opinions? Choose all that apply.
   A. At least nine of the thirteen states approved the Constitution.
   B. The Constitution was a great American achievement.
   C. The purpose of the Supreme Court is to ensure that laws are constitutional.
   D. The nationalists did their best to convince people to support the Constitution.

posttests_____

FICTION POSTTEST
Treasure Island (Excerpt)
by Robert Louis Stevenson

A [1]We had thus proceeded for about half a mile, and were approaching the brow of the plateau, when the man upon the farthest left began to cry aloud, as if in terror. [2]Shout after shout came from him, and the others began to run in his direction.

B [3]"He can't 'a' found the treasure," said old Morgan, hurrying past us from the right, "for that's clean a-top."

C [4]Indeed as we found when we also reached the spot, it was something very different. [5]At the foot of a pretty big pine, and involved in a green creeper, which had even partly lifted some of the smaller bones, a human skeleton lay, with a few shreds of clothing, on the ground. [6]I believe a chill struck for a moment to every heart.

D [7]"He was a seaman," said George Merry, who, bolder than the rest, had gone up close and was examining the rags of clothing. [8]"Leastways, this is good sea cloth."

E [9]"Aye, aye," said Silver, "like enough; you wouldn't look to find a bishop here, I reckon. [10]But what sort of a way is that for bones to lie? [11]'Tain't in natur'."

F [12]Indeed, on a second glance, it seemed impossible to fancy that the body was in a natural position. [13]But for some disarray (the work perhaps of the birds that had fed upon him, or of the slow-growing creeper that had gradually enveloped his remains), the man lay perfectly straight—his feet pointing in one direction, his hands raised above his head like a diver's, pointing directly in the opposite.

G [14]"I've taken a notion into my old numskull," observed Silver. [15]"Here's the compass; there's the tiptop p'int o' Skeleton Island, stickin' out like a tooth. [16]Just take a bearing, will you, along the line of them bones."

H [17]It was done. [18]The body pointed straight in the direction of the island, and the compass read duly E.S.E. and by E.

I [19]"I thought so," cried the cook; "this here is a p'inter. [20]Right up there is our line for the Pole Star and the jolly dollars. [21]But, by thunder! if it don't make me cold inside to think of Flint. [22]This is one of his jokes, and no mistake. [23]Him and these six was alone here; he killed 'em, every man; and this one he hauled here and laid down by compass, shiver my timbers! [24]They're long bones, and the hair's been yellow. [25]Aye, that would be Allardyce. [26]You mind Allardyce, Tom Morgan?"

J [27]"Aye, aye," returned Morgan, "I mind him; he owed me money, he did, and took my knife ashore with him."

DIRECTIONS: Choose or write the best answer to each of the following questions using the evidence presented in the passage. When required, list specific sentence numbers or paragraph letters from the story to support the answer.

1. Morgan thought that the man who shouted could not have found the treasure. Why did he think this?
   A. The man was deep in the vegetation, not in the clearing.
   B. What the man had found was too new to be the treasure.
   C. Morgan knew the treasure should not be near a skeleton.
   D. The treasure was supposed to be on the plateau.

2. Why did Silver say you "wouldn't look to find a bishop here"?

   _____

   _____

   _____

3. According to the narrator, if the bones were not laid out perfectly straight, what were the probable causes? (Choose all that apply.)
   A. birds
   B. men
   C. vines
   D. rocks

   Give the number of the sentence that best supports the answer. _____

4. When Silver got an idea about the bones in paragraph G, what did he suggest they do?

   _____

   _____

   _____

5. In sentence 22, what was the joke that Flint probably played?

   _____

   _____

   _____

6. Based on paragraph I, the conclusion can be made that Allardyce had been: (Choose all that apply.)
   A. slender.
   B. bearded.
   C. tall.
   D. blond.

   Give the number of the sentence that best supports the answer. _____

7. Number the following events in the order in which they most likely occurred.

   _____ Morgan's knife is taken.

   _____ The men discover the bones.

   _____ Flint kills Allardyce.

   _____ The body is arranged to align with the island.

8. Label each of the following sentences as F for fact or O for opinion.

   _____ They had proceeded for about half a mile.

   _____ The dead man wore good sea cloth.

   _____ Flint intended to lay out the bones as a pointer.

   _____ The bones pointed in the direction of the island.

9. The mood of the passage is shown by the men's sense of:
   A. hope.
   B. happiness.
   C. confusion.
   D. dread.

   List the numbers of the 4 sentences that best support the answer.

   _____, _____, _____, _____

10. Which of the following was a key event of the passage?
    A. They approached the brow of the plateau.
    B. They found that the body pointed in the direction of the island.
    C. The man was recognized as Allardyce.
    D. The man was determined to be a seaman rather than a bishop.

NONFICTION POSTTEST—
How Money Has Changed

A [1]What is money? [2]It can be anything people want it to be—literally.

B [3]It is easy to think of money as dollar bills and quarters, but money is anything that a majority of people can agree on as a means of exchange. [4]If enough people in one town are willing to accept donuts as money, then donuts *are* money—at least for the people in that town. [5]They might run into trouble when they try to spend those donuts in other towns, however.

C [6]Before coins or paper money, people exchanged (traded) fish for stone tools or leather goods for wood. [7]This method of exchanging one thing for something else is called *barter*. [8]It is still in use today: Sue might agree to fix Ramon's electrical wiring if Ramon agrees to figure Sue's income tax. [9]They've exchanged services, not goods, but they've still bartered.

D [10]The difference between barter and money is the situation. [11]Money can be used in most situations; in a barter, each individual must have something to exchange that the other individual needs or wants. [12]Sue and Ramon can agree to swap electrical work for accounting, but Harold, another accountant, might insist on being paid in dollars and cents. [13]Harold may not need any electrical work done, and he can spend dollars anywhere.

E [14]Money in coin form has been around since about 600 B.C. [15]When the Greek and Roman civilizations—the dominant economies and civilizations of the times— began accepting coins as money, most of the rest of the world went along. [16]Coins are still accepted today, but usually as percentages of paper money. ([17]A quarter is one quarter of a dollar, etc.)

F [18]The first paper money was issued

Money: The Savers' Favorite

Money is the most popular means of exchange because it is easily spent just about  anywhere. However, people also like it because it can be saved and then spent later—unlike, say, fresh fish. This feature of money—that it can be saved and spent later— is called the *asset value* of money. As a good banker will always say, "Better save than sorry."

in China in the 13th century. [19]The concept didn't catch on in the West until about 400 years later. [20]The paper dollar appeared in the United States after the Revolutionary War and slowly became the national standard of value.

G [21]Most of the common forms of money today—including checks, money orders, stock certificates, and government bonds, just to name a few—are based on the dollar. [22]Going back to our definition, we can say that the dollar is money because a majority of people in the country (and even the world) accept it as a means of exchange. [23]In historical terms, the dollar is a new form of money, yet it is accepted almost everywhere in the world.

H [24]An even newer form of money is *electronic money*. [25]With the widespread use of computers today, a great many monetary transactions are electronic. [26]No physical money changes hands, and paper records are optional. [27]The dollars and cents are represented by bits and bytes. [28]The standard hasn't changed, just the method of exchange.

DIRECTIONS: Choose or write the best answer to each of the following questions using the evidence presented in the passage. When required, list specific sentence numbers or paragraph letters from the story to support the answer.

1. What needs to happen for a particular object to be accepted as money?

    _____

    _____

    _____

    Give the number of the sentence that best supports the answer. _____

2. Which of these exchanges is a barter?
    A. dollars for donuts
    B. quarters for a dollar
    C. babysitting for help with studying
    D. shoveling the sidewalk for checks

    Give the letter of the paragraph that best supports the answer. _____

3. In general, money CANNOT be described as:
    A. taking many forms.
    B. being accepted everywhere.
    C. having a long history.
    D. being almost anything.

4. Label each of these statements as a fact (F) or an opinion (O).

    _____ Barter has not vanished; it is still in use today.

    _____ The dollar is recognized around the world, so it is the best currency to use.

    _____ If enough people will accept paper clips as money, then paper clips will become money.

    _____ Computers can keep accurate accounts of transactions.

5. What kind of trouble might the people who accept donuts as money run into if they try to spend those donuts in a neighboring town?

    _____

    _____

    _____

    _____

    Give the number of the sentence that best supports the answer. _____

6. Why did most people begin accepting coins?

    _____

    _____

    _____

    _____

    _____

    Give the number of the sentence that best supports the answer. _____

7. Explain why $10 of money has a higher *asset value* than $10 worth of fresh fish.

    _____

    _____

    _____

    _____

    _____

8. What inference can be made about what Sue and Ramon might think about their barter?
   A. that they needed a record of their exchange
   B that they were ignoring the value of money
   C. that they each got what the other wanted from the exchange
   D. that they each believed the exchange was in their interest

9. Compare what Harold and Ramon would probably be willing to accept for their accounting services from Sue the electrician.

   _____

   _____

   _____

   _____

   _____

   List the numbers of the 2 sentences that best support the answer. ____, ____

ANSWERS

The answer key provides the following information: a copy of the student passage with superscripted numbers, questions with the reading skill in parentheses, the correct answers given in bolded text, the numbers or letters of the evidence sentences or paragraphs if asked, and an explanation of the answers (when necessary).

Although we give a recommended answer choice for each question, teachers should discuss any different responses with students to clarify their reasoning. If the teacher feels a student has made a good case for a response, based on the evidence in the passage, the teacher may want to accept the student's answer, also.

For the short answer questions, students do not have to follow the suggested wording exactly as long as they include the key information needed to answer the question. The literature and fiction stories, in particular, are open to greater interpretation than the nonfiction as to author meaning. The primary focus of this program is to get students to think about what they read and to improve their understanding of the material. You may find your student involved in a lively debate as to which is the best answer to a question. By all means, encourage this!

FICTION PRETEST

Billy Brussels Sprouts (p. 2)

1. How often were Brussels sprouts on the menu? (reading for detail)

   They were on the menu about once every two weeks.

   1 best evidence sentence: **10**

2. Why did the author describe Billy's fellow students as "friends" in sentence 10? (author's purpose/irony)

The students were not really being Billy's friends when they gave him their sprouts.

Explanation: The author put the word in quotes to emphasize that it was being used in a different, or ironic, way.

3. In general, Billy is the kind of person who: (generalization)
   A. **wants to be liked.**
   B. likes to get into trouble.
   C. prefers to eat healthy foods.
   D. backs away from a challenge.

   2 best evidence sentences: **7, 27**

   Explanation: Sentence 7 says he doesn't want the guys to think he's a wimp. Sentence 27 says he wants Maria to see that he's the guy for her. Both of these instances support the idea that he wants to be respected. D is contradicted by the fact that Billy takes up the challenge. The passage has no evidence to support B or C.

4. Which of these best describes why Billy agreed to *finish eating* all of the Brussels sprouts? (conclusion, cause/effect)
   A. He valued his friendship with Sevy.
   B. He wanted to make his mother proud of him.
   C. **He wanted money to buy a present for Maria.**
   D. He thought other people would look at him differently.

   2 best evidence sentences: **26, 27**

   Explanation: C is directly supported by sentences 26 and 27. It can be argued that A and D are correct answers, but C is the best one based on the evidence presented.

5. Label these phrases from paragraphs F and G as fact (F) or opinion (O).

O They smell bad.

F They are little cabbages.

F They contain vitamins.

O Good nutrition will be as easy as ABC.

Explanation: The first and last sentences are value judgments—an indicator of an opinion. The other two sentences are facts.

6. What does the word *coercion* mean, as used in sentence 24? (vocabulary)

Coercion means he felt he was forced into doing it.

1 best evidence sentence: **25**

Explanation: Sentence 25 supports the definition of coercion; it says Billy wanted to tell Maria that he was forced into it.

7. Number the following according to the actual time order of events. (sequence events)

3 Billy agrees to eat a plate full of Brussels sprouts.

4 Billy blames his mother.

1 Billy's mother praises the nutritional value of Brussels sprouts.

6 Teachers step in.

2 Sevy claims Billy can eat 16 brussels sprouts at one sitting.

5 Maria Hernandez tells her friend how gross the whole thing is.

8. What is meant by the phrase "on to them," as used in sentence 29? (figurative language: idiom)
    A. They wanted to watch.
    B. They were attacking them.
    C. They discovered what was going on.
    D. They were counting along with the crowd.

Explanation: Once the teachers were "on to them," they acted to break up the action, so they must have discovered what was going on. A, B, and D don't make sense in the context of the passage.

9. What does it mean that Billy wanted to "collect his winner's wage" (sentence 30)? (inference)

Billy wanted to eat all of the Brussels sprouts so he could win the bet and collect the $16.

2 best evidence sentences other than 30: **7, 31**

NONFICTION PRETEST

The Hidden Cost of Buried Treasure
(p. 6)

1. The word *extract* means to draw or pull out. Explain the meaning of the words "price it extracts from us," as used in sentence 3. (inference)

The phrase means *what it takes from us* or the *cost to us* to retrieve the treasure.

Explanation: Paragraphs B–E describe the price, or costs, in time and lives, of hunting treasure. Sentence 25 reinforces the idea of costs.

2.   The author's main purpose is to: (author's purpose)
   A. persuade you that searching for treasure may cost a lot.
   B.   give examples of times and locations of finding treasure.
   C.   entertain you with the adventures of treasure seekers.
   D.   describe the details of difficulties suffered by particular men.

   1 best evidence sentence from paragraph A: **3**

   Explanation: We can tell by the author's question in sentence 3, and the subsequent examples, that she intends to show that searching for treasure has been costly to the seekers. B, C, and D are simply byproducts of the main purpose.

3.   According to paragraphs B through E, all of the following were lost as a result of seeking treasure EXCEPT: (reading for detail)
   A.   money.
   B.   lives.
   C.   effort.
   D. land.

4.   The word *heeded*, as used in sentence 4, most nearly means: (vocabulary)
   A.   refused to hear.
   B.   looked for.
   C. paid attention to.
   D.   required.

   Explanation: Since the author goes on to describe what happened to people who did follow the treasure, choice C makes sense, and A is contradicted. It makes no sense for people to look for or require the *call* of the gold; it is the gold they look for or think they require, so B and D make no sense.

5.   Write the phrase in sentence 12 that show personification. (figurative language)

   hole that refuses

   Explanation: An inanimate object is incapable of *refusing*, something requiring thought; therefore, *hole* is being personified.

6.   What cause and effect are suggested in sentence 6? (cause/effect)

   Digging through the crater's rim causes the lake to drain.

7.   Choose the best summary for the passage. (summary)
   A. Many of us are attracted to treasure, but whether in a lake, a cave, a shaft, or at the bottom of the sea, finding a fortune can carry a high price tag.
   B.   Some people do find money and live happily ever after, but chances are strong that most of us will never even have the opportunity to hunt for treasure.
   C.   Though it costs a lot to find buried or hidden riches, human greed has remained the same from the 1500s to the 1900s.
   D.   If you are tempted to search for hidden fortunes, it is best not to go looking in lakes, caves, shafts, or shipwrecks.

8.   What made Tom Gurr's search different from the other treasure hunts? (compare/contrast)
   A.   He got to keep all the money.
   B.   No treasure was found.
   C. No people were killed.
   D.   The treasure was underwater.

   3 best evidence sentences from paragraphs B, C, and D: **8, 13, 18**

9. Based on the examples given, what generalization is the author trying to convey? (generalization)
   A. Treasure hunting is a successful activity.
   B. Most buried treasure lies in the oceans.
   C. Seeking hidden treasure is not worth the effort.
   D. Treasure is always hidden intentionally.

   Explanation: All four paragraphs support choice C. Choice A is contradicted by all four. There is no support for choice D in paragraphs B (gold is thrown in the lake as an offering, not to hide it) and E (there is no reason to assume the ship was wrecked for the purpose of hiding its treasure). There is no evidence for choice B.

10. Explain why the first statement is a fact but the second is an opinion: (fact/opinion)
    A. Some treasure hunts have ended in death.
    B. Treasure hunting is not worth the cost.

    A is a fact because it can be proven. B is an opinion because someone might believe that it is worth the effort.

LITERATURE

1. The Cay (p. 10)

1. What natural disaster does the passage describe? (conclusion)
   A. a tornado
   B. a hurricane
   C. an avalanche
   D. an earthquake

   Explanation: In paragraph A, sentence 1

describes the increasing wind. Sentence 2 refers to a storm, which rules out choices C and D. Paragraph B describes the waves crashing against the trees, so this rules out a dust storm.

2 best evidence paragraphs: **A, B**

2. The narrator proved that he was: (character trait)
   A. resourceful.
   B. helpless.
   C. lucky.
   D. adventuresome.

   Explanation: The narrator is able to wriggle out of tight, wet ropes; release Timothy from similar bonds; and drag him onto the sand. All of these support A and contradict B. C could be argued, but A has more support in the passage based on the actions of the narrator. There is no evidence for D.

3. Put the following events from the story in their proper time order. (sequence events)
   5 Narrator unties Timothy. (28)
   1 Narrator stands against palm tree. (1)
   6 Narrator holds Timothy's hand. (30)
   2 Wind dies down. (11)
   4 Narrator unties himself. (23)
   3 Narrator regains consciousness. (11)

4. Explain how the roles of the narrator and Timothy changed from the beginning of the passage to the end. (literary device: irony)

   In the beginning, Timothy was taking care of the narrator. At the end, the narrator was taking care of Timothy.

5. What caused the narrator and Timothy to faint? (cause/effect)
   A. being tied to a tree
   B. being struck by waves
   C. being battered by wind
   D. being so close together

   1 best evidence paragraph: **B**

6. Which of these does the narrator probably feel toward Timothy? (inference)
   A. anger
   B. jealousy
   C. indifference
   D. compassion

   1 best evidence paragraph: **J**

   Explanation: D is supported by sentences 30 and 31. The narrator stays with Timmy and holds his hand to make him feel better. This also contradicts choice C. There is no evidence for A or B.

7. Name two things that made it difficult for the narrator to untie the ropes around Timothy and himself. (setting, cause/effect)

   Timothy's weight was against them, and the rope was soaked.

   2 best evidence sentences: **26, 27**

8. Explain the simile used in sentence 31. (figurative language)

   The narrator thinks holding Timothy's hand might make the injured man better, like medicine.

2. ***Sparrow Hawk Red*** (p. 12)

1. In paragraph C, what bothered Ricky? (inference, conflict)
   A. He wanted to go home.
   B. He was barely noticed.
   C. He was worried about the girl.
   D. He didn't like the attention.

1 best evidence sentence: **10**

Explanation: Sentence 10 explains that he felt invisible, like a piece of dirt. There is no evidence for A or C. D is contradicted by sentence 4, people hardly noticed him.

2. Which of the following statements can be made about Soledad? (generalization)
   A. She is familiar with street life.
   B. She cares only for herself.
   C. She lives alone.
   D. She likes Spanish music.

   3 best evidence paragraphs: **F, I, K**

   Explanation: In paragraph F, Soledad has little fear of being hit by a car. In paragraph I, she knows where the garbage cans are behind the restaurant. Paragraph K suggests that she has eaten like this before—she doesn't hesitate and she is afraid of being caught. B is contradicted by the fact that she offers Ricky the fullest can. There is no evidence for C or D.

3. List the numbers of the three sentences that best support the idea that Soledad did not like the car racing towards her and honking. (supporting detail)
   17, 18, 19

4. Which of the following is NOT a key event of the passage? (key event)
   A. Ricky watches Soledad eat food from the garbage.
   B. Ricky is bothered by his appearance.
   C. Soledad leads Ricky to the restaurant.
   D. Ricky catches up to Soledad.

5.   Write the sentence that uses a simile in paragraph C. Underline the simile. (figurative language)

Here he felt invisible, <u>like a piece of dirt on the street.</u>

6.   Why was Ricky surprised when Soledad headed for the back of the restaurant? (inference)

He expected her to go into the restaurant since she said they would eat there. (Also acceptable: He didn't see how they could afford to eat there.)

1 best evidence sentence: **24**

7.   Compare Soledad's attitude about eating from the trash with Ricky's attitude. (compare/contrast, point of view)

Soledad had no problem with eating food out of a garbage can. Ricky seemed shocked by the whole experience.

8.   Describe the Restaurante del Sol. (setting)

Restaurante del Sol is a fancy restaurant with Spanish music playing inside. Blinking lights surround the restaurant sign. Behind the restaurant are garbage cans swarming with flies.

2 best evidence paragraphs: **G, I**

3. *El Güero* (p. 14)

1.   What does Don David's search for his son suggest about his character? He was: (character trait)
A.   an indifferent father.
B.   a cruel man.
C.   a good provider.
D.   a determined man.

Explanation: D is supported by his

long search to find his missing son, especially sentences 27 and 30. There is no evidence for A, B, or C.

2.   What did Papa mean when he said David "must learn to be white"? (inference)
A.   He must learn to live among his own people.
B.   He must change his skin color.
C.   He must learn how to cook.
D.   He must learn to speak his family's language.

Explanation: A is supported by sentences 33 and 34. David seemed more Indian than white. There is no evidence for B or C. Learning to speak his family's language is only one part of what he needs to do to recapture his heritage. This makes A a better choice.

3.   What does the reference to David's *blood* mean in sentence 33? (vocabulary)

It means that David was born of non-Indian parents.

4.   Why was David afraid to go with his father? (inference)

He was probably afraid because he did not know his father. He had not seen him since he was a baby.

3 best evidence sentences: **21, 26, 27**

Explanation: From 21, we know that the child was taken when he was an infant. Sentence 26 says he was brought up by the tribe. Sentence 27 lets us know that it was more than 7 years before his father found him.

5.   Why was the narrator surprised when David called the Indians *his* people? (inference)

David was white.

1 best evidence sentence: **10**

6. Where does most of the story take place? (setting)
   A. San Diego
   B. Mexico
   C. Spain
   D. Canada

   2 best evidence sentences: **23, 24**

   Explanation: In sentence 23, the use of the word *border* tells us there are two countries involved; the sentence also refers to the Americans on the other side of the border, which eliminates A. In sentence 24, Don David went north to America, which eliminates Canada as the country he came from. There is no evidence for C.

7. Why did it take Don David so long to find his son? (cause/effect, conclusion)

   The tribes moved often and were unwilling to give white men any information.

   1 best evidence sentence: **28**

8. Which of the following is a good summary of young David's (El Coyote's) history? (summary, sequence events)
   A. When his mother died, his father went to look for gold, and the Indian nurse took him to live with her tribe.
   B. While his father was gone, his mother and sister died, but the Indian nurse stayed until his father returned.
   C. While his father was gone, his mother died. His sister left to find their father, and the Indian nurse took him to live with her tribe.
   D. While his father was gone, the Indian nurse took the boy to live with her tribe. Then his mother died.

4. *The Moon by Night* (p. 16)

1. What probably caused the shivering mentioned in paragraph A? (cause/effect)

   An earthquake probably caused the shivering.

   Explanation: Sentence 4 mentions the ground shivering, 9 says the ground heaves, and 26 mentions tremors, which are associated with earthquakes.
   (Also acceptable: **a landslide**)

2. Fill in the following blanks to describe the metaphor used in sentence 11. (figurative language)

Metaphor	Represents
A horse	the planet
The mane	**the grass**

3. Explain what two things are being compared in the analogy given in sentence 6. (literary device: analogy)

   The jerk the narrator felt is compared to the feeling you get when you are water-skiing and the boat slows or stops then speeds up again.

4. The narrative form of the passage could best be classified as: (literary form)
   A. humorous.
   B. tragic.
   C. suspenseful.
   D. fantastic.

   Explanation: The events described create tension and make us wonder if things will come out all right, so choice C is appropriate. We don't know that anything tragic has happened, so B is incorrect. Nothing is humorous, so choice A is incorrect. Though the events described are not typical, they could really occur and are therefore not considered fantasy.

5. In paragraph E, the words "the mountain was much closer to me" mean that: (conclusion, inference)
   A. she had moved towards the mountain.
   B. the mountain had literally moved towards her.
   C. she was speaking figuratively.
   D. the field had risen into a mountain.

Explanation: The mountain's being much closer made her realize that most of the mountain had fallen into the field (sentence 24). Also, according to sentence 22, the top was gone.

6. Based on paragraph F, where is Zachary most likely to be found? (predict outcome)

under the rock pile

2 best evidence sentences: **30, 31**

7. Which of the following most likely describes the narrator's point of view? (point of view)
   A. The earth is a monster she must tame.
   B. The earth is a partner; she is at ease with it.
   C. She is vulnerable to the earth's terrifying forces.
   D. She is not affected by the natural forces of the earth.

Explanation: The description of the ground moving under her and her feelings of sickness (paragraphs A, B), her feeling like she was riding something veering out of course (sentence 11), and the fact that she felt terror (sentence 19) support choice C and contradict choices B and D. There is no evidence that she feels she should tame the earth, so A is incorrect.

8. Number the following events in the order of the narrator's experience. (sequence events)
   5 Looked for Zachary. (29)
   2 Heard loud noises. (12)
   3 Felt like vomiting. (19)
   1 Clung to the grass. (10)
   4 Saw the mountain was closer. (24)

9. How does the narrator compare herself Earth in paragraph D? (compare/contrast)

The earth heaves, and she also feels like heaving (throwing up).

5. *The Giver* (p. 18)

1. What is the Sameness? (reading for detail)

The Sameness is the lack of color in Jonas's world.

2 best evidence paragraphs: **D, K**

2. The Giver's role in this dialogue seems to be to: (point of view)
   A. lecture Jonas about what is correct.
   B. advise Jonas on what he should do.
   C. listen to Jonas and question him.
   D. argue with Jonas.

3. What could be the result of people's making their own choices? (cause/effect)

They might make wrong choices.

1 best evidence sentence: **29**

4. It can be inferred that in Jonas's world: (inference)
    A. **decisions are made for you.**
    B. people make their own choices.
    C. people are allowed to vote.
    D. decisions are made by The Giver.

    2 best evidence paragraphs: **M, R, also accept K.**

    Explanation: A is correct because both paragraphs M and R tell us that Jonas's society thinks it is too dangerous for people to make choices of their own. B is contradicted by sentence 35. There is no evidence for C or D.

5. In sentence 40, what does the word *absurdity* most nearly mean? (vocabulary)
    A. seriousness
    B. sadness
    C. **silliness**
    D. emptiness

    Explanation: C is supported by the fact that Jonas almost laughs. There is no evidence for choices A, B, or D.

6. Why is Jonas still frustrated at the end of the passage? (inference)

    He still wants to decide something for himself.

    1 best evidence paragraph: **C**

    Explanation: In the beginning, Jonas wanted to decide things for himself. By the end of the passage he had talked himself into believing people shouldn't make their own choices, but he still felt that he was missing something.

7. Based on the passage, you could say that Jonas: (conclusion, character trait)
    A. accepted his life without question.

    B. **was questioning his society's rules.**
    C. was ready to change his life completely.
    D. wanted The Giver to tell him what to do.

    Explanation: Throughout the passage, Jonas is questioning his life, which supports B as the best choice and makes A incorrect. There is no evidence for D. C is contradicted by paragraphs M and R in particular: he wasn't ready for people to make their own choices.

8. What is the primary conflict for Jonas? (conflict)

    The primary conflict is between Jonas's desire to have choices and his fear of making the wrong choice.

    2 best evidence paragraphs: **C, R**

9. What is the theme of the passage? (theme)
    A. Life is full of choices.
    B. **Learning to think for yourself involves making difficult choices.**
    C. People need to make their own choices.
    D. Life is not always fair.

    Explanation: B is supported by the fact that Jonas is wanting to make his own choices (C) but realizes that doing so would mean choosing a mate or a job (O, P). There is no evidence for A or D. C is the basis of the discussion between Jonas and The Giver but is not completely the theme of the passage. Jonas is also struggling to think for himself, which includes making decisions.

6. *Under the Blood-Red Sun* (p. 20)

1. What is the theme of the passage? (theme)
   A. Power is the reason people fight wars.
   B. Power is a quality admired in world leaders.
   C. Power is the ability to read whatever you want.
   D. Power is the freedom to make your own choices.

   1 best evidence sentence: **34** (Also acceptable: **15**)

2. What actual situation triggers the class discussion? (inference)
   A. a war
   B. a movie
   C. an argument
   D. an assignment

   3 best evidence sentences: **1, 2, 7**

   Explanation: References are made to Japan and Adolf Hitler.

3. Describe what Mr. Ramos's relationship is to the other characters. (reading for detail)

   Mr. Ramos is a schoolteacher. The other characters are his students.

   1 best evidence paragraph: **C**

4. Who is the narrator? (inference)

   The narrator is a student in Mr. Ramos's class.

   1 best evidence sentence: **10**

5. Explain the difference between the two situations Mr. Ramos mentions in paragraph J. (compare/contrast)

   The difference between the two situations is that choice is possible

in one of them. **He compares a job you like and choose for yourself with one in which you have to work late and can't talk.**

6. Name the two things being compared by the analogy in paragraph A. (literary device: analogy)

   The analogy compares power to a drug. Some men get hooked on power, as if it were a drug.

   3 best evidence sentences: **2, 3, 4**

7. Is sentence 21 a fact or an opinion? Explain your answer. (fact/opinion)

   It is an opinion. The sentence cannot be proven as a fact. It is something Mr. Ramos believes.

8. In sentence 20, Mr. Ramos reaches out his open hand and closes it into a fist. What does this gesture symbolize? (inference, literary device: symbolism)

   The gesture symbolizes the grabbing of power, or just power.

7. *The View From Saturday* (p. 22)

1. What do you think the narrator means in sentence 9 when she says her dad can't swing? (figurative language)
   A. He is not a very good dancer.
   B. He is not good at home repairs.
   C. He has gotten too old.
   D. He doesn't fit the single life.

2. In sentence 10, what does the word *hovered* mean? (vocabulary)
   A. flew past
   B. remained near
   C. disappeared
   D. lectured

   Explanation: B is supported by the comparison with the Goodyear blimp, which usually flies above the stadium during a game.

3. In paragraph C, what is the main conflict between the narrator and her dad? (conflict)
   A. **They don't know what to do with each other.**
   B. They are constantly fighting and arguing with each other.
   C. She doesn't want to visit him.
   D. They both like to talk a lot.

   Explanation: A is supported by sentence 11. Her father kept hovering over her because he didn't know what to do with her. There is no evidence for B, C, or D.

4. From paragraph E, it can be inferred that Grandpa Izzy's eyes: (inference)
   A. see very poorly.
   B. look empty.
   C. **reveal his feelings.**
   D. are dark brown.

   2 best evidence sentences: **15, 16**

   Explanation: Sentence 15 explains how Grandpa's eyes reveal his feelings about his wife's death. In 16, his eyes indicate his happiness. There is no evidence for A or D. B is contradicted by sentences 15 and 16.

5. From paragraph A, you can guess that the narrator lives with: (inference)

   her mother

   1 best evidence sentence: **1**

6. In sentence 7, what does the narrator means when she describes her dad as "terminally nervous?"
   (character trait, inference)

   She means that his nervousness has gotten worse, like a terminal illness, and there is no hope that it will get better.

7. What has brightened Grandpa's eyes again? (cause/effect)

   His marriage to Margaret.

   1 best evidence sentence: **16**

8. How would you describe the narrator's attitude towards her dad? (tone)
   A. adoring
   B. fearful
   C. **annoyed**
   D. scornful

   Explanation: Choice C is supported by paragraph C, especially the fact that she did not enjoy his hovering and told him to stop. There is no evidence for A, B, or D.

8. *The Trolley to Yesterday* (p. 24)

1. Which of these is a true statement about the tunnel? (conclusion)
   A. It is full of water.
   B. **It is underground.**
   C. It ends outside a forest.
   D. It is too small to walk through.

   1 best evidence sentence: **7**

2. What time of day is it at the end of the passage? (inference, setting)
   A. morning
   B. noon
   C. afternoon
   D. **evening**

   2 best evidence sentences: **12, 13**

3. What is the tunnel ceiling made of?
   (reading for detail)
   A. dirt
   B. moss
   C. wood
   D. **stone**

   1 best evidence sentence: **4**

4. Which of these words is closest in meaning to *doggedly*, as used in sentence 11? (vocabulary)
   A. easily
   B. stubbornly
   C. suddenly
   D. excitedly

   Explanation: The sentence also says that he knew it was the only way out. Johnny was doing what he had to do, even though he was scared.

5. What might cause Johnny to slip and fall while walking in the tunnel? (prediction)

   He could slip and fall because the tunnel floor was wet, muddy, and covered with moss in places.

   1 best evidence sentence: **2** (or **4**)

6. Which of these is NOT a key event of the plot? (key event)
   A. They arrive in the forest.
   B. They walk through a tunnel.
   C. They climb up the well shaft.
   D. They wade through some water.

   Explanation: Even though they do wade through water, that action does not trigger or directly lead to any other action. D is just a detail of B.

7. In sentence 9, why was Johnny terrified? (cause/effect)

   He was afraid that he would fall and die.

   1 best evidence sentence: **10**

8. Describe the change in mood from the beginning of the passage to the end. (mood)

   The mood is tense at the beginning and relieved at the end.

9. **"How the Rhinoceros Got His Skin"** (p. 26)

1. Which of the following is a form of literature that *best* describes the passage? (literary form)
   A. science fiction
   B. fantasy
   C. biography
   D. nonfiction

   Explanation: The elements of whimsy and logical impossibility classify it as fantasy.

2. Why did the Parsee put cake-crumbs in the rhinoceros's skin? (inference, cause/effect)

   The Parsee probably wanted to get back at the rhinoceros for eating all of the Parsee's cake.

   1 best evidence sentence: **3**

3. Which of these key events is NOT described in detail? (key event)
   A. the rhinoceros's taking off of his skin
   B. the rhinoceros's eating of the Parsee's cake
   C. the Parsee's putting cake-crumbs into the rhinoceros's skin
   D. the Parsee's finding of the rhinoceros's skin

4. Give two reasons why cake-crumbs were available for the Parsee to put in the rhinoceros's skin. (cause/effect)

   1) The Parsee ate only cake.
   2) He never swept out his camp.

   1 best evidence sentence: **7**

5. Name one thing about the rhinoceros that changed in the story and describe the change. (compare/contrast)

His skin changed. He now has great folds in his skin and the buttons are gone. (Also acceptable: **He gained a very bad temper.**)

1 best evidence sentence: **14** or **17**

6. Which of these facts about rhinoceroses in general is NOT listed in the story? (generalization, illustration use)
   A. They have a single horn.
   B. They have bad tempers.
   C. They have great folds in their skin.
   D. They can blow bubbles through their nose.

   Explanation: A is the only choice not listed in the story. It is reinforced, however, by the illustration, which shows a horn.

7. Put the following events in the order in which they occurred in the passage. (sequence events)

   1   rhinoceros takes off his skin. (1)

   2   Parsee puts cake-crumbs in rhinoceros's skin. (8)

   5   rhinoceros rubs against tree. (13)

   4   rhinoceros rolls in sand. (12)

   3   Parsee climbs to top of palm tree. (9)

8. Which of these would be a good moral for the story? (inference, theme)
   A. One good turn deserves another.
   B. Don't count your chickens till they're hatched.
   C. You get what you pay for.
   D. The punishment can be worse than the crime.

   Explanation: The rhinoceros ate all of the Parsee's cake, most likely creating a temporary situation. But the Parsee gave the rhinoceros a permanent skin change.

10. **Face to Face** (p. 28)

1. In sentence 4, the word *alluring* means: (vocabulary)
   A. unusual.
   B. shiny.
   C. dirty.
   D. attractive.

   Explanation: D is supported by the rest of sentence 4 in that the books seemed new to him. It is also supported by sentence 5; the room was inviting. There is no evidence for A, B, or C.

2. Based on paragraph A, his room in the mirror world seemed: (inference)
   A. different.
   B. frightening.
   C. annoying.
   D. drab.

   3 best evidence sentences: **1, 3, 4**

   Explanation: Sentence 1 states that his bed looked like a stranger's bed. Sentence 2 states his trophy and ribbons were shinier, which contradicts D. Sentence 4 states his books looked mysterious. There is no evidence for B or C.

3. Why did Michael think he could reach through the mirror in his room? (cause/effect)

   He thought that if he closed his eyes, he could reach into the mirror because it was made of nonsolid atoms.

   2 best evidence sentences: **9, 10**

4. From paragraph E, the conclusion can be made that a farm boy is: (conclusion)
   A. independent.
   B. practical.
   C. silly.
   D. unrealistic.

5. The mood of the passage is: (mood)
    A. lighthearted.
    B. sad.
    C. angry.
    D. thoughtful.

    Explanation: The whole passage focuses on Michael's thoughts about mirrors and life. There is no evidence for A, B, or C.

6. In sentence 8, it can be inferred that Michael and his father? (inference)

    Michael and his father are or were separated.

7. In paragraph A, how did the images in the mirror differ from the real objects? (compare/contrast)

    The trophies and ribbons seemed shinier and brighter. The books seemed mysterious and alluring.

    2 best evidence sentences: **3, 4**

8. When Michael was younger, the hidden place where the mirror image stopped had symbolized:
    (literary device: symbolism)
    A. his desire for a place to play.
    B. his fear of small spaces.
    C. his desire to see his father.
    D. his need for a place to hide.

    1 best evidence paragraph: **C**

    Explanation: The fact that he thought his father was waiting to be found in the mirror indicates his wish that his father wanted to see him. There is no evidence for A, B, or D.

11. *The Bronze Bow* (p. 30)

1. Which of the following best describes the setting? (setting)
    A. the valley
    B. a mountain path

    C. Rome
    D. another world

    Explanation: B is supported by sentence 1. Since Daniel is looking down at the valley, A is incorrect. Rome is described as "far off," so C is incorrect. There is no evidence for D.

2. Which of these words best describes how Daniel is feeling? (character trait)
    A. misunderstood
    B. fearless
    C. anxious
    D. forgetful

    1 best evidence sentence: **9,** also accept **11**.

    Explanation: In sentence 9, Daniel is described as uneasy. There is no evidence for A or D. Sentence 11 explains that Daniel was fearful of discovery, so B is incorrect.

3. Based on the information in paragraph A, which of the following can be said about Daniel: (reading for detail)
    A. Daniel is no longer a boy.
    B. Daniel can be a fierce patriot.
    C. Daniel is angry.
    D. Daniel's people are unsettled.

    2 best evidence sentences: **3, 4**

    Explanation: Sentence 3 describes how Daniel's eyes can light with fierce patriotism. Sentence 3 also says that he can become angry, not that he is, so C is incorrect. A is incorrect because he is described as a boy. D does not refer to Daniel specifically.

4. Based on the author's description of Daniel, what prediction can be made about how he might react to the two strangers if he is seen?
    (predict outcome)

A. **He will stand his ground and confront them.**
B. He will cower and hope they do not harm him.
C. He will ignore them.
D. He will ask them about the people in his village.

Explanation: A is the best answer because sentences 10 and 11 explain that Daniel thinks the strangers are "foolhardy" for approaching the mountain. Although he is fearful, he is unwilling to let them out of his sight. Based on sentences 3 and 4, Daniel is too proud to cower, so B is incorrect. C is incorrect because Daniel seems intent on watching them; he will probably not ignore them. D is incorrect because Daniel resents being reminded of the village, so he will probably not ask them about it.

5. The word *unreconciled* in sentence 4 means: (vocabulary)
   A. **unaccepting.**
   B. disagreeing.
   C. unaware.
   D. recalling.

Explanation: We know from the last phrase in sentence 4 that Palestine refuses to acknowledge the emperor. Therefore, we can determine that *unreconciled* probably means that the Galileans are *unaccepting* of being a conquered nation.

6. What is the author trying to convey about the history of Daniel's people? (author's purpose)
   A. His people have been living in peace for the last five years.
   B. His people were once violent and restless.
   C. **His people have been conquered by the Emperor Tiberius.**
   D. His people are at war with Rome.

1 best evidence sentence: **4**

Explanation: From sentence 4, we do know that his people have been conquered, so C is correct. There is no evidence for A. B is incorrect because the Galileans are violent and restless. The Galileans refuse to acknowledge the Emperor as their leader, but we do not really know if they are still at war with Rome, so D is incorrect.

7. During what season does the story take place? (setting)

   spring

   1 best evidence sentence: **6**

8. What inner conflict is Daniel dealing with in paragraph C? (conflict)

   He is afraid of being noticed, but he cannot stop watching them.

   1 best evidence sentence: **11**

FICTION

12. Head Chef at 14 (p. 34)

1. To be allowed to cook, what was the one thing that Rajiv *had* to do? (reading for detail)

   He had to let his brother help.

   1 best evidence sentence: **6**

2. How many times does Rajiv check the pork chops? (reading for detail)
   A. one
   B. two
   C. **three**
   D. four

   2 best evidence sentences: **13, 21**

   Explanation: Sentence 13 says he checked them twice in a minute; 21 indicates he was going to check them again. B could be acceptable, but it is more likely that Rajiv did check the pork chops a third time as he intended.

3. What likely happened to the honey butter? (inference)

    Sanjay poured it on the vegetables.

    2 best evidence paragraphs: **O, Q**

4. Put these steps in their proper order. (sequence steps)

    4 Bake potatoes

    2 Boil potatoes

    3 Put cheese on top of potatoes

    1 Peel potatoes

5. Compare how Rajiv's parents viewed his cooking. His mother was eager to try it; his father was: (point of view, compare/contrast)

    unsure whether he wanted to try it.

    1 best evidence sentence: **12**

6. Which of these statements can be made about Rajiv's mother? (character trait)
    A. She is proud.
    B. She is trusting.
    C. She likes to cook.
    D. She likes dessert.

    Explain your answer.

    She lets the two boys cook a meal together without supervision.

    The passage contains no evidence for A, C, or D.

7. In general, it can be said that Sanjay: (generalization)
    A. likes to cook.
    B. likes his brother.
    C. doesn't follow directions well.
    D. doesn't know how to make apple pie.

    Explain your answer.

    Sanjay puts too much cheese on the potatoes and spreads honey butter over the vegetables.

    Explanation: C is supported by evidence throughout the passage, especially sentences 20 and 22–24. B is suggested by the passage, but not definitely stated. There is no evidence for A or D.

13. Love From Camp Gitchigoomi (p. 36)

1. How does Arthur's point of view compare with the actual events? (point of view, compare/contrast)

    Arthur thought camp was wonderful and exciting. However, he seemed to cause one accident after another.

2. In paragraph B, what kind of animal did Arthur try to pet? (inference)

    A skunk.

    2 best evidence sentences: **7, 8**

    Explanation: Sentences 7 suggests that the animal left a stink that isn't going away. Sentence 8 tells you the animal was black and white.

3. What caused the canoes to tip over? (cause/effect)

    The canoes tipped over when Arthur leaned over to help Chad.

    1 best evidence sentence: **17**

4. Based on events mentioned in the letter, what prediction can be made about what might happen at the cookout? (prediction)

Arthur will probably cause another accident, possibly setting something on fire.

3 best evidence paragraphs: **B, C, D**

5. Arthur could be characterized as: (character trait)
   A. angry.
   B. unhappy.
   C. positive.
   D. disinterested.

   2 best evidence paragraphs: **A, E**

   Explanation: No matter what happens, Arthur always seems to have a cheerful outlook. There is no evidence for A, B, or D.

6. Why is it important to Arthur that Mary not be mad at him? (inference)

   He likes her.

   1 best evidence sentence: **23**

   Sentence 21 also supports this idea but does not state it as directly.

7. In sentence 2, what does "on the go" mean? (figurative language: idiom)

   It means to be always doing something or keeping busy.

8. What is the best explanation for Mr. Purdy's writing to Arthur's parents? (conclusion)
   A. He writes to all the campers' parents.
   B. He wants them to know how much he likes Arthur.
   C. He wants them to know the problems Arthur is causing.

D. He is going to ask if Arthur can stay an extra week.

1 best evidence paragraph: **F**

Explanation: Paragraph F suggests that it is unusual for the director to write to parents, and Arthur is assuming that Mr. Purdy is impressed with his skills. Given the problems that Arthur has caused, it seems highly unlikely that Mr. Purdy would want him to stay longer. C seems most likely based on sentences 30 and 31. There is no evidence for A, B, or D.

14. Race for Pepper (p. 38)

1. It can be inferred that the reason Janelle is in a wheelchair is that: (inference)
   A. she had an accident.
   B. she had a broken leg.
   C. she was born disabled.
   D. she was borrowing it.

   1 best evidence sentence: 1

2. In sentence 1, the word *confidant* most likely means: (vocabulary)
   A. an enemy.
   B. a nurse.
   C. a close friend.
   D. a neighbor.

   Explanation: C is supported by sentences 1 and 2. She confides in Pepper. Sentence 7 eliminates choice B, and there is no evidence for A or D.

3. Why did Janelle have to start the race after the runners? (cause/effect)

   She had to start later so the wheelchair wouldn't create an obstacle for the runners.

   1 best evidence sentence: **24**

4. Why wasn't it important for Janelle to win the race? (reading for detail)

    Runners collected donations based on how many miles they completed, not how quickly they ran.

    1 best evidence sentence: **18**

5. Which of these best describes Janelle? (character trait)
    A. She was unsure of herself.
    B. She seemed shy and withdrawn.
    C. She didn't give up easily.
    D. She was friendly to everyone.

    1 best evidence paragraph: **D**

6. Why did Janelle have to raise the money herself? (supporting detail)

    Her parents were still paying for her medical bills.

    1 best evidence sentence: **14**

7. What do you think will be the outcome of this story? (predict outcome)

    Janelle will finish the race and get Pepper the surgery he needs.

    Explanation: Janelle has accomplished all of her goals so far. Her determination will ensure the outcome.

    1 best evidence paragraph: **F**

8. Which of the following gives the theme of the story? (theme)
    A. Friendship is important.
    B. People are unreliable.
    C. Animals make good friends.
    D. Persistence pays off.

    Explanation: Most of the story emphasizes Janelle's determination to help her dog, in spite of her own

problems. There is no evidence for B. Both A and C are true, but they are not the main focus of the story.

15. Sea Otter Attack (p. 40)

1. Number the following events in the order they actually occurred. (sequence events)

    3 Kyra grabs the boy's swim trunks.

    1 A sea otter grabs hold of Wyatt.

    5 Kyra goes to the hospital.

    2 Kyra swims out to get Wyatt.

    4 Abrahm swims into the ocean.

2. Which of these traits best describes Kyra? (character trait)
    A. playful
    B. protective
    C. unpredictable
    D. vicious

    4 best evidence sentences: **6, 7, 8, 10**

3. Using paragraphs F–I, list three sentences that support the idea that sea otters can be aggressive. (supporting detail)

    Sentences **13, 16, 22**

4. Mark the following statements F for fact or O for opinion. (fact/opinion)

    O The otter attacked the boy because it was protecting its young.

    F Kyra was attacked by the sea otter.

    O Kyra considers Wyatt one of her own.

    F The boy was swimming about 1/4 mile out from the beach.

Explanation: The first and third statements cannot be proven; therefore, they are opinions. The second and last statements are facts because they can be proven by a reliable source (the newspaper reporter).

5. Why do you think the witness didn't get to the children before the dog? (inference)

   She probably couldn't tell who or where the cries were coming from.

   2 best evidence sentences: **4, 5**

6. How might Kyra respond if she detected a burglar trying to crawl into Wyatt's room? (prediction)

   Kyra would probably respond by attacking the burglar because she is a protective dog.

7. Describe the time and place of the attack. (setting)

   The attack took place on a Friday afternoon at Guardian Beach. The children and the otter were about 1/4 mile out from the shore.

   1 best evidence paragraph: **A**

8. What is the best explanation for what might have caused the sea otter to attack the boy? (cause/effect)
   A. It was provoked by the dog.
   B. **It was protecting its young.**
   C. It was hungry.
   D. It was sick and wounded.

   2 best evidence sentences: **22, 23**

16. He Said, She Said (p. 42)

1. Which of the following statements best summarizes the story? (summary)
   A. **Luisa has a party and her brother interrupts it.**
   B. Luisa has a party with her mother's permission.
   C. Jose eavesdrops on the girls and then gets chased out.
   D. The girls play Rumor and discover Keesha's secret.

   Explanation: A is correct because it summarizes the main events of the story. B, C, and D are only details of the story; they don't summarize the main events.

2. List the following events in the order in which they occurred. (sequence events)
   1 The doorbell rang.
   3 Jose ran to his room.
   2 Moesha whispered the secret.
   4 The girls hit Jose with pillows.

3. How did the blanket and the entryway to the living room affect the events of the story? (setting)

   The blanket kept Jose hidden. The entryway allowed him to hear what was going on.

4. Which of the following inferences is best supported by the passage? (inference)
   A. Jose is Luisa's little brother.
   B. **The girls are having a good time.**
   C. Luisa's mom is in her bedroom.
   D. The girls are in love with Jose.

   1 best evidence paragraph: **K**

   Explanation: B is the best answer because the girls are laughing, playing games, and enjoying each other's company. K is the best paragraph choice because laughter is a strong indication that people are having a good time. There is no direct evidence for A, C, or D.

5. List the paragraph from the story that supports the idea that the secret Keesha began with in paragraph I got misinterpreted. (supporting detail)

Paragraph **J**

6. Luisa's mom probably decided to keep Jose out of the living room because (conclusion/inference)
    A. she knew he was contagious.
    B. there wasn't enough room for him.
    C. **her daughter pleaded with her.**
    D. she knew he wouldn't want to be there anyway.

1 best evidence paragraphs: **C**

Explanation: We can infer that Luisa's mom probably listened to her daughter's pleas because she agreed to keep Jose out of the living room after hearing Luisa's whimpering "puh-leeze."

7. What probably caused Jose to peek his head out from under the blanket and make himself known? (inference, cause/effect)

He wanted to tease the girls and let them know that he had been eavesdropping on them.

1 best evidence paragraph: **M**

8. In general, Jose can be described as: (character trait, generalization)
    A. shy.
    B. **mischievous.**
    C. loud.
    D. serious.

3 evidence paragraphs: **L, M, P**

Explanation: Jose was told to stay in his room, but he sneaked out and then eavesdropped on the girls while they were playing Rumor. He also teased them by telling them they thought he looked like a Greek god.

9. In sentence 32, two things are being compared using figurative language. What is that comparison and what does it mean? (figurative language)

Jose's reflexes are compared to lightning. It means that Jose's reflexes were really fast.

17. My Most Embarrassing Day (p. 44)

1. At about what time does the story take place? (setting)
    A. 3:00 p.m.
    B. **6:30 p.m.**
    C. 8:30 p.m.
    D. 7:30 p.m.

2 best evidence sentences: **6, 18**

Explanation: From sentence 6, we know that it is dark outside. Since Meagan's mom is going to pick her up at 8:30 and movies normally last about 2 hours, you can infer that the story probably takes place about 6:30.

2. What caused Meagan's mother to turn up the radio and tune Meagan out? (cause/effect)

She'd had enough of Meagan's arguing.

1 best evidence sentence: **9**

3. How do you predict Meagan will act the next time her mother drops her off where her friends will be? (prediction)

Meagan probably will be more comfortable when her mother is around.

1 best evidence sentence: **32**

4. Who is the girl Meagan refers to in sentence 32? (inference)

herself

1 best evidence sentence: **13**

Explanation: In sentence 13, we learn that Meagan is wearing a turtleneck sweater. This same sweater is referred to in sentence 32.

5. List the numbers of the three sentences within the passage that support the idea that Meagan's mom is concerned about her. (supporting detail)

Sentences **6, 15, 20**

6. How did Meagan's point of view change by the end of the story? (point of view, inference, compare/contrast)

She realized that her behavior towards her mother was what was really embarrassing.

1 best evidence sentence: **32**

7. What is the main reason Meagan wanted to walk to the theater alone? (conclusion)
   A. She wanted to go in the back entrance.
   B. She saw Bret in the back parking lot with his mom.
   C. **She didn't want Bret to see her with her mom.**
   D. The music coming from the car was embarrassingly loud.

1 best evidence paragraph: **A**

Explanation: Meagan was embarrassed about being seen with her mother (1). There is no evidence for A or B. Meagan was embarrassed to be seen with her mom before she turned up the music, so

D is incorrect. She also says it wasn't her mother that embarrassed her anymore, meaning her mother had embarrassed her at one point (32).

8. Compare Meagan's treatment of her mother to Bret's treatment of his mother. (compare/contrast)

Meagan is embarrassed to be seen with her mother and wants her to drop her off in the back parking lot. Bret does not appear to be embarrassed to be seen with his mother. He wants to introduce her to Meagan.

18. **The Game Winner** (p.46)

1. List three words the author uses to suggest that the three baserunners ran fast. (supporting detail)

The baserunners were "sprinting"; Maria "sped" (and "zoomed"); Maria "tore."

3 best evidence sentences: **14, 17, 22**

2. What does paragraph B suggest about how Maria felt? (inference)
   A. She was tense.
   B. She was scared.
   C. **She was confident.**
   D. She was inexperienced.

What event in the story supports your answer?

She stared down the pitcher (5).

3. What had the Eagles done between the first two outs and Maria's turn at bat? (sequence events)

    They had gotten three singles and scored a run.

    1 best evidence sentence: **8**

4. One of the sentences in paragraph A contains a simile. Write that sentence below and then underline the simile. (figurative language)

    The runners on first and second were ready to run <u>like the wind</u> at the sound of contact (3).

5. Give three examples from paragraphs D and E of how the author describes the sounds of the game. (setting: imagery)

    the crack of the bat, the roar of the crowd, the thump of the ball into the catcher's mitt

    1 best evidence sentence for each example: **14, 15, 24**

6. Why did the infielders hope for a catch, as described in sentence 18? (conclusion)

    If the right fielder caught the ball, that would be the third out, the game would be over, and the Bearcats would win.

    1 best evidence sentence: **10**

7. What was the score when the new pitcher took over for the Bearcats? (reading for detail)

    The score was 4–1.

    2 best evidence sentences: **2, 7**

8. Why was the pitcher "helpless," as described in sentence 16? (cause/effect)

    The ball went too high or too wide for him to reach; it was now up to the outfielders to try to catch the ball and make the out.

9. Which of these was NOT a key event in the story? (key event)
    A. Maria's base hit
    B. the roar of the crowd
    C. the arrival of a new pitcher
    D. the scoring of the winning run

    The passage contains no evidence that the roar of the crowd affected the action on the field, as did the other three events.

19. A Test of Friendship (p. 48)

1. Based on paragraphs A and B, there is NO evidence to support the idea that John: (inference)
    A. is a top player.
    B. is friends with Ed.
    C. is good in history.
    D. likes to win.

    Explanation: You can infer from sentence 2 that John was in danger of not passing history. There is evidence to support A, B, or D.

2. In paragraph B, what kind of figurative language does the writer use? Write the sentence. (figurative language: simile)

    In sentence 9, the writer uses a simile: John's mind was still as blank as his notepad.

3.   Why did Mr. Fessler assume it was John who got help with the paper? (conclusion)

Since Ed had received an A on his last paper, there is no reason that Ed would copy John's paper. Also, John was in danger of not passing history.

2 best evidence sentences: **2, 14**

4.   Which of the following was a key event in the plot? (key events)
A.   John and Ed went to the library.
B.   John copied Ed's paper.
C.   John read Ed's paper.
D.   Mr. Fessler handed back the papers.

Explanation: By copying Ed's paper, John made a deliberate decision that triggered further events in the story. A, C, and D are details in the story. Reading Ed's paper was not significant because John could have put the paper back down. Passing back the papers was not significant; not passing back John's and Ed's papers was a key event.

5.   Why is it ironic that John got an F on his paper? (literary device: irony)

John cheated in order to get a passing grade. Instead, he ended up getting an F.

2 best evidence sentences: **37, 46**

6.   What was the primary conflict in the story? (conflict)

The primary conflict was John's inner struggle with himself about whether or not he should copy Ed's paper.

1 best evidence paragraph: **G**

Explanation: In sentence 29, John tries to convince himself that what he's doing isn't cheating. In sentence 32, he tells himself that Ed wouldn't mind, but if that was true he would have just asked Ed if he could copy his paper. In sentencee 34 he still feels uneasy.

7.   Which of the following best states the theme of the story? (theme)
A.   Winning is important, no matter what the cost.
B.   It pays to be honest.
C.   Cheating can have painful consequences.
D.   It is important to rely on our friends.

Explanation: John got himself and Ed in trouble by cheating and felt bad when Mr. Fessler penalized Ed. He didn't intend to hurt his friend, so winning at any cost was not the most important thing. There is also no evidence for D.

8.   Based on paragraphs A and B, John could described as: (character trait)
A.   organized.
B.   relaxed.
C.   worried.
D.   bored.

Explanation: C is supported by, and B is contradicted by, John's concerns about playing in the game and finishing his paper. Sentence 10 says he is starting to panic. There is no evidence for A or D.

9.   Why do you think John felt queasy in sentence 41? (inference)

John realized that Mr. Fessler knew he had copied Ed's paper.

Sentence 42 uses the exclamation, "Mr. Fessler knew!"

10. What will John do to help his friend Ed? (predict outcome)

John will probably explain to Mr. Fessler that Ed didn't know John copied his paper.

In sentence 49, we know John is going to do something to "make things right."

20. Old Woman of the Oak (p. 50)

1. What resulted from pressing the tree knot in paragraph B? (cause/effect)

The rope ladder came down.

2. Paragraph B suggests that Meg's speech is: (character trait)
   A. brief.
   B. lengthy.
   C. mean.
   D. descriptive.

1 best evidence sentence: 6

3. In sentence 9, *gnarled* most likely means: (vocabulary)
   A. green.
   B. twisted.
   C. tall.
   D. flat.

Explanation: Since *gnarled* is contrasted with the liveliness of her eyes, the author probably wants to show that Meg's body is aged, like a tree with knots and twisted branches.

4. Why did Jude need to be careful in climbing to Meg's home? (reading for detail)

The rope was wet.

5. In sentence 24, "came home to me" means: (figurative language: idiom)
   A. became clear to me.
   B. entered my house.
   C. confused me.
   D. made me sad.

Explanation: A is supported by sentence 27, where he spells out what she meant. Choice B makes no sense; "dark mood" indicates that Jude got the meaning and it made him sad, so C is unlikely. It would be repetitive to say "my mood darkened as her meaning made me sad," so D is unlikely.

6. Jude is most likely to make a plan to: (predict outcome)
   A. force Meg to move.
   B. move in with Meg.
   C. get the Oak Log.
   D. stop the bulldozing.

2 best evidence sentences: **13, 14**

Explanation: Choice D is supported by sentences 13 and 14, which show that Jude has strong feelings against the bulldozing. B is unlikely because there is no evidence that moving in with Meg would help. Since Meg is already going to give Jude the Oak Log, C is incorrect. A is a possibility, but is unsupported.

7. Which of the following is probably NOT a conflict implied in the passage? (compare/contrast)
   A. Jude wanted to stop the bulldozing, but Meg was against stopping it.
   B. Meg loved her home but also thought it was time to let go.
   C. Jude wanted to help Meg but felt that he could do nothing.
   D. Jude respected the journal, but felt bad about Meg's giving it to him.

Explanation: Paragraph J contradicts the idea that Jude could do nothing, so choice C is not a conflict. Paragraphs D, E, and F confirm A. Paragraphs G and H support B. Paragraph I supports D.

8. Describe where the oak tree was located. (setting)

    The oak tree was outside of town, through bushes, past a stream, in a field or clearing. It was near a rocky coast.

    3 best evidence sentences: **1, 21, 29**

9. In sentence 23, what is the darkening of the sky used to symbolize? (literary device: symbolism)

    The darkening of the sky is used to symbolize Jude's darkening mood as he becomes aware of Meg's meaning.

    1 best evidence sentence: **24**

    Explanation: Sentence 24 states that Jude's mood darkened with the sky.

10. In sentence 24, what does Jude infer from Meg's comments? (inference)

    He probably infers that Meg thinks her time has come to leave or die or both.

    1 best evidence sentence: **27**

21. **Middle School: First Day Survival**
    (p. 52)

1. What is the main purpose of Adam's speech? (main idea)
    A. to show new students how to get around campus
    B. to tell new students how nervous he was about his first day of school
    C. **to minimize the fear new students might have about middle school**
    D. to let new students know how different middle school is going to be

    1 best evidence sentence: **2**

2. Compared to Adam's middle school, his elementary school: (conclusion)
    A. **had fewer students.**
    B. had more buildings.
    C. had more students.
    D. had fewer buildings.

    1 best evidence sentence: **18**

3. Which of the following character traits best describes Adam now? (character trait)
    A. shy and insecure
    B. **confident and outgoing**
    C. mistrustful and secretive
    D. slow and cautious

    2 best evidence paragraphs: **A, H**

4. Compare Adam's attitude in the beginning of his first day of school to his attitude by the end of the first day. (compare/contrast)

    In the beginning, he was nervous. By the end, he knew that middle school was going to be all right.

5. What type of figurative language is used in sentence 19? (figurative language)

    a metaphor

    Explanation: The writer is comparing the kids to insects crawling out of the cracks.

6. List two things Adam did to help ease his transition into middle school. (supporting detail)

    He taped his schedule and a map of the school to his binder. He begged his mom to drop him off at school an hour early so he could find his classes.

7. Which direction would you go if you were in the art building and had to get to the English building?
    (use of illustration)
    A. northwest
    B. southeast
    C. southwest
    D. northeast

8. The "X" on the map represents Adam on his first day. Third period has just ended, and Adam is lost. Give him accurate directions to his next class.
    (use of illustration)

    You need to go northeast to the social studies building, which is across the field.

9. How do you predict Adam will feel about his first day of high school? (prediction)

    He might be a little nervous, but he will get through the day.

10. What probably caused Mrs. Jelica to smirk? (cause/effect)

    Adam called her class "the best," and then kidded that he wasn't just saying it because she was in the room.

22. A Dramatic Plea (p. 54)

1. How many members have left the club since last spring? (conclusion)
    A. twenty-five
    B. nearly fifty
    C. more than twenty-five
    D. about a third

    1 best evidence sentence: **18**

    Explanation: According to sentence 18, over 50 percent (more than half) of the members have left the club. Since there are currently 25 members, this means that more than 25 left, making C correct and B and D incorrect. A is incorrect because it is exactly 50%.

2. Explain why the name of the club includes the words "Two Face."
    (inference)

    The club uses the words "Two Face" because two faces are used as symbols for drama.

    Also, since actors play different kinds of roles at different times, you could say they have more than one "face."

3. The title of Jason's news article (Now Is the Time to Act!) really has two meanings. Explain them. (inference)

    By saying "Now is the time to act," Jason could mean that you must take action and join the club quickly. He could also mean it is time to act, as in a play.

4. Give an example of how the writer applies each of the following techniques to persuade us to join the club. (author's style)

Grabbing attention: **Now is the Time to Act! (article title). The club offers great benefits.**

Listing benefits: **Help decide on plays, audition for plays, take acting classes, develop leadership and organizational skills.**

Giving gifts: **free movie ticket.**

Giving a warning: **may lose funds if you don't join, don't miss out—sign up today.**

5. How is Jason setting an example for one of the members' responsibilities? (application)

He is recruiting new members.

1 best evidence sentence: **12**

6. If you join, you can definitely: (reading for detail)
   A. get a part in a play.
   B. receive free lessons.
   C. get free movie tickets.
   D. be elected to an office.

1 best evidence sentence: **7**

Explanation: B is supported by "Take free acting classes!" in sentence 7, which is included in a list of benefits. Though you can audition for parts (6), there is no guarantee you will get one, so A is incorrect. Likewise, getting free tickets (13) is guaranteed to only the first five new members. There is no evidence for D.

7. Label each of the following as F for fact or O for opinion. (fact/opinion)

O The club offers great benefits.

F The first 5 new members will get free tickets.

O It's important to join now.

F Grease Monkeys was performed.

Explanation: "Great" in the first sentence and "important" in the third sentence are both indicators of an opinion.

8. What threatens the functions of the drama club? (reading for detail)

The school will not support them by giving them money and plays will be cancelled if they don't get 30 members by October 1. They have only 25 now.

1 best evidence sentence: **19**

9. Describe both the cause and the effect implied in sentence 19. (cause/effect)

(Accept either answer)

Cause: **Membership increases to 30 before October 1.**

Effect: **The school will continue to fund the club, and the club will not cancel all plays.**

OR

Cause: **Membership does not increase to 30 before October 1.**

Effect: **The school will not fund the club, and the club will cancel all plays.**

23. The Way of the Wild   (p. 56)

1. List the numbers of the four sentences from the story that give clues to the ending. (literary device: foreshadowing)

    Sentences **6, 13 (or 9), 18, 19**

2. Contrast Emily's attitude about the attack with Juma's attitude. (compare/contrast)

    Emily is worried about the giraffe and feels uneasy about watching without helping it. Juma doesn't want to interfere because he considers the attack "the way of the wild."

    2 best evidence paragraphs: **M, N**

3. Write the simile that is used in paragraph A. (figurative language)

    like an old rusty hinge

4. Give the letter of the paragraph that best describes where the story takes place. (setting)

    Paragraph **A**

5. What caused the impalas to run? (cause/effect)

    They heard the sound of breaking twigs.

    1 best evidence sentence: **31**

6. List three examples of how the author uses sound to build tension in the story. (plot)

    (Accept any three)

    1. The quiet is eerie. 2. A roar interrupts the silence. 3. Emily whispers with excitement. 4. Juma hushes Emily and tells her to wait. 5. Emily cries out. 6. Breaking twigs scare off the impalas.

7. Why were the animals unwilling to drink at the watering hole? (inference)

    They were afraid of being eaten by the lion.

    1 best evidence sentence: **19**

    Explanation: We know that the animals will not dip their heads to drink from the watering hole. Sentence 19 explains that the fear of capture was too much.

8. What do Juma's words and actions reveal about his character? (character trait)
    A. He is unfamiliar with wild animals.
    B. He worries about helpless animals.
    C. He understands wild animals.
    D. He is unsure of himself.

    4 evidence paragraphs: **B, D, G, N**

    Explanation: Juma sensed that the animals were hesitating at the watering hole because a lion was nearby (B). He knew something would happen as the sun was setting (G). He also understood that there was nothing they could do (N). These paragraphs contradict the other choices.

9. What most likely happened to the giraffe? (predict outcome)

    The giraffe was most likely eaten by the lion.

    3 best evidence sentences: **35, 36, 38** (Also acceptable: **40**)

10. How do Emily's feelings about watching the animals change? (conclusion)

    At first, Emily enjoys watching the animals and worries that she won't be able to see them when the sun goes down. At the end, Emily looks

away because she does not want to see the lion kill the giraffe.

24. Amazon Adventure (p. 58)

1. In sentence 15, how does the author use personification to describe the volcano? (figurative language)

   She talks about the volcano's yawning mouth and appeasing its angry outbursts.

2. In sentence 10, what does the word vortex most likely mean? (vocabulary)
   A. a landslide
   B. a whirlpool
   C. a crater
   D. a river

   Explanation: The definition is supported by the description of the vortex as swirling. Also, in sentence 12, Sirah finds himself spinning. There is no evidence for A, C, or D.

3. In sentence 9, why did Sirah throw down the game controller? (inference)
   A. He was hoping to stop the game.
   B. He got tired of playing.
   C. He was angry for losing.
   D. He couldn't hold on to it.

   Explanation: Since he was being sucked inside the game at this point, he probably hoped that dropping the controller would stop the game. This idea is reinforced by the statement in sentence 9 that "it was too late." There is no evidence for B, C, or D.

4. Which of the following is NOT a reason the natives might be angry? (prediction, inference)
   A. They did not like strangers.
   B. They thought he was stealing the treasure.
   C. They considered him to be trespassing.
   D. They were eager to share the treasure.

   Explanation: If they were hoping to share the treasure, they would be happy to see him bringing it up from the volcano.

5. Sirah's attitude at the end of the passage could be described as: (character trait)
   A. unhappy
   B. enthusiastic
   C. realistic
   D. amused

   Explanation: Sentence 22 tells us that Sirah knows what he has to do to escape the game and return home. There is no evidence to support the other choices.

6. Why was there treasure inside the volcano? (cause/effect)

   The natives had thrown their gold and jewels into the volcano.

   1 best evidence sentence: **15**

7. The mood of the story could be described as: (mood)
   A. peaceful.
   B. hilarious.
   C. exciting.
   D. tragic.

   Explanation: C is supported by the fact that Sirah is playing an adventure game when he suddenly becomes an active participant in the adventure. A is contradicted by the events in paragraphs B, C, and D. There is no evidence for B or D.

8. What event was linked to Sirah's being pulled into the game? (key event)

the eruption of the volcano

1 best evidence sentence: **5**

9. What literary form is this story? (literary form)
    A. comedy
    B. mystery
    C. science fiction
    D. fable

Explanation: Video games and virtual reality are scientific facts. However, becoming part of a video game is still fictional. Therefore, science fiction is the best choice of form. There is no evidence for A or D. The only mystery is finding the treasure, but this is not the primary focus of the story.

25. Sketches of Summer (p. 60)

1. At what time of day does the story take place? (setting)

sunset

1 best paragraph: **I**

2. Give two examples of how this girl compares to his idea of girls in general. (compare/contrast)

Accept any two points of comparison: 1. She takes his sketches seriously and understands them. Other girls do not understand his drawings. 2. She does not ask or say anything. Other girls act silly. They giggle and lie. 3. She does not always hang out in a group. Other girls stick together.

2 best evidence paragraphs: **C, D**

3. In telling a story, an author sometimes describes events out of the actual order of occurrence. (The author may use flashback to tell of a previous event.) Number the following paragraphs according to the actual sequence of events within the characters' lives. (literary device: flashback; sequence)

2   A and B
1   D and E
3   F and G
4   H and I

Explanation: The beginning of the story is in present time. In paragraph C, the author starts relaying previous events to give us some background information. Paragraphs D and E continue to describe what happened before. In paragraph F, we are brought back to the present.

4. Who drew the picture the boy found in his sketch pad? (conclusion, inference)

The girl who was leaving drew the picture.

1 best evidence sentence: **25**

Explanation: Sentence 25 says that he never smiled like he did in the picture unless he was smiling at her; therefore, we can conclude that she drew the picture.

5. In sentence 17, what was meant by "language he could share"? (conclusion)

The language they shared was the meaning of his drawings.

2 best evidence sentences: **12, 16**

6. What message do you think the boy understood from the cartoon, and why? (inference)

He concluded that the girl would return to see him next summer because 1) the boat was heading toward him, 2) the name of the boat was NEXT SUMMER, and 3) she wrote "See you!"

Explanation: Sentences 25–27 suggest that a boat is heading toward the boy. Sentence 28 implies that this action will happen next summer. Her words "See you" support this.

7. Why does it say "he saw her" in sentence 31? (inference)
   A. He actually saw her on the boat, though he couldn't see the sail.
   B. She was on the shore because she had decided not to go after all.
   C. He was looking at a picture of her that he had drawn.
   D. He was able to imagine her after getting her message.

8. How is the plot resolved? (predict resolution)
   A. She finally leaves on a ship.
   B. He decides to let her go.
   C. He learns of her plan to return.
   D. He learns to like girls.

Explanation: Sentence 32 suggests a resolution supported by the previous sentences in the paragraph that imply that she'll come back.

26. 15 Minutes of Fame (p. 62)

1. Who was the "she" of paragraph B? (inference)
   A. the performer
   B. an audience member
   C. a dreamer
   D. an office worker

Explanation: Sentence 12 says she was breathing heavily, which would support A. There is no evidence for choices B, C, or D.

2. The audience consisted of: (inference)
   A. regular people.
   B. famous people.
   C. projected images.
   D. dummies.

1 best evidence sentence: **19**

Explanation: Sentence 19 explains that the company will provide you with audiences using holograms, which are projected images (see caption).

3. The word *boisterous*, as used in sentence 22, most likely means: (vocabulary)
   A. reserved.
   B. polite.
   C. rude.
   D. noisy.

Explanation: The context implies that there is a contrast in meaning between being reserved and being boisterous. The best contrast for reserved is D.

4. Much of the first paragraph describes: (use of illustration)
   A. a performance by a real superstar.
   B. an illusion created by special effects.
   C. a vivid and detailed dream.
   D. a rock concert at a large arena.

Explanation: Sentences 16 and 17 support the sales information in the brochure. The brochure describes a service in which holograms are used to create the illusion of an audience.

5. By paragraph B, the room where the performance had taken place was: (inference)
    A. empty.
    B. clean.
    C. crowded.
    D. enormous.

    Explanation: You can infer, by putting together information from the brochure with paragraphs A and B, that the room referred to in sentence 12 is the same room where the performance took place.

6. Describe the setting of the story. (setting)

    It took place in a room used by a business. Holograms were used to give the illusion of many people, a stage, and a band.

7. Two lasting things were promised at the end of the brochure. Explain whether or not they were fulfilled. (conclusion)

    The experience gave the girl a thrill, but not confidence.

    Explanation: Sentence 17 shows that she considered the experience a thrill; sentence 18 seems to contradict the idea of confidence.

8. Describe the use of personification in paragraph B. (figurative language)

    In sentence 14, the author compares dustballs to people by saying they "danced" across the floor.

9. Describe the metaphor used in sentence 18, and explain what is meant by "unfurnished." (figurative language)

    The "place in her mind where esteem would live" is being compared to an empty or unfurnished room. Since that place is empty, she must not have any esteem.

27. A Flood of Help (p. 64)

1. Which of these statements best captures the main idea? (main idea)
    A. Rain threatens a town.
    B. A river overflows its banks.
    C. People from a neighboring town help out.
    D. Neighbors work together to save two houses and farms.

    Explanation: Only D encapsulates the main idea. A and B are details; C is true but doesn't specify how the people worked together.

2. How would the loss of the farms affect the rest of the community? (inference)

    The people would have to try to get their vegetables somewhere else.

    1 best evidence sentence: **17**

3. The mood of the people of Carruth is: (mood)
    A. hopeless.
    B. thoughtful.
    C. determined.
    D. overwhelmed.

    2 best evidence sentences: **1, 26**

4. Why were the Miller house and the Mendes cottage threatened? (cause/effect)

    The land surrounding the two houses was washing away.

    1 best evidence sentence: **12**

5. The author suggests that the people aren't sure they will save the houses. Give two phrases from paragraph I to support that idea. (supporting detail)

desperate eyes, grim looks

(Also acceptable: **prayers answered** implies that prayers were offered)

6. What does *torrent* mean, as used in sentence 28? (vocabulary)
    A. windstorm
    B. thunderstorm
    C. heavy rain
    D. heavy flooding

    Explanation: The sentence says the torrent becomes a drizzle, so rain is the likely choice.

7. What is the condition of the houses other than Millers' and Mendes' in Carruth? (conclusion)
    A. They have been washed away.
    B. They have been abandoned.
    C. They have been secured.
    D. They have been demolished.

    2 best evidence sentences: **4, 12**

8. Based on information in the passage, it can be said that, in general, the people of Carruth are: (generalization)
    A. helpful.
    B. unfriendly.
    C. secretive.
    D. unprepared.

    Explanation: The people pitch in to help their neighbors. The passage contradicts B and D and provides no evidence for C.

9. Explain how the people of Carruth are like the apple trees. (compare/contrast)

Both had taken a beating but were still standing.

1 best evidence sentence: **33**

(Also acceptable: **both are wet; both have heavy limbs; both will recover**)

28. Diving In   (p. 66)

1. How does sentence 2 give the reader a clue as to what might happen later? (literary device: foreshadowing)

It suggests that the narrator feels as if he is in the picture. He smells the sea and hears the seagulls. Later in the story, he actually does enter the painting.

This early suggestion of a later event may be considered foreshadowing.

2. Explain what is meant by the figurative language used in sentence 3. (figurative language)

"Out of that sleeve grew a sword" is a way of saying the sword looked like it was growing naturally out of the sleeve, though it is really being held in the hand.

3. In general, picture diving requires all of the following EXCEPT: (conclusion)
    A. confidence.
    B. focus.
    C. running.
    D. precision.

3 best evidence sentences: **7, 8, 9**

Explanation: The only item that is not listed as necessary for picture diving in general is D. Precision is necessary only for diving into a specific character within a picture.

4. Match each point of view to the character to whom it most likely belongs. Use each letter only once. (point of view)

    B 1. Phineus is a foe to be conquered.

    A 2. I'm an outside observer.

    D 3. I'm defending the captain's honor.

    C 4. I must defend my ship.

    A. Narrator before picture diving

    B. Red Rooster

    C. Captain Phineus

    D. Narrator in the picture

5. The word *fetid*, as used in sentence 15, most likely means: (vocabulary)
    A. foul.
    B. sweet.
    C. encouraging.
    D. inspiring.

    Explanation: The word *stench* is used to refer to Rooster's breath. Also, the breath makes the narrator want to push him away. Therefore, only A makes sense.

6. Why did a new scar appear on Rooster's face in the picture (sentence 35)? (inference)

    As the narrator slid through the rails inside the picture, his sword snapped up and scratched Rooster's cheek.

    1 best evidence sentence: **30**

7. The main conflict in the story is between: (conflict)
    A. Rooster and himself.
    B. the narrator and himself.
    C. Phineus and the narrator.
    D. Rooster and the narrator.

8. The story could be classified as any of the following EXCEPT: (literary forms)
    A. fantasy.
    B. nonfiction.
    C. mythical.
    D. adventure.

    Explanation: Since this story is not true to reality, it would not be classified as nonfiction (true story). A and C are nonrealistic kinds of stories; either of these forms could apply to this story. The story does have elements of adventure, so D could apply.

9. Why was the narrator panicked paragraphs C and D? (inference)

    He realized that Phineus had died in the fight and that he would too if he couldn't get out of the picture.

    2 best evidence sentences: **20, 21**

29. The Comeback Can (p. 68)

1. It can be inferred from his presentation that Alexander: (inference, character trait)
    A. is easily confused.
    B. has a sense of humor.
    C. is very shy.
    D. acts stuck-up.

    3 best evidence sentences: **6, 29, 30**

    Explanation: B is the best answer because Alexander jokes with the class. There is no evidence that he is confused, so A is incorrect. He appears to be knowledgeable but not arrogant, so D is incorrect. C is contradicted by Alexander's wit and poise during his presentation.

2. Number the following steps in the order they should occur. (sequence steps)

5   Fasten the rubber band to the plastic top with a paper clip

2   Pierce two holes in the can: one on top, one on bottom

4   Tie a weight to the rubber band

3   Pull a rubber band through the hole in the bottom of the can

1   Get a coffee can, rubber band, and weight

3.   Explain why Alexander whispered into his can "Good job, Mickey." (inference)

He was probably joking with the class by pretending that there was actually a mouse in the can doing all the work.

4.   The main purpose of Alexander's science project was most likely to: (main idea)
   A.   **demonstrate a scientific principle.**
   B.   joke about the mouse trick.
   C.   get the class involved.
   D.   answer questions from the class.

3 best evidence sentences: **1, 22, 23**

Explanation: A is supported because Alexander states that he is performing a "demonstration" (1). He also ends his demonstration by stating Newton's First Law of Motion (22, 23). Choices B, C, and D are all part of the project but not the main purpose.

5.   What caused the can to roll backwards? (cause/effect)

When Alexander pushed the can forward, the rubber band was twisted forward by the weight, increasing the tension. This tension eventually caused the rubber band to begin untwisting in a backwards

direction, causing the can to also move backwards.

6.   What do you predict would happen if Alexander placed the can at the bottom of a slightly elevated ramp and then twisted the lid away from the ramp? Explain your answer. (prediction, application)

The can would probably roll uphill. Turning the lid backwards increases the tension of the rubber band. The tension would be released as the can rolled uphill.

7.   What type of figurative language does the author use in sentence 9? Explain your answer. (figurative language)
   A.   simile
   B.   **metaphor**
   C.   idiom
   D.   irony

Explanation: In sentence 9, the narrator calls the questions a flood that comes pouring in.

8.   Label each of these statements either F for fact or O for opinion. (fact/opinion)
   O   "That's a good guess..."
   F   "The can moved forward when I pushed it with my hand."
   F   "When I rolled the can across the tabletop, the rubber band twisted in a forward direction."
   F   The class applauded Alexander's science demonstration.

Explanation: The first statement includes the word "good," which ascribes value and is thus an opinion. The second and last two statements present events that did occur in the story.ki

30. The Prime Suspect (p. 70)

1. What famous event in American history is the background for the story? (setting)

   The Civil War is the background.

   4 best evidence sentences: **7, 10, 12, 25**

2. Which of these words best describes Courteney Baker? (character trait)
   A. unkind
   B. unpatriotic
   C. secretive
   D. cooperative

   2 best evidence sentences: **2, 23**

3. Why do you think "the Southern troops continued to know exactly where to strike," as described in sentence 25? (cause/effect)

   The Southern troops had copies of the Union troop reports and reinforcement schedules.

   3 best evidence sentences: **7, 8, 10**

4. Which of these paragraphs gives the strongest evidence for why Pinkerton thought Courteney Baker was a spy? (supporting detail)
   A. Paragraph F
   B. Paragraph B
   C. Paragraph J
   D. Paragraph D

5. Identify the idiom used in paragraph B. (figurative language: idiom)

   The idiom used in paragraph B is "in the dead of the night."

   Explanation: The idiom means when night is at its stillest.

6. Describe the difference in attitudes of Courteney Baker and Detective Pinkerton in paragraphs F and G. (character trait, compare/contrast)

   Courteney Baker doesn't seem to care. Pinkerton does care. He demands that she answer his questions.

7. What is the primary mystery of the story? (conclusion)
   A. what was in the stolen plans
   B. where the plans were stolen
   C. what Pinkerton knew about the stolen plans
   D. what Courteney Baker knew about the stolen plans

   3 best evidence sentences: **1, 11, 19**

8. If, as a result of the battle, Detective Pinkerton decided to question Courteney Baker again, what would be the probable outcome? (predict outcome)

   She would probably tell him nothing.

   4 best evidence sentences from paragraphs A and H: **2, 20, 22, 23**

31. A Week in Ancient Greece (p. 72)

1. Which phrase best describes what most influenced ancient Greek society in the story? (theme)
   A. cultural masterpieces
   B. philosophical arguments
   C. the birth of democracy
   D. the exchange of ideas

   2 best evidence sentences: **2, 12**

2. Antigone is a famous Greek play about a woman who speaks out against the government and is sentenced to death because of it. Which of these people probably wrote Antigone? (conclusion)
A. Aristotle
B. Aristophanes
C. Socrates
D. Sophocles

1 best evidence sentence: **20**

3. In general, the Greeks placed the highest value on: (generalization)
A. individual enlightenment.
B. cultural enrichment.
C. collective achievement.
D. democratic government.

2 best evidence sentences: **2, 26**

4. How could an ancient Greek stay in government for more than one year? (conclusion)

He could draw the right number more than once.

1 best evidence sentence: **9**

5. Which of these sentences from the passage contains BOTH a fact and an opinion? (fact/opinion)
A. Every male citizen could serve in the assembly and vote on laws and policies.
B. Ancient Greece must have been a fascinating place to live.
C. I'm glad they also gave us the Olympics.
D. They also fought many wars, but in those times who didn't?

Explanation: Only D contains both a fact (They also fought many wars) and an opinion, or judgment (but in those times who didn't). A, B, and C are facts.

6. Explain the difference between Greek comedy and Greek tragedy. (compare/contrast)

Greek tragedy told a story of a main character who came to a bad end. Greek comedies were mostly satires, which poked fun at important people.

3 best evidence sentences: **21, 22, 23**

7. Which of these sets of statements is a syllogism? (application)
A. All mice have families. Stuart is a mouse. Therefore, Stuart has a sister.
B. All mice wear shoes. Stuart is a mouse. Therefore, Stuart wears shoes.
C. All dogs run. Simon runs Therefore, Simon is a dog.
D. All dogs have tails. Simon is a dog. Therefore, Simon eats dog food.

NONFICTION

32. Put Your Heart Into It (p. 76)

1. The main idea of the story is that exercise can: (main idea)
A. build your overall muscle mass.
B. lower your blood pressure.
C. keep your body healthy.
D. increase oxygen in your blood.

1 best evidence sentence: **21**

2. Using examples from the passage, list how each of the three categories of exercise affects your blood flow. (reading for detail)

Aerobic **creates a more regular flow of oxygen into and carbon dioxide out of the blood**

Strength **builds large muscles so more blood flows to them**

Flexibility **helps get blood flowing around areas you want to exercise**

1 best evidence sentence for each answer: **6, 8 (or 9), 11 (or 15)**

3. Muscles at rest: (inference)
    A. are usually the body's larger muscles.
    B. require a large amount of weight resistance to work them properly.
    C. need more exercise than muscles in use.
    D. have less blood flowing around them than the same muscles in use.

    2 best evidence sentences: **11 (or 15), 13**

4. Which of these best sums up the benefit of exercise described in sentence 23? (inference)
    A. improved respiration
    B. rest and relaxation
    C. strength and endurance
    D. improved fitness

    Explanation: Only B is a benefit that applies to sentence 23.

5. What happens when you do not stretch your legs after running? (prediction/inference)

    Your muscles stay tight and don't relax.

    2 best evidence sentences: **17, 18**

6. Which of these functions of a plant is the direct opposite of what the human body does? (compare/contrast)

    A. It absorbs sunlight and converts it to energy.
    B. It serves as a producer in the food chain.
    C. It makes its own food through photosynthesis.
    D. It takes in carbon dioxide and gives off oxygen.

    1 best evidence sentence: **6**

    Explanation: A plant takes in carbon dioxide and gives off oxygen; in contrast, the human body takes in oxygen and gives off carbon dioxide. A, B, and C discuss food production, of which the article makes no mention.

7. How is the article organized? (organization of material)
    A. by topic
    B. by time order
    C. as an argument
    D. as a comparison

    Explanation: The article compares the benefits of three different types of exercise. Neither a time order nor an argument is given, so B and C are incorrect. A is possible, but D is the best answer.

33. Galileo's Vision (p. 78)

1. Which of these best explains why people before Galileo hadn't seen moons around Jupiter? (cause/effect)
    A. They hadn't looked in the right place.
    B. They hadn't turned the telescope toward the night sky.
    C. They thought Jupiter didn't have moons.
    D. They thought Earth was the center of the universe.

    1 best evidence sentence: **8**

2. Which of these words best describes the process that Galileo introduced to scientific theory? (conclusion)
    A. visualization
    B. determination
    C. argumentation
    D. experimentation

    1 best evidence sentence: **12**

3. The author's purpose in writing the passage was probably:
    (author's purpose)
    A. to discuss modern astronomy.
    B. to show how to use a telescope.
    C. to prove Galileo's theories about the universe.
    D. to show Galileo's contributions to science.

4. Scientists before Galileo proved theories by making arguments. This kind of proof can best be described as:
    (inference)
    A. theoretical.
    B. historical.
    C. natural.
    D. technical.

    Explanation: Sentences 12 and 13 says Galileo was the first scientist to prove theories using evidence. Scientists before him, then, must have relied on untested theories. There is no evidence for B, C, or D.

5. Compare the two scientific theories described in Paragraph F.
    (compare/contrast)

    The old theory was that Earth was the center of the universe and that planets and moons circled it. Copernicus's theory said the sun was the center of our solar system and that Earth circled the sun.

6. Explain one way that Galileo changed the way people thought about the moon.
    (reading for detail)

    (Accept either)

    **1. Before Galileo, people thought the moon was perfectly smooth and round and that it gave off its own light.
    2. Galileo proved that the moon had craters and was not its own source of light.**

    1 best evidence paragraph: **D**

7. Which of these statements about the passage is an opinion? (fact/opinion)
    A. The moon is filled with craters.
    B. Galileo put the telescope to good use.
    C. Galileo discovered four moons of Jupiter.
    D. People didn't believe Copernicus's theory at first.

    Explanation: B contains the word "good," which is a value judgment—an indicator of an opinion. A, C, and D are facts.

34. Goalsetting (p. 80)

1. Compare how Jan's evenings were spent at the beginning of the passage and how they were probably spent at the end of the passage.
    (inference, compare/contrast)

    At first, Jan would watch TV. By the end she was probably tutoring, doing homework, and practicing basketball.

    3 best evidence sentences: **1, 32, 33**

2. Which set of steps is most important to the main idea of the passage? (supporting detail)
   A. getting drums, practicing, finding musicians
   B. setting a goal, identifying steps, breaking them down
   C. looking in the paper, checking drums, earning cash
   D. taking a "Do It Yourself" course, practicing, being responsible

3 best evidence paragraphs: **D, E, F**

Explanation: B is broad enough to encompass the ideas given. A and C are too specific to be the broad ideas of the story. There is no evidence for D.

3. According to the passage, which of the following is most important for success? (supporting detail)
   A. setting goals to do what you enjoy
   B. listing the obstacles to the goal
   C. having faith you can reach the goal
   D. moving toward your goal every day

1 best evidence sentence: **23**

4. The word *emboldened*, as used in sentence 29, means: (vocabulary)
   A. encouraged.
   B. foolish.
   C. too bold.
   D. loud.

Explanation: A works best within the context of the passage. (Sentence 30 says you will build confidence to achieve your dream.) Choice D makes no sense; there is no evidence for B or C.

5. Which of the following is most likely the author's point of view? (point of view)
   A. Anyone can be successful.
   B. You get only one chance to believe in yourself.
   C. Success is a matter of chance.
   D. Belief in yourself comes only after taking steps toward the goal.

1 best evidence sentence: **9**

Explanation: When a writer talks to "you," as in sentence 9, she means "anybody who reads this." There is no evidence for choices B and C. Paragraph G indicates that taking steps can increase belief, but it is not stated that you can't believe before taking steps.

6. Jan's newfound success is a result of her: (cause/effect)
   A. getting sick of being in a rut.
   B. being told she has to pass math.
   C. wanting to be a tutor.
   D. being inspired by taking a course.

1 best evidence sentence: **5**

Explanation: Sentence 5 says Jan did the things in paragraph A before taking the course. By the end, we find she has changed.

7. Number the following steps to become a writer in the order the author would suggest. (sequence steps, prediction, application)

   3 Identify publishers of the type of writing you choose to do.
   2 Buy a reference book of publishers.
   1 Decide what kind of writer you want to be.
   4 Request writing guidelines from appropriate publishers.

8. Write a one- or two-sentence summary of the information in the passage. (summary)

To accomplish something, make a goal, break it into steps, and start doing them. It's important to believe you can accomplish your goal.

Explanation: To be considered correct, the answer must include the following ideas: (1) make goal, (2) break goal into steps, (3) start doing the steps, and (4) believe you can achieve.

35. The Long and Short of Color (p. 82)

1. In white light, if a book appears to be red, which of these are true about the book? (Choose all that apply.) (cause/effect)
    A. It is absorbing red light.
    B. It is absorbing all colors of light except red.
    C. It is reflecting the shortest wavelengths of visible light.
    D. It is reflecting the longest wavelengths of visible light.

    1 best evidence paragraph: **D**

    Explanation: You can use the information in sentences 16–18 and 8 and apply the principles derived from the example of the blue chair to conclude that red objects reflect red; then use the information that red light has the longest wavelength.

2. Which of the following best describes the *sequence* of events as portrayed in the passage? (sequence events)
    A. Light strikes an object, the object reflects light, the viewer sees the object's reflected light as its color.
    B. A viewer sees a colored object, the object reflects light, light strikes the object.
    C. Light strikes an object, the viewer sees the object's color, the object reflects the color.
    D. The object reflects colored light, a viewer sees the light, the light strikes the object.

    1 best evidence paragraph: **D**

    Explanation: Sentences 15–18 describe the sequence of choice A.

3. How does the prism affect the yellow light differently from how it affects the blue light? Use the passage and the illustration to answer. (cause/effect, compare/contrast, diagram use)

    The waves of yellow light are bent less.

    2 best evidence sentences: **6, 9**

    Explanation: Sentences 6 and 9, along with the illustration, indicate that the yellow light waves are shorter and would be bent less.

4. How is violet light different from orange light? (compare/contrast)
    A. It is closer to yellow.
    B. Its wavelength is greater.
    C. Its wavelength is shorter.
    D. It is not absorbed.

    Explanation: Using sentences 9–10, the colors are listed in order of wavelength from longest to shortest.

5. Let's say we start with light that has no blue in its spectrum. We shine the light on an object that can reflect only blue. What color will the object appear to be? (prediction)
    A. blue
    B. black
    C. white
    D. red

1 best evidence paragraph: **E**

Explanation: According to paragraph E, the object is capable of reflecting only blue, but there is no blue to reflect; it absorbs the other colors. If it doesn't reflect anything, according to sentence 20, it must appear black.

6. As used in sentence 18, the word reflected most nearly means: (vocabulary)
    A. bent around.
    B. allowed through.
    C. bounced back.
    D. absorbed.

Explanation: Since light that is reflected is not absorbed by the object but is received at our eyes (17–18), it must be bounced from the object.

7. Which of these is a generalization that can be made from the information given in the passage? (generalization)
    A. Without light, there is no color.
    B. White light contains the eight basic colors.
    C. A chair that reflects blue absorbs the other colors.
    D. The number of wavelengths has no limit.

Explanation: Sentences 18 and 6 imply that the definition for "color" is the reflected light our eyes receive. If there is no light, none can be reflected; therefore, there is no color.

8. The author's purpose is to: (author's purpose)
    A. describe the wavelengths of light.
    B. show how light is bent with a prism.
    C. convince you that the world is magic.
    D. explain why things appear colored.

Explanation: The question in sentence 2 asks why things appear colored, and the rest of the passage answers that question.

36. Making Apple Pie (p. 84)

1. Why does the dough get divided into two pieces? (conclusion)

You do this to make a top crust and a bottom crust.

1 best evidence sentence: **20**

2. Contrast the use of water in preparing the crust and in preparing the unbaked pie. (compare/contrast)

In making the crust, you use the water to form moist clumps. In finishing the pie, you brush the edges of the bottom crust with water to help seal the top and bottom crusts together.

2 best evidence sentences: **5, 14**

3. What is the reason for cutting slits in the pie crust? (cause/effect)
    A. so the juices can bubble
    B. so steam can escape
    C. so the crusts won't burn
    D. so the pie can cool more quickly

1 best evidence sentence: **22**

4. Put the following steps in order. (sequence steps)

    1 Add butter to dry mixture (4)

    5 Cut slits in crust (22)

    3 Refrigerate dough (8)

    6 Bake pie (24)

    4 Put filling into pie plate (16)

    2 Divide dough into two pieces (7)

5. Why shouldn't all the sugar go into the filling mixture? (conclusion)

    You should save some sugar to sprinkle on the crust.

    1 best evidence sentence: **15**

6. What does the word *crimp* mean, as used in sentence 21? (vocabulary)
    A. press together
    B. cut off
    C. add sugar to
    D. remove top from

    Explanation: The words "to seal" give a clue to the meaning; you use your fingers to seal the edges together.

7. If LaTonya lost her measuring tablespoon, about how many teaspoons of ice water would she use to make the crust? (reading for detail, diagram use)

    about 15

    Explanation: Recipe calls for about 5 tablespoons; diagram says 1 tbsp = 3 tsp. 5 × 3 = 15

8. What is the purpose of separating the crust directions from the filling directions? (author's purpose)

    The two sets of directions are separated because the author wants you to follow each one in order and not mix ingredients.

9. How many ounces of sugar will you use to prepare the crust? (reading for detail, diagram use)

    1/2 ounce

    Explanation: The diagram says 1 cup is 16 tbsp, or 8 ounces. Therefore, 1 tbsp = 1/2 ounce. The recipe calls for 1 tbsp of sugar for the crust.

37.   Making Mountains   (p. 86)

1. What are the similarities and differences between a volcano and a dome mountain? (compare/contrast)

    Both are formed by magma from beneath the earth's crust. A volcano forms when the magma erupts through the earth's surface. A dome mountain forms when magma lifts the crust, but does not break through the earth's surface.

    2 best evidence paragraphs: **B, C**

2. The Black Hills are an example of: (supporting detail)
    A. dome mountains.
    B. volcanic mountains.
    C. fold mountains.
    D. block mountains.

    1 best evidence sentence: **16**

3. The main idea of the article is: (main idea)

    to describe how mountains are formed.

    1 best evidence paragraph: **A**

4. From the passage, it can be inferred that: (inference)
   A. **mountains can begin forming undersea.**
   B. mountains form only on land.
   C. mountains are formed all at once.
   D. mountains occur only in warm climates.

1 best evidence sentence: **12**

Explanation: A is supported by sentence 12; islands are mountains that form from beneath the sea. There is no evidence for B or D. C is contradicted by sentence 6.

5. A mountain is the result of: (cause/effect)

   movement in the earth's crust

1 best evidence sentence: **2**

6. A volcano is built from: (reading for detail)
   A. crust.
   B. **lava and ash.**
   C. rock and ash.
   D. magma.

1 best evidence sentence: **10**

7. When blocks of rock move diagonally towards each other, it is called: (diagram use)
   A. a tear fault.
   B. a normal fault.
   C. **a reverse fault.**
   D. a block fault.

8. The folding of rocks occurs when: (cause/effect)
   A. two plates slide in opposite directions.
   B. two plates pull apart from each other.
   C. two plates are thrust downward.

   D. **two plates are pushed together.**

1 best evidence paragraph: **E**

Explanation: D is correct based on sentences 21 and 23. A is incorrect based on paragraph D. There is no evidence for B. C is incorrect based on paragraph E.

9. From the article, the conclusion can be made that mountains: (conclusion)
   A. stop growing once they are formed
   B. **continue to grow and change**
   C. change only after an earthquake
   D. grow a specific amount every year

1 best evidence paragraph: **A**

Explanation: B is supported by paragraph A. There is no evidence for A, C or D.

38. Researching the Rennaissance
(p. 88)

1. The passage about Michelangelo supplies evidence that he did all of the following except: (reading for detail)
   A. sculpt a statue.
   B. design a church dome.
   C. paint a religious painting.
   D. **keep a scientific notebook.**

3 best evidence sentences: **13, 14, 16**

2. Which of these did Leonardo probably also study? (conclusion)
   A. history
   B. politics
   C. **anatomy**
   D. languages

1 best evidence sentence: **5**

3. The word *Renaissance* means "rebirth." The Renaissance was a rebirth of interest in the early civilizations of Greece, Rome, and Israel. Name two examples of art listed in the story that support this idea. (supporting detail)

Israel: Michelangelo's *David* and Greece: Raphael's *School of Athens*

(Also acceptable: ***Israel: The Last Supper, The Last Judgment,* the *Sistine Madonna,* and St. Peter's Church.**)

4. Is the underlined part of the following sentence a cause or an effect? "He is also famous for painting the *Mona Lisa*." (cause/effect)

The underlined part is the cause.

Explanation: The painting was part of the cause of his fame.

5. Based on sentences 9 and 17, which of the following general statements could be made about all three men? (generalization)
   A. Their work survives them.
   B. Their peers admired them.
   C. Their reputation preceded them.
   D. Their work still inspires people.

Explanation: The main idea of the story is that the works of these three artists still inspire people, as evidenced in 9 and 17. A is true, but is not as specific as D. The story contains no evidence for B or C.

6. Name three things that all three men had in common. (compare/contrast) (Accept any three.)

**They painted religious paintings.
They were sculptors.
They were from Italy.
They painted people as realistic.**

7. Which of these sentences is the best summary of the article? (summary)
   A. The Renaissance was a time of great artists, long wars, and political unrest.
   B. During the Renaissance, great artists produced beautiful paintings, sculptures, and buildings.
   C. Artists of the Renaissance focused on religion and realism above all else.
   D. The Renaissance featured famous men who were masters in the fields of art, architecture, and science.

Explanation: D provides the most comprehensive summary of the article. B and C are details; A is outside information.

39. Soccer's Deadly Weapon: Mia Hamm (p. 90)

1. Based on paragraph B, how did Mia's family help to develop her interest in soccer? (inference)

She played soccer with her older brothers and sisters. Her father was a soccer coach and referee.

2. Mia won her first Olympic medal: (sequence events)
   A. while still in college.
   B. after she graduated from college.
   C. while still in high school.
   D. before she joined the U.S. women's national team.

2 best evidence sentences: **10, 17**

3. Mia's personal goal for playing soccer is
    to: (point of view, reading for detail)
    A. win as many awards as possible.
    B. always improve.
    C. play to be recognized.
    D. do only what's necessary.

    1 best evidence sentence: **16**

    Explanation: Mia's comment supports B
    and contradicts C. There is no evidence
    that she believes A or D.

4. Sentence 17 suggests that Mia is a
    person who: (character trait, inference)
    A. puts herself first.
    B. is easily discouraged.
    C. craves attention.
    D. does not quit.

5. Why is Mia considered the U.S. team's
    all-time leading scorer?
    (reading for detail)

    She has scored 107 goals so far.

    1 best evidence sentence: **21**

6. Why was the attendance at the 1999
    Women's World Cup significant?
    (supporting detail)

    **It was the highest attendance at
    any women's sporting event in the
    world.**

    1 best evidence sentence: **19**

7. Based on this passage, it can be
    concluded that Mia: (conclusion)
    **A. has contributed to the
        growth of women's soccer.**
    B. is best at playing goalie.
    C. is determined to win as many
        awards as possible.
    D. has a desire to one day coach
        soccer.

Explanation: Mia has supported
women's soccer through her active
participation and achievements in
the sport, and her establishment of a
foundation to encourage young female
athletes. Mia usually plays forward,
so B is incorrect. C is contradicted by
sentence 16. There is no evidence for D.

8. Based on paragraph F, the conclusion
    can be made that interest in women's
    soccer has: (conclusion)
    A. decreased.
    B. stayed the same.
    C. increased.
    D. varied.

    Explanation: Attendance at the 1999
    World Cup game was even greater than
    the attendance at the 1996 Olympics
    game, supporting an increase in interest.
    There is no evidence for A, B, or D.

40. Measuring Time (p. 92)

1. How does our hour contrast with that of
    the Babylonians? (compare/contrast)

    **Our hour doesn't change. It is
    always 60 minutes. The Babylonian
    hour did change. It was shorter
    in the winter and longer in the
    summer.**

    2 best evidence sentences: **12, 13**

2. Why are there 13 lines marked on the
    sundial?
    (diagram use, reading for detail)

    **The spaces between the 13 lines
    mark off 12 daylight "hours."**

    1 best evidence sentence: **10**

3. What caused the hands of a water clock to turn? (cause/effect)

    The hands were attached to wooden ducks that floated on the water's surface. As the water level went down, the ducks went lower, pulling the hands down.

    2 best evidence sentences: **22, 23**

4. How did the early Egyptian water clock measure time?
    (reading for detail, diagram use)

    Marks were made inside the pot to show how much time passed as the water ran out.

5. How might a water clock get clogged?
    (inference, prediction)

    Pebbles or leaves could fall into the pot and clog the drain. (Also acceptable: mold, algae, etc.)

6. What were the advantages of using sand in a clock? (supporting detail)
    A. Sand didn't freeze or clog as easily.
    B. Sand passed more quickly than water.
    C. Sand was easier to find than water.
    D. Sand clocks were sturdier.

    Explanation: A is supported by sentence 26. There is no evidence for B, C, or D.

7. How did the design of the hourglass make it portable?
    (diagram use, conclusion)

    (Accept either answer.)

    Since it was smaller, it was easier to move around. Since it was sealed, it wouldn't spill. (26)

8. In general, NONE of the early clocks indicated: (generalization)
    A. how many hours had passed.
    B. the length of the sun's shadow.
    C. how many minutes had passed.
    D. the number of daylight hours.

    2 best evidence sentences: **8, 16**

    Explanation: None of the earliest clocks measured time in minutes; they all used some form of hour.

9. What is the main idea of the article?
    (main idea)
    A. Man relied on the sun to keep track of time.
    B. Time was unimportant to early man.
    C. Early clocks measured only daylight.
    D. Man invented different ways to measure time.

    Explanation: D is supported by the descriptions of different types of clocks in the passage. A and C are details. There is no evidence for B.

41. ElectroMagic (p. 94)

1. What is the author's main purpose?
    (author's purpose)

    The author's main purpose is to show what an electromagnet is and how it can be used to make an electromagnetic motor.

    1 best evidence sentence: **5**

2. Which of the following are necessary to make the electromagnet spin in an electromagnetic motor? (Choose all that apply.) (reading for detail)
   A. **the reversal of the flow of current**
   B. the continuous switching of the poles of the permanent magnet
   C. **the attraction of opposite magnetic poles**
   D. the disconnection of the current source

   1 best evidence paragraph: **D**

3. What is the first step in buidling an electromagnet? (sequence steps)
   A. Send current through a wire.
   B. Place an electromagnet between poles of a permanent magnet.
   C. **Coil wire around an iron bar.**
   D. Connect both ends of a wire.

   1 best evidence sentence: **13**

4. Let's say you set up the magnet as described in the passage, but you place the electromagnet between the south poles of two different permanent magnets. Predict the results. (prediction)

   The electromagnet would not spin.

   Explanation: According to paragraph D, each end of the electromagnet (e.m.) attracts the opposite pole of the permanent magnet (p.m.). It is logical to assume the north pole of e.m. will be halfway between the p.m. poles. (Also, the e.m. south pole will equally repel those south poles.) This should remain true when the current is reversed:

5. What generalization can be made from the information given? (generalization)
   A. Magnetism requires the flow of electric current.
   B. **Electromagnetic motors are used to perform different types of work.**
   C. No work can get done without alternating current.
   D. All electromagnets must be spinning electromagnetic motors.

   1 best evidence paragraph: **A**

6. What is the main difference between a permanent magnet and an electromagnet? (compare/contrast, diagram use)
   A. **Permanent magnets do not need electricity to produce a magnetic field.**
   B. Electromagnets need alternating current.
   C. In permanent magnets, poles are attractive to opposite poles of another magnet.
   D. Electromagnets attract best without current.

   1 best evidence sentence: **6**

7. It can be inferred that alternating current: (inference, diagram use)
   A. changes direction only once.
   B. **keeps reversing its direction of flow.**
   C. runs both directions at the same time.
   D. flows without changing direction.

   2 best evidence sentences from paragraph D: **20, 21**

42. Sports Stats (p. 96)

1. According to the passage, which basic math task is NOT used in computing statistics? (supporting detail)
   A. addition
   B. subtraction
   C. multiplication
   D. division

   3 best evidence sentences: **4, 5, 6**

2. Name two ways coaches use statistics. (reading for detail)

   Coaches use statistics to compare performances of players and to estimate probability.

   2 best evidence sentences: **7, 25**

3. In the first 10 games, a player made 50 of 100 shots. In his latest game, he was 15-for-20. What was his shooting percentage before the latest game, and what is it now? (inference)

   His shooting percentage was 0.50; now, it's 0.54.

   Explanation: (50+15 = 65; 100+20 = 120; 65/120= 0.54)

4. Rank these players according to their shooting percentages. Use 1 for the highest and 4 for the lowest. (application)

2 Kidd	9-for-12	(75%)
4 Jamison	11-for-22	(50%)
3 Iverson	7-for-10	(70%)
1 Webber	9-for-10	(90%)

5. Kobe Bryant's shooting percentage suddenly drops from 63 to 59 percent. What probably caused this? (cause/effect)

   He missed a higher percentage of shots.

   1 best evidence paragraph: **E**

6. If Shaquille O'Neal improved his free throw shooting, which of these would most likely be true of his teammates? (prediction)
   A. **They would want to pass him the ball more.**
   B. They would want to improve their own free throw shooting.
   C. They would want him to play better defense.
   D. They would want to know their probability of making free throws.

   4 best evidence sentences: **28, 29, 30, 31**

7. Which of these statements best describes the main idea? (main idea)
   A. to teach the value of probability
   B. to teach the calculation of percentages
   C. **to show how math is used in sports**
   D. to show how much math athletes need to know

   1 best evidence paragraph: **A**

8. According to the diagram, the Blazers: (diagram use)
   A. are first on the list in defense.
   B. are last on the list in shooting.
   C. **have made a higher percentage of shots than their opponents.**
   D. have made more shots than they have missed.

43.   Secrets of Special Effects   (p. 98)

1.   What is the main idea of this article?
(main idea)
**A.   Computer-generated special
effects have significantly
changed film animation.**
B.   Computers are being used in
many aspects of filmmaking.
C.   Computer-generated images can
now be blended with live-action
footage in films.
D.   Computers can be used to create
three-dimensional images.

Explanation: The main idea is that
the use of the computer has provided
filmmakers with new ways to create
special effects. Choices C and D are
supporting detail of this idea. There is
no evidence for choice B.

2.   After the wire-frame is built, the next
step is to: (sequence steps)
A.   add facial expressions.
B.   mold the muscles.
C.   paint the skin texture.
D.   move the muscles.

1 best evidence sentence: **13**

3.   A "wire-frame" is composed of:
(reading for detail)

**digital lines connecting key body
parts**

1 best evidence sentence: **9**

4.   What was the author's purpose in
writing this article? (author's purpose)
A.   to explain how cartoons are made
B.   to describe how a film uses
special effects
C.   to compare different kinds of
special effects
**D.   to explain how computer images
are used in special effects**

Explanation: The author explains
the process of creating a computer
generated image and how it is used in
films. There is no evidence for A, B, or
C.

5.   What effect can a filmmaker hope to
achieve by blending the computer image
with the live-action footage?
(cause/effect)

**To give the illusion that the
computer image is part of the live
action.**

1 best evidence sentence: **20**

(Also acceptable: **18**)

6.   A wire-frame is a kind of: (diagram use)
A.   outline.
B.   body cast.
C.   grid.
D.   sculpture.

Explanation: The wire-frame image is
made of lines joined together to form
a framework of the object. There is no
evidence to support A or B. A sculpture
is an object, not an image, so D is
incorrect.

7.   In contrast to early cartoon figures,
computer images appear to be:
(compare/contrast)
A.   three-dimensional.
B.   able to move.
C.   two-dimensional.
D.   in full color.

1 best evidence sentence: **8**

Explanation: Computer images are
more realistic because they look three-
dimensional. Choices B, C, and D are
true for earlier cartoon figures.

8. Why was the film *Toy Story* important in filmmaking history? (supporting detail)

It was the first full-length film done completely with computer animation.

1 best evidence sentence: **21**

44. Emperor Kublai Khan (p. 100)

1. From the passage, the conclusion can be made that the emperors who ruled after Khan and his son: (conclusion)
    A. upheld the dynasty.
    B. strengthened the dynasty.
    C. bankrupted the dynasty.
    D. weakened the dynasty.

    2 best evidence sentences: **28, 29**

    Explanation: Explanation: Sentence 28 explains that succeeding emperors were ineffective; this probably weakened the dynasty. The fact that a peasant rebellion brought down the dynasty also supports the idea that the emperors who ruled after Khan and his son weakened the empire (29). A and B are contradicted by sentence 29: the emperors were considered ineffective, so they did not uphold or strengthen the dynasty. There is no evidence for C.

2. The main purpose of the passage is to: (author's purpose)
    A. explain how the Yuan dynasty fell.
    B. present the artistic achievements of the Yuan dynasty.
    C. explain how Kublai Khan ruled China.
    D. compare Mongol rule of China to Chinese rule.

    Explanation: A and B mention details within the passage, not the main purpose. There is no evidence for D.

3. We can infer that Khan wanted to be accepted by the: (inference)
    A. peasants.
    B. Chinese.
    C. Mongols.
    D. soldiers.

    1 best evidence paragraph: **B**

    Explanation: Sentence 6 explains that Khan wanted the Chinese to believe he had been given the Mandate of Heaven, a divine approval.

4. Number the following events in their correct order. (sequence events)
    4 Khan's son rules. (27)
    1 Khan declares himself emperor. (2)
    5 The Yuan dynasty ends. (29)
    3 Khan is buried. (23)
    2 Some people come to believe Khan has received the Mandate of Heaven. (22)

5. What caused some people to believe that Khan had received the Mandate of Heaven? (cause/effect)

    The achievements in art, science, and religion proved to many that he had received the Mandate of Heaven.

    1 best evidence sentence: **22**

6. What four things did Khan do to help farmers? (supporting detail)

    1) He restored the farmlands that had been destroyed. 2) He gave them larger plots to farm. 3) He gave them seeds. 4) He established grain reserves.

    3 best evidence sentences: **13, 14, 15**

7. What do Kublai Khan's actions tell you about his character? (character traits)
   A. He was artistic.
   B. He was tolerant.
   C. He was merciless.
   D. He was unsure of himself.

2 best evidence paragraphs: **B, D**

Explanation: Paragraph B explains that Khan wanted to work with the Chinese, not against them. He followed Chinese ways by appointing Confucians, or Chinese advisors. Paragraph D explains how art, science, and various religions flourished under Khan's rule. He wanted to be accepted by people of all religious beliefs. There is no evidence for A or C. D is contradicted by sentence 20.

45. Is the Earth Heating Up? (p. 102)

1. How does cutting down forests increase CO_2 in the atmosphere? (cause/effect)

Trees absorb carbon dioxide from the atmosphere. If there were no trees, the CO_2 would stay in the atmosphere.

1 best evidence sentence: **17**

2. What is the main idea of the article? (main idea)
   A. Global warming is good for the earth's environment.
   B. The Greenhouse Effect is a factor in global warming.
   C. The Greenhouse Effect is caused by increasing carbon dioxide.
   D. Global warming is caused by cutting down forests.

Explanation: There is no evidence for A or C. D is a detail in the passage.

3. What causes higher levels of methane in the atmosphere? (reading for detail)

Methane is released during coal mining and from garbage in landfills.

1 best evidence sentence: **19**

4. How does gas in the atmosphere function similarly to the glass or plastic in a greenhouse? (compare/contrast)

They both let in sunlight and then trap heat energy.

2 best evidence sentences: **10, 11**

5. Why are increasing methane levels in the atmosphere a concern? (conclusion)

Methane traps heat better than carbon dioxide.

1 best evidence sentence: **21**

Trapped heat causes global warming.

6. How does the amount of the gases in the atmosphere affect the amount of heat energy in the atmosphere? (cause/effect)

As the amount of gases increases, so does the amount of heat they absorb.

1 best evidence sentence: **12**

7. Why might levels of carbon dioxide have begun to increase during the Industrial Revolution, as indicated in sentence 16? (conclusion)

As more large factories were built, they burned more fossil fuels.

1 best evidence sentence: **15**

8. According to the diagram, both heat energy and sunlight are: (diagram use)
   A. reflected into space.

B. trapped in the atmosphere.

C. reflected back to Earth.

D. absorbed by gases.

46. Gimme Some Latitude! (and a little longitude wouldn't hurt) (p. 104)

1. The main purpose of the passage is to: (author's purpose)
   A. show the usefulness of latitude and longitude.
   B. show how to track someone down.
   C. describe the positions of geographical locations.
   D. convince you to solve problems.

   1 best evidence sentence: **1**

2. If someone were to walk along the Prime Meridian to the North Pole and beyond, that longitude line would become:
   (Choose all that apply.)
   (conclusion)
   A. the International Dateline.
   B. the equator.
   C. 0° longitude.
   D. 180° longitude.

   1 best evidence sentence: **14**

3. Which of the following is NOT reasonable to conclude? (conclusion)
   A. The eastern and western hemispheres have different days.
   B. The day changes as you cross the International Dateline.
   C. It is a day earlier in the western hemisphere than in the eastern.
   D. The day changes as you cross the Prime Meridian.

   Explanation: There is nothing in the passage to indicate that the day in the western hemisphere is earlier than the day in the eastern. In fact, the opposite is true (it was an arbitrary

decision). Choices A and B follow from the information in sentences 15 and 16. D can be concluded thus: if the day changes at the International Dateline and the eastern and western hemispheres have different days, then your day must change as you cross the Prime Meridian as well.

4. Label the following as T for true or F for false. (reading for detail, diagram use)

   F 0° longitude is the equator.

   T 90° N is the North Pole.

   F 0°, 0° is where the equator crosses the International Dateline.

   F 30° N, 75 W° is in Asia.

   Explanation: 0° *latitude* (not longitude) is the equator. The first position in coordinates gives latitude, the second gives longitude. Therefore, 0°, 0° must be where the equator (0° latitude) intersects the Prime Meridian (0° longitude). The facts that 90° N is the North Pole and 30° N, 75° W is not in Asia can be confirmed by consulting a globe or atlas.

5. Explain why coordinates are given in place of the verb in sentence 24. (diagram use, inference)

   The coordinates are for Rome, Italy. The word *roam* means to wander.

6. Label each of the following F for fact or O for opinion. (fact/opinion)

   F Tahiti is located at 17° N, 139° W.

   F The International Dateline and Prime Meridian separate the world into halves.

   O Latitude/longitude is the best system for locating people or things.

   F Cairo is on the Nile River.

Explanation: The first, second, and fourth sentences can be proven by consulting a map. The word *best*, in the third sentence, is a clue that it cannot be proven but is an opinion.

7. Describe one way in which the lines of latitude and longitude are different and one way in which they are alike. (compare/contrast, diagram use)

(Accept any one difference and one similarity.)

Examples of Differences:

1) Latitude lines are parallel, running east/west. Longitude lines are not parallel and run north/south, meeting at the poles. 2) Latitude lines are different lengths. Longitude lines are all the same length. 3) Latitude lines are marked in degrees up to 180, while longitude lines are marked in degrees up to 90.

Examples of Similarities:

1) Latitude and longitude are both lines used to form a grid on the globe for pinpointing locations. 2) They are both marked off in degrees.

Explanation: It can be concluded from sentences 6–10 and by looking at the diagram that the latitude lines are different lengths. From sentence 11 and the diagram, we can conclude that the longitude lines are all the same length.

8. The word *groveling*, as used in sentence 23, most likely means: (vocabulary)
   A. dancing.
   B. acting snobby.
   C. knowledgeably.
   D. acting humble.

Explanation: If they realize the error of their ways, as described in sentence 23,

they are most likely to be humble. There is no evidence for choices A, B, or C.

9. The phrase "gets the goods," as used in sentence 3, most likely means: (figurative language: idiom)
   A. retrieves the couple.
   B. finds information.
   C. picks up packages.
   D. extracts a confession.

Explanation: Choice B makes the most sense in the context of the passage. If a private investigator "gets the goods" from an informant, she or he probably gets information.

47. Finding the Career for You (p. 106)

1. What is the author's viewpoint on how to choose a career? (point of view)
   A. Take whatever job you're offered.
   B. Research a career path based on interests and abilities.
   C. Evaluate your options to make the best career choice.
   D. Try out several careers and then choose the best one.

Explanation: B is the best choice because the author's view is that students should research their interests and skills and then research different career choices based on these. There is no evidence for A or D. C is only part of the process involved.

2. Number the steps that Ali should take in the order in which the author of the article would advise. (sequence steps)

   2 Ali talks to a family member.

   5 Ali makes a list and rates each option.

   4 Ali volunteers at a local elementary school.

   1 Ali brainstorms different career options.

3　Ali takes an aptitude test and discovers she's creative.

3.　In sentence 31, what does the author mean when she suggests that you "test the waters"?
(figurative language: idiom)

She means that you should try out a career before you actually decide to get into it.

4.　Label the following statements F for fact or O for opinion.　(fact/opinion)

O　It's perfectly acceptable to change your mind about a career.

F　The public library's reference section has information on careers.

O　Now is a good time to start researching a career.

Explanation: The first and last statements are opinions because they use words that signify value, like "acceptable" and "good." The second statement is a fact because it can be proven.

5.　What two things does the article mention will happen if you successfully research a career before you have to find a job?　(reading for detail)

1. You will know what classes to take in high school and college.

2. You will know what types of jobs you may be interested in.

1 best evidence sentence: **26**

6.　Pablo can't decide if he wants to become a veterinarian, a writer, a pharmacist, or a horse trainer. According to the passage, what should he do?　(reading for detail)

He should make a list of options and rate them pro or con.

1 best evidence paragraph: **G**

7.　You are trying to decide if you want to become a social worker. There are two very important cons and two important pros. According to the passage, should you still consider becoming a social worker? Explain your answer.
(application)

No. The cons outweigh the pros because they are "very important" and the pros are only "important."

1 best evidence paragraph: **G**

48.　Training for the Ballet　(p. 108)

1.　The main idea is to describe:
(main idea)
A.　what is done during *barre* and exercises *au milieu.*
B.　how difficult it is to become a professional dancer.
C.　**the training of a ballet dancer.**
D.　the structure of a ballet company.

2.　What type of work must be done before center work?　(sequence steps)

barre work

2 best evidence sentences: **4, 6**

3.　Label the following statements F for fact or O for opinion.　(fact/opinion)
F　Male ballet dancers do weight lifting exercises.
F　The professional ballet dancer learns the *pas de deux.*
O　The life of a dancer is fascinating.
O　The principal dancer has the most desireable position within the ballet company.

Explanation: The first two statements are facts and can be proven by a reliable source. The last two statements are opinions because they use words that signify personal value, like "fascinating" and "desirable."

4. Which of the following inferences is supported in the passage? (inference)
   A. There are fewer principal dancers than *corps* dancers.
   B. There are fewer *corps* dancers than soloists.
   C. There are more principal dancers than soloists.
   D. There are fewer male dancers than female dancers.

1 best evidence sentence: **18**

Explanation: Sentence 18 states that the company's largest group of dancers is the *corps*. From this, you can infer that the other groups of dancers (soloists and principals) are smaller.

5. If the dancer shown *en pointe* were to lower her heels directly onto the floor, which position would her feet be in? (diagram use)
   A. first
   B. second
   C. fourth
   D. fifth

6. What is the *pas de deux*? (reading for detail)

   The *pas de deux* is a dance done with two people, usually a male and a female.

2 best evidence sentences: **10, 11**

7. List the different levels of dancers and the order in which the levels progress. (reading for detail, sequence steps)

   **corps de ballet—beginning
   soloist—middle
   principal—top**

3 best evidence sentences: **18, 19, 20**

8. In the illustration, which movement shows the dancer standing on one leg with the other leg elevated behind? (diagram use)

   arabesque

9. In general, the training of someone who wants to be a dancer requires: (generalization)
   A. a demanding instructor.
   B. an education in music and fine arts.
   C. a long-term commitment.
   D. a large financial strain.

3 best evidence sentences: **2, 3, 13**

Explanation: C is correct because ballet dancers must begin their careers early and continue training for almost a decade before they can begin a professional career. (Note: Training continues throughout a dancer's career.)

49. From Superman to X-Men (p. 110)

1. How is the story organized? (organization of material)
   A. in order of importance
   B. in time order
   C. by type of comic book
   D. by type of superhero

2. Based on the article, the conclusion can be made that the business of publishing comic books has been: (conclusion)
   A. a great success.
   B. inconsistent.
   C. a great failure.
   D. steady.

Explanation: The article states two different times in the history of comic books that publishers have gone bankrupt. The article also notes that each time there was something that brought comic book sales back up again; thus, you can make the conclusion that the comic book business is inconsistent.

3. Sequence the following events in the order in which they occurred. (sequence events)

   2 Superhero comic books become a big hit. (4)

   6 "Teenage Mutant Ninja Turtles" are the big rage. (25)

   1 "Yellow Kid" makes its first appearance. (2)

   3 WWII ignites the popularity of soldier and spy heroes. (8)

   5 Science fiction superheroes revive the comic book industry. (18, 20)

   4 Crime and horror comics gain popularity. (11)

4. What do the words "spun off," as used in sentence 26, most likely mean? (vocabulary)
   A. resulted
   B. halted
   C. picked out
   D. combined

   Explanation: A is correct because we know that a movie and television miniseries resulted from the comic book. B, C, and D don't make sense within the context of the sentence.

5. What caused people in the early '50s to take a closer look at comic books? (cause/effect)

   Parents and lawmakers began questioning how crime and horror comic books were affecting children.

   1 best evidence sentence: **14**

6. What is the major change from the superhero of the past to the superhero of today? (compare/contrast)

   Superheroes of the past enjoyed their superhero abilities. Superheroes today don't always enjoy these abilities, and many have very human problems.

   1 best evidence sentence: **21**

7. In general, it could be said that the image of the superhero is: (generalization)
   A. unpopular.
   B. realistic.
   C. unchanging.
   D. changing.

   3 best evidence sentences: **8, 21, 23**

   Explanation: D is the best answer because the image of the superhero is changing. A is contradicted by the fact that there are many successful comic books in publication today (paragraph G). War heroes might be considered realistic, but they are not technically "superheroes"; thus, B is incorrect. C is contradicted by the many changes the superhero has undergone.

8. It can be inferred that comic books are: (inference)
   A. usually about war and crime.
   B. very short stories.
   C. influenced by politics.
   D. read and enjoyed by everyone.

   2 best evidence paragraphs: **C, E**

   Explanation: C is correct because comic books were influenced by WWII and in the early '50s, by what people felt was acceptable content. A is contradicted by the fact that there are other categories of comic books—superhero, horror, etc. There is no evidence for B. We know that comic books are popular, but we do not know if everyone finds them enjoyable, so D is incorrect.

50. Secret Codes (p. 112)

1. What is the author's purpose? (author's purpose)

to describe three types of secret codes

2. As used in sentence 21, the word *template* most likely means: (vocabulary)
A. grid.
B. cardboard.
C. holes.
D. guide.

Explanation: Sentences 20–23 indicate the template is being used as a guide. (Sentence 21 describes how to use a cardboard cutout, implying that it is the cutout that is a template.)

3. Which of the following provides the best summary of the article? (summary)
A. Secret codes include camouflage (letter hiding), substitution (letter replacing), and repositioning (letter rearranging), among others.
B. Someone had to make up all those codes, including camouflage and repositioning, and substitution, and yours may be just as good as those.
C. Everyone from children to adults finds it useful to know how to use secret codes at one time or another.
D. The best known secret code involves an alphabet substitution, though there are also two other main types.

Explanation: Choice A is supported by paragraph A; the rest of the passage describes and gives examples of the three types of codes. There is no evidence for B and C. D is contradicted by paragraph I.

4. Suppose you are given the message FAILNEDX and the key of 2 (meaning to take the first letter then every second letter) to get FIND ALEX. What type of code would that be? (conclusion)
A. camouflage
B. substitution
C. repositioning
D. none of the above

2 best evidence sentences: **15, 16**

Explanation: In the code given, the letters are rearranged. Sentences 15 and 16 indicate that a repositioning code mixes or rearranges the letters, so C is correct. There is no evidence for choices A, B, or D.

5. As used in sentence 10, what does the word *decoding* mean? (diagram use)

To decode is to figure something out, the opposite of putting something in a code.

(Accept anything similar, including descramble or unlock.)

6. Write the word CAT using the substitution code in paragraph C but with letters that are offset by two places, not one. (inference, application)

ECV

7. Using the substitution code at the top left in the illustration, translate the following message: 223511531155 (diagram use)

GO AWAY

8. What is the message given in the repositioning code at the lower left in the illustration? (application, diagram use)

LETS MEET AT ONE IN THE CABIN.

Explanation: Reading as directed, you take the letter in the lower right corner, then loop back and forth diagonally.

9. From sentences 11, 19, and 25, you can generalize that in order to interpret a message, the receiver needs: (generalization)
   A. **a tool to decode the message.**
   B. information on where to start.
   C. a template.
   D. a code word.

51. The Making of the Constitution
(p. 114)

1. Why were many of the delegates surprised when they first heard Edmund Randolph's plan for a new government? (inference)
   A. They were expecting something more drastic.
   B. **They were not expecting to change the current system of government.**
   C. They didn't realize Randolph was a nationalist.
   D. They thought the current system of government was working well.

   2 best evidence sentences: **3, 4**

2. Why did the delegates agree to a national government but avoid describing it as "national"? (inference)

   Most people during this time feared a national government. They had only recently won their freedom from Great Britian.

   1 best evidence sentence: **4**

3. Why was a bill of rights added to the Constitution? (cause/effect)

   A bill of rights was added to protect the rights of individuals.

   Explanation: Some delegates feared the new president would become like a king and the rights of individuals would be in danger.

   1 best evidence sentence: **16**

4. If 60 of the 100 members of the Senate voted to override the president's rejection, what would happen to the bill? (application)

   It would not be passed. (The president's rejection would stand.)

   The bill requires a 2/3 majority—66 of 100.

5. When first approved, the Constitution had a bill of rights. True or False? (reading for detail)

   False

   1 best evidence sentence: **17**

6. Why would small states have been at a disadvantage according to Randolph's plan? (conclusion)

   Congress would have been represented by population only. Therefore, large states with larger populations would have greater influence and control over the government.

   2 best evidence sentences: **10, 11**

7. Give one view of the nationalists that differed from the view of the people who were unsure of the Constitution. (compare/contrast)

(Accept either one.)

1. The nationalists wanted a single government that would be higher than the states. The people who were concerned about the Constitution thought that states needed to be equally represented.

2. The people concerned about the Constitution feared the power of the President and wanted a bill of rights to be included with the Constitution.

2 best evidence sentences: **6, 10 (or 15, 16)**

8. Which of the following statements are opinions? Choose all that apply. (fact/opinion)
   A. At least nine of the thirteen states approved the Constitution.
   B. The Constitution was a great American achievement.
   C. The purpose of the Supreme Court is to ensure that laws are constitutional.
   D. The nationalists did their best to convince people to support the Constitution.

Explanation: B states that the Constitution was a "great" achievement, which is a value statement. D is a value statement because it uses the word "best" to describe how the nationalists convinced the people. A and C are facts that can be proven.

FICTION POSTEST

Treasure Island (p. 118)

1. Morgan thought that the man who shouted could not have found the treasure. Why did he think this? (figurative language: idiom)
   A. The man was deep in the vegetation, not in the clearing.
   B. What the man had found was too new to be the treasure.
   C. Morgan knew the treasure should not be near a skeleton.
   D. The treasure was supposed to be on the plateau.

By "for that's clean a-top" in sentence 3, Morgan meant that the treasure was on the plateau.

2. Why did Silver say you "wouldn't look to find a bishop here"? (inference)

He meant you wouldn't expect to find a religious person here.

Explanation: The setting is an island frequented by pirates (one of whom is later hinted to be a cold-hearted killer). In paragraph C, a chill strikes because of the sight of a skeleton.

3. According to the narrator, if the bones were not laid out perfectly straight, what were the probable causes? (Choose all that apply.) (cause/effect)
   A. birds
   B. men
   C. vines
   D. rocks

1 best evidence sentence: **13**

4. When Silver got an idea about the bones in paragraph G, what did he suggest they do? (reading for detail)

    He suggested they "take a bearing," or measure the direction in which the bones were pointing.

    Explanation: Silver's suggestion is given in sentence 16, and the result is described in sentence 18.

5. In sentence 22, what was the joke that Flint probably played? (inference)

    His joke was to take the bones of a man he'd killed and use them as a pointer to the treasure.

6. Based on paragraph I, the conclusion can be made that Allardyce had been: (Choose all that apply.) (conclusion)
    A. slender.
    B. bearded.
    C. tall.
    D. blond.

    1 best evidence sentence: **24**

7. Number the following events in the order in which they most likely occurred. (sequence events)

    1 Morgan's knife is taken. (27)

    4 The men discover the bones. (1)

    2 Flint kills Allardyce. (23)

    3 The body is arranged to align with the island. (23)

8. Label each of the following sentences as F for fact or O for opinion. (fact/opinion)

    F They had proceeded for about half a mile.

    O The dead man wore good sea cloth.

    O Flint intended to lay out the bones as a pointer.

    F The bones pointed in the direction of the island.

    Explanation: The first and last sentences are verifiable. That the dead man wore good sea cloth cannot be proved, as *good* implies a value judgment. Also, though the bones are aligned with the island, no one can prove the intentions of the one who laid them out. It is possible the alignment was unintentional.

9. The mood of the passage is shown by the men's sense of: (mood)
    A. hope.
    B. happiness.
    C. confusion.
    D. dread.

    4 best evidence sentences: **6, 7, 21, 23**

10. Which of the following was a key event of the passage? (key event)
    A. They approached the brow of the plateau.
    B. They found that the body pointed in the direction of the island.
    C. The man was recognized as Allardyce.
    D. The man was determined to be a seaman rather than a bishop.

    Explanation: Choice B was a key event because the body was determined to be a pointer toward the treasure they were seeking. A, C, and D are minor events of the passage.

NONFICTION POSTTEST

How Money Has Changed (p. 122)

1. What needs to happen for a particular object to be accepted as money? (main idea)

   A majority of people have to be willing to accept something as money before it can be considered money.

   1 best evidence sentence: **3**

2. Which of these exchanges is a barter? (application)
   A. dollars for donuts
   B. quarters for a dollar
   C. baby-sitting for help with studying
   D. shoveling the sidewalk for checks

   1 best evidence paragraph: **C**

   Explanation: Only C is a barter. A, B, and D involve a monetary exchange for a good or service.

3. In general, money CANNOT be described as: (generalization)
   A. taking many forms.
   B. being accepted everywhere.
   C. having a long history.
   D. being almost anything.

   Explanation: Only B is unsupported in the passage. See sentences 4, 5, 11, 15, 22.

4. Label each of these statements as a fact (F) or an opinion (O). (fact/opinion)

   F   Barter has not vanished; it is still in use today.

   O   The dollar is recognized around the world, so it is the best currency to use.

   F   If enough people will accept paper clips as money, then paper clips will become money.

   F   Computers can keep accurate accounts of transactions.

   Explanation: The second sentence uses the word "best," which is a value judgment—an indicator of an opinion. The rest are facts.

5. What kind of trouble might the people who accept donuts as money run into if they try to spend those donuts in a neighboring town? (prediction, inference)

   If the people in a neighboring town don't accept donuts, the people who do will have to pay with something else in that town.

   1 best evidence sentence: **3** (or **4**)

6. Why did most people begin accepting coins? (inference, cause/effect)

   The Greek and Roman civilizations began accepting coins, so most other people went along because Greece and Rome were the primary economic influence of their times.

   1 best evidence sentence: **15**

7. Explain why $10 of money has a higher *asset value* than $10 worth of fresh fish. (conclusion, diagram)

   Money can be saved and spent later; it does not spoil. Fresh fish does spoil and must be used right away.

8. What inference can be made about what
    Sue and Ramon might think about their
    barter? (inference)
    A. that they needed a record of
        their exchange
    B. that they were ignoring the value
        of money
    C. that they each got what the
        other wanted from the exchange
    **D. that they each believed
        the exchange was in their
        interest**

    Explanation: Sentences 9 and 12 say Sue
    and Ramon agreed to swap services.
    Neither sentence says anything about
    dissatisfaction or further exchange. C
    is contradicted by sentence 9, which
    implies that each got what he/she
    wanted; neither A nor B has support in
    the article.

9. Compare what Harold and Ramon
    would probably be willing to accept for
    their accounting services from Sue the
    electrician. (compare/contrast)

    **Ramon would probably be willing
    to accept a barter**, such as Sue's
    helping him with his electrical
    work. **Harold**, on the other hand,
    would probably want to be paid with
    money.

    2 best evidence sentences: **9** (or **12**),
    13

GLOSSARY OF TERMS

analogy: A comparison between two things that are normally quite different.

character trait: A person's individual qualities, such as greed or kindness.

conflict: The tension or opposition between two characters, or between a character and some opposing force, such as society.

fact/opinion: Facts are statements of truth that can be proven with evidence. Opinions are judgments that may be based on interpretations of facts but are not in themselves provable.

figurative language: Words and phrases used to compare two unlike things or to mean something other than their actual meaning. Similes and metaphors are types of figurative language.

flashback: A description of events that happened at an earlier time. A jump from the present to the past.

foreshadowing: A hint or clue of what is going to happen later in the story; an early suggestion of things to come.

generalization: A broad statement that is made about a group of things in general, based on one or more samples from the group.

idiom: Words or phrase meaning something other than their literal meaning. Examples are "keep tabs on" or "lost track of."

inference: Information that is suggested in a story but not directly stated.

irony: Contradiction or unexpected occurrence. When something is ironic, things are not as they seem, they do not turn out as they should, or there is a discrepancy between the intent and the effect.

literary device: A method used to create a particular effect on the reader. Examples are flashback, foreshadowing, irony, and symbolism.

metaphor: A comparison between two things which says that one thing is another. Example: The flowers were bright flags heralding the return of spring.

mood: The feeling a story gives the reader. The mood can be cheerful, thoughtful, depressed, etc.

narrator: The person or character who is telling the story.

GLOSSARY OF TERMS (continued)

opinion: (See fact/opinion)

personification: Giving human traits to inanimate objects or ideas. For example, the tree boughs nodded sleepily in the warm breeze.

plot: The structure of the story around which events occur. Most plots begin with a problem or conflict that builds to a high point and is then resolved.

point of view: The narrator's focus in telling the story. In a first person viewpoint, the narrator is a character in the story. In a third person viewpoint, the narrator is observing the story characters.

resolution: Solving the problem or conflict in a story.

setting: The particular time and place in which a story occurs.

simile: A comparison of two things, using the words like or as.
Example: His nose glowed like a lantern in the night.

summary: A brief description of what the passage is about; a summary combines main ideas, supporting ideas, and a conclusion and may be stated in one or more sentences.

symbolism: The use of an object, event, or relationship to represent a broader idea. A rock may be used to represent, or symbolize, strength.

theme: The underlying meaning of the story. It is a comment or view about life or human nature in general that is woven throughout the story. It may be stated directly or revealed through the character's words and actions and the story's events.

tone: The author's attitude about the writing. The tone can be humorous, serious, objective, etc.

LITERATURE CITATIONS

The Cay
From THE CAY by Theodore Taylor. Copyright (c) 1969 by Theodore Taylor. Used by permission of Doubleday, a division of Random House, Inc.

Sparrow Hawk Red
From SPARROW HAWK RED by Ben Mikaelsen. Text © 1993 Ben Mikaelsen. Published by Hyperion Books for Children.

El Güero
Excerpt from Chapter 19 from EL GÜERO by Elizabeth Borton de Trevino. Copyright © 1989 by Elizabeth Borton de Trevino.

The Moon by Night
Excerpt from THE MOON BY NIGHT by Madeleine L'Engle. Copyright © 1963 by Madeleine L'Engle. Copyright renewed 1991 by Madeleine L'Engle.

The Giver
Excerpt from THE GIVER. Copyright (c) 1993 by Lois Lowry. Reprinted by permission of Houghton Mifflin Co. All rights reserved.

Under the Blood-Red Sun
From UNDER THE BLOOD-RED SUN by Graham Salisbury. Copyright (c) 1994 by Graham Salisbury. Used by permission of Delacorte Press, a division of Random House, Inc.

The View from Saturday
Reprinted with the permission of Atheneum Books for Young Readers, an imprint of Simon & Schuster Children's Publishing Division from THE VIEW FROM SATURDAY by E.L. Konigsburg. Copyright © 1996 E.L. Konigsburg.

The Trolley to Yesterday
From THE TROLLEY TO YESTERDAY by John Bellairs, copyright (c) 1989 by John Bellairs. Used by permission of Dial Books for Young Readers, a division of Penguin Putnam Inc.

Face to Face
Excerpt from FACE TO FACE by Marion Dane Bauer. Copyright (c) 1991 by Marion Dane Bauer. Reprinted by permission of Houghton Mifflin Co. All rights reserved.

The Bronze Bow
Excerpt from THE BRONZE BOW. Copyright (c) 1961 by Elizabeth George Speare. Reprinted by permission of Houghton Mifflin Company. All rights reserved.